Communications in Computer and Information Science 2695

Rationale

The CCIS series is devoted to the publication of proceedings of computer science conferences. Its aim is to efficiently disseminate original research results in informatics in printed and electronic form. While the focus is on publication of peer-reviewed full papers presenting mature work, inclusion of reviewed short papers reporting on work in progress is welcome, too. Besides globally relevant meetings with internationally representative program committees guaranteeing a strict peer-reviewing and paper selection process, conferences run by societies or of high regional or national relevance are also considered for publication.

Topics

The topical scope of CCIS spans the entire spectrum of informatics ranging from foundational topics in the theory of computing to information and communications science and technology and a broad variety of interdisciplinary application fields.

Information for Volume Editors and Authors

Publication in CCIS is free of charge. No royalties are paid, however, we offer registered conference participants temporary free access to the online version of the conference proceedings on SpringerLink (http://link.springer.com) by means of an http referrer from the conference website and/or a number of complimentary printed copies, as specified in the official acceptance email of the event.

CCIS proceedings can be published in time for distribution at conferences or as post-proceedings, and delivered in the form of printed books and/or electronically as USBs and/or e-content licenses for accessing proceedings at SpringerLink. Furthermore, CCIS proceedings are included in the CCIS electronic book series hosted in the SpringerLink digital library at http://link.springer.com/bookseries/7899. Conferences publishing in CCIS are allowed to use our online conference service (Meteor) for managing the whole proceedings lifecycle (from submission and reviewing to preparing for publication) free of charge.

Publication process

The language of publication is exclusively English. Authors publishing in CCIS have to sign the Springer CCIS copyright transfer form, however, they are free to use their material published in CCIS for substantially changed, more elaborate subsequent publications elsewhere. For the preparation of the camera-ready papers/files, authors have to strictly adhere to the Springer CCIS Authors' Instructions and are strongly encouraged to use the CCIS LaTeX style files or templates.

Abstracting/Indexing

CCIS is abstracted/indexed in DBLP, Google Scholar, EI-Compendex, Mathematical Reviews, SCImago, Scopus. CCIS volumes are also submitted for the inclusion in ISI Proceedings.

How to start

To start the evaluation of your proposal for inclusion in the CCIS series, please send an e-mail to ccis@springer.com

Qingsong Wen · Yongfeng Zhang · Zhiwei Liu ·
Julian McAuley · Hua Wei · Linsey Pang ·
Wei Liu · Philip S. Yu
Editors

AI Agent for Information Retrieval: Generating and Ranking

Agent4IR International Workshops: Agent4IR 2024@CIKM 2024; Agent4IR@AAAI 2025; and Agent4IR@KDD 2025
Revised Selected Papers

Editors
Qingsong Wen
Squirrel AI Learning
Seattle, WA, USA

Zhiwei Liu
Salesforce AI Research
Palo Alto, CA, USA

Hua Wei
Arizona State University
Tempe, AZ, USA

Wei Liu
University of Technology Sydney
Sydney, NSW, Australia

Yongfeng Zhang
Rutgers University
New Brunswick, NJ, USA

Julian McAuley
UC San Diego
San Diego, CA, USA

Linsey Pang
Salesforce
San Francisco, CA, USA

Philip S. Yu
University of Illinois at Chicago
Chicago, IL, USA

ISSN 1865-0929 ISSN 1865-0937 (electronic)
Communications in Computer and Information Science
ISBN 978-3-032-11476-1 ISBN 978-3-032-11477-8 (eBook)
https://doi.org/10.1007/978-3-032-11477-8

This Springer imprint is published by the registered company Springer Nature Switzerland AG
The registered company address is: Gewerbestrasse 11, 6330 Cham, Switzerland

Preface

The field of information retrieval is being significantly transformed by the integration of AI technologies. AI agents, especially those leveraging LLMs, and vast computational power, are revolutionizing information retrieval, processing, and presentation. LLM agents, with advanced memory, reasoning, and planning capabilities, are able to perform complex tasks, engage in coherent conversations, and provide personalized responses. Despite these advancements, challenges such as ensuring relevance and accuracy, mitigating biases, providing real-time responses, and maintaining data security remain.

The AI Agent for Information Retrieval (Agent4IR) workshop aimed to explore these challenges, share innovative solutions, and discuss future directions. It provided a platform that brought together researchers and practitioners to discuss the latest theoretical advancements and practical implementations of AI agents in information retrieval. Topics included AI in search, recommendation, and personalization systems. By gathering a diverse group of experts, the workshop sought to deepen understanding of AI agents in information retrieval, advance the field, and enhance its societal impact. Participants gained insights into cutting-edge research and emerging trends, and fostered knowledge exchange and collaboration within the community. This workshop was successfully held at CIKM 2024, AAAI 2025, and KDD 2025.

Agent4IR workshop topics included, but were not limited to: Agentic Retrieval Systems; Agentic Conversational Recommendation; AI Agents for Personalization; AI Agents for Sequential Recommendation; AI Agents for Contextual Information Retrieval; AI Agents for Cross-lingual and Multimodal Retrieval; Retrieval-Augmented Generation Systems; Optimization of AI Agent Retrieval Models; Bias Mitigation in AI-Driven Information Retrieval; Interpretable Generative Retrieval Systems; Adversarial Attacks and Defenses in Agentic Retrieval Systems; Ethical Considerations in Agentic Information Retrieval; Human-AI Collaboration in Information Retrieval; Evaluation for Agentic Information Retrieval; and Scalability and Efficiency in AI Agent Retrieval.

The Agent4IR workshop used a single-blind peer review process. Paper submissions included full papers and short papers. Full papers could not exceed 9 pages, including an appendix, plus unlimited references. Short papers could not exceed 4 pages, plus unlimited references. For the Agent4IR workshops held at CIKM, AAAI, and KDD, the total number of submissions was 38, of which 21 were accepted. Eleven of these papers are included in these proceedings.

Organization

Chairs

Qingsong Wen	Squirrel Ai Learning, USA
Yongfeng Zhang	Rutgers University, USA
Zhiwei Liu	Salesforce AI Research, USA
Julian McAuley	University of California, San Diego, USA
Hua Wei	Arizona State University, USA
Linsey Pang	Salesforce, USA
Wei Liu	University of Technology Sydney, Australia
Philip S. Yu	University of Illinois Chicago, USA

Program Committee

Yuyang Ye	Rutgers University, USA
Dezhi Yu	University of California, Berkeley, USA
Yingzhou Lu	Stanford University, USA
Shiyu Zhao	Stanford University, USA
Ce Zhou	Michigan State University, USA
Dachun Sun	University of Illinois Urbana-Champaign, USA
Dongji Feng	Gustavus Adolphus College, USA
Mingyang Wan	Texas A&M University, USA
Karen M. D'Souza	Purdue University, USA
Juntao Tan	Salesforce AI Research, USA
Sujitha Pasumarty	Albertsons Companies, Inc, USA
Chen Wang	University of Illinois Chicago, USA
Yu Wang	Netflix Research, USA
Yong Liu	Salesforce, USA
Tianyi Zhang	University of Southern California, USA
Ling Yue	Rensselaer Polytechnic Institute, USA
Shengjie Liu	Amazon, USA
Deep Narayan Mishra	Walmart, USA
Fuheng Zhao	University of California, Santa Barbara, USA
Ze Yang	University of Illinois Urbana-Champaign, USA
Haifang Li	Mayo Clinic, USA

Contents

Assessing Performance of Large Language Models in Generating Local and Trending Query Auto-completions

Srichandra Chilappagari, Rishab L. N. U., Kedhar Nath Narahari, R. G. Karthik, Manish Gupta(✉), and Puneet Agrawal

Microsoft, Hyderabad, India
{srichandrac,rishablnu,kedharn,karrg,gmanish,punagr}@microsoft.com

Abstract. Query Auto Completion (QAC) plays a pivotal role in streamlining search engine interactions for users. By suggesting relevant query completions, QAC acts as a gateway to efficient search formulation, allowing users to swiftly express their search intent. Traditional QAC systems rely on curated tries derived from historical query logs to provide timely and context-aware query completions. In this study, we explore the integration of Large Language Model (LLM)-generated query completions into the QAC system. Broadly, the huge inference latency of LLMs renders them unsuitable as an *online* tool for improving quality of QAC which require rapid response times. Hence, our study investigates query completions using LLMs within two offline contexts: local intent and trending queries. We leverage GPT-3.5 to generate query completions and incorporate these completions into our existing production system. The goal is to improve relevance and address the coverage gap by providing relevant query completions to users. Over an extended period, we rigorously assessed user engagement with these GPT-driven completions by leveraging metrics such as click-through rates and key strokes saved per query.

Our insights shed light on how effectively GPT provided relevant query completions to users. Furthermore, we investigate the positive influence of GPT-generated completions on users' acceptance rates, contributing to the effectiveness of GPT-based query completions in real-world query auto-complete scenarios.

Keywords: Query Auto Completion (QAC) · Large Language Model (LLM) · Bing Autosuggest · User Engagement · GPT3.5

1 Introduction

Query Auto Completion (QAC) [10] mechanisms have revolutionized the search experience by predicting and suggesting completions to users' queries as they type. This predictive feature not only accelerates the search process but also

Q. Wen et al. (Eds.): Agent4IR 2025/2024, CCIS 2695, pp. 1–11, 2026.
https://doi.org/10.1007/978-3-032-11477-8_1

enhances user satisfaction by offering relevant query completions. Bing Autosuggest, a key component of Microsoft's Bing search engine, serves billions of keystrokes everyday across hundreds of languages in less than 100 ms.

Traditional QAC systems adopt a two-stage approach: Candidate retrieval and Candidate ranking [3]. In the candidate retrieval stage, a set of query completions is retrieved from a pool of query completions. This retrieval process is typically supported using a trie data structure, which records complete suggestions along with their historical popularity scores computed over a specific time window. When a user types a query prefix, the system traverses the tries to retrieve matching query completions. Various signals, such as region, language, location-based affinities, popularity, and user history, are used to rank the retrieved query completions. Finally, top-N ranked candidates are shown to the user. Additionally, there are various components to handle defects, perform spell correction on the user's prefix, and suggest non-prefix match query completions.

While these systems have proven effective in leveraging historical data for query completion, the emergence of Large Language Models (LLMs) [36] has opened up new possibilities for enhancing the relevance and scope of query completions. LLMs, such as OpenAI's GPT-3.5, can generate high-quality text based on contextual understanding, making them ideal candidates for enriching QAC systems with more relevant and diverse query completions. However, the inference latencies of these LLMs are much higher than the low latency requirements of QAC. QAC systems need to compete with the typing speed of the users. Hence, online generation of QAC suggestions using LLMs is not practically feasible.

In this paper, we explore the integration of GPT-3.5 [33] generated completions into the Bing Autosuggest QAC system in an offline manner. Addressing the challenges of presenting relevant local query completions and trending query completions has been complex within the QAC domain. Hence, we focus on these two specific contexts: (1) local intent queries, which relate to geographical or regional relevance, and (2) trending queries, which capture current topics of interest. These scenarios pose unique difficulties. For local intent queries, the expression of intent in query completions is limited. This limitation can be attributed to weaker signals from users and query log sparsity in particular regions. In the case of trending queries, we lack sufficient freshness signals due to a time lag in organic trending. By incorporating GPT generated completions tailored to these contexts, we aim to provide users with more relevant and engaging query completions, thereby enhancing their search experience.

2 Related Work

Query Auto Completion (QAC) is the first service that search users interact with. Ranking for QAC systems is typically supported by several modules such as most popular completion [32], time sensitive suggestions [25,30], location sensitive suggestions [1,31], ghosting [22], session co-occurrences [2] and non-prefix matches [8]. Besides these, suggestion ranking in QAC has also been studied using traditional Machine Learning (ML) methods [5,11,27] and deep learning (DL) methods like convolutional latent semantic model [18], LSTMs [29] and BERT and BART [19]. To make QAC more effective, personalization has been studied using traditional ML methods [24] as well as using DL methods like Hierarchical RNN Encoder-decoder [26] with pointer generator [4], GRUs with user and time representations [7] and Transformer-based hierarchical encoder [35]. While showing suggestions it is important to not show defective suggestions and prefixes. To avoid defects, researchers have used LSTMs for inappropriate query suggestion detection [34], A* search and Markov noisy channel models for online spell correction [6], and character RNNs [28]. Lastly, although generating suggestions using NLG methods can be complicated [20], there have also been efforts to generate suggestions using RNNs with character and word embeddings [21], LSTMs with subword embeddings [13], hierarchical RNN encoder-decoder [12,27] and next phrase prediction with T5 [14]. NLG methods conditional on trie suggestions have also been proposed [17]. Recently, there has also been some work on detoxification of suggestions [15,16]. Refer to [10] for more details about QAC systems. In this work, we focus on the local intent and fresh intent aspects of QAC systems.

3 Approach

In this investigation, we delve into two separate scenarios, one centering on local-intent queries and the other on trending queries. Customized prompts [23] were employed to address the unique requirements of each scenario.

Metrics including *Click Through Rate (CTR)* which is the proportion of clicks where query completions were displayed and *Keystrokes Saved Per Query (KSPQ)* indicating the fraction of keystrokes saved when users accept query completions, were tracked to assess the impact of GPT-3.5 generated completions on user behavior and search efficacy.

3.1 Local Intent Queries

Local intent queries refer to search queries that have a geographical focus, i.e., queries about local products, services, or locations. We meticulously selected location-based search queries, discerning them by their inclusion of phrases such as 'near me' or 'around me,' from one-month (August 2023) archive of historical Bing search logs. Among the extracted queries are examples like *doctors near*, *pizzahut near me*, and *plumbers around me*. Various filters were put in place to exclude irrelevant, harmful, or misleading queries. In total, we compiled ~200K English queries, originating from users across various locations in the world accessing Bing through different endpoints.

Employing GPT-3.5, we generated five completions for each query encompassing generic inquiries related to the input query. An excerpt from the customized prompt goes as follows: *"..You must generate relevant completions around generic questions related to the prefix and in the language same as the input language..”*

The inputs to GPT were Query, Language, Country and the prompt. It is expected to generate 5 relevant query completions. For instance, if the input query is *Dominos near* with *English* as Language and *India* as the country, the generated query completions are *dominos near me, dominos near me open now, dominos near me contact number, dominos near me menu, dominos near me delivery.* To control the model's generative behavior and prevent harmful outputs, we employed a combination of few-shot examples, strict prompts, and stop tokens.

These query completions were then ingested into Bing Autosuggest's candidate retrieval system alongside conventional query completions derived from historical query logs. All the generated query suggestions were assigned equal scores during their ingestion.

3.2 Trending Intent Queries

The analysis of trending intent queries is closely tied to real-time traffic dynamics. The emergence of a trending item is often accompanied by relatively weaker signals, resulting in a discernible gap in user experience, especially when the intent is a previously unseen [17] one and have not been a part of historical query logs. To address this, we leveraged the Bing News API[1] to procure real-time news articles by utilizing Real Time User Search logs across diverse categories and geographical regions.

The extracted articles encompass a spectrum ranging from the latest news articles specific to different regions to those directly associated with user queries related to real-time events, reflecting trending signals. Additionally, the dataset includes articles pertaining to popular categories such as Sports, Technology, Politics, Business, Entertainment, among others, which amount to ~10K articles world-wide, every hour.

To enhance user engagement and provide timely and relevant suggestions, we employed GPT-3.5, utilizing a customized prompt and the extracted news articles as input. The input titles are on an average eight words long and titles are partial descriptions which are roughly 35 words long. An excerpt from the used customized prompt goes as follows: “*...You must generate completions only on the main intent of the input news article. Extract important keywords, people, events and organization names and generate highly interesting user queries surrounding these extracted phrases and return them in a prioritized order based on the importance that users would prefer or engage with more...*”. The complete prompt used for this experiment was about 1100 tokens long.

The suggestions are generated by giving supporting documents to the GPT-3.5 model for each of the news categories. For suggestions adhering to the trending news topics, authoritative news articles along with the highly searched

[1] https://www.microsoft.com/en-us/bing/apis/bing-news-search-api.

queries (queries belonging to the top ten percent of the trending queries) pertaining to the news article is provided as a context to the GPT-3.5 [9], the addition of 8 to 10 news articles as supportive documents helps in validating the suggestion being generated is more related to the current real-world context along with the knowledge on which the GPT-3.5 model was trained on.

Trending topics can also be divided into two categories: previously seen topics and unseen topics. For previously seen topics, the generated suggestion may or may not overlap with the existing production suggestion set, but if there is an overlap, we promote these suggestions over other suggestions as it is likely to be more relevant to the user. If there is no overlap, we boost the ranking of these GPT-generated suggestions but at a lower rank than the overlapping suggestions.

For unseen topics, the generated suggestions help the users to get to their queries faster (as seen by the KSPQ metric). We add it in range such that these suggestions come up when user has entered a prefix which is long enough to match the context of the generated suggestions. These ranges are selected using the probability distribution of all the suggestions of a particular region, and we boost these suggestions towards the head of the distribution artificially.

4 Experiments and Results

4.1 Local Intent Queries

We deployed the refined QAC system to a representative user sample (Treatment). The time-period of this experiment panned over a week in Fall 2024 and for 10% of the Bing Users across all regions with their language set to English. Since the scale is of millions, any positive or negative movement in our key-metrics gave a strong indication of the user preferences. We then monitored their interactions during this period and compared them with a standard user group (Control). Encouragingly, we observed positive trends *CTR +0.06 % and KSPQ +0.14 %* supported by a *p-value of 0.049* in these metrics leading to the system's extension to all users. Among various regions, the United States has experienced the highest KSPQ increase of +0.32%.

Subsequently, we broadened this method to encompass all users and closely monitored their acceptance. Following a thorough evaluation spanning 10 weeks from September to Mid-November 2023, we meticulously assessed user engagement to gain insights into the integration of GPT-3.5 generated completions into the Bing Autosuggest QAC system. Table 1 illustrates the acceptance rate and effectiveness of these completions as perceived by users.

An acceptance rate of 43.33% (in contrast to the global rate 35.5 %) signifies a substantial improvement in the relevance and diversity of query completions. Notably, GPT-3.5 generated completions adeptly captured the nuanced intricacies of potential query completions, reflecting contemporary trends and thereby elevating the overall quality of QAC systems.

Table 2 compares Bing QAC query completions for the query *breakfast buffet near* by a user in *Hyderabad, India* before and after integrating GPT-generated

Table 1. Acceptance Metrics Overview for Local Intent Queries

Metric	Value
Total GPT-3.5 Completions Added	1 Million
Completions Shown to User[a]	0.90 Million
Completions Accepted by User	0.39 Million
Completions Acceptance Rate	43.33%

[a]This number can be less than the total completions added as all the completions are not guaranteed to come up alongside traditional completions from QAC system

Table 2. Comparison of Bing QAC Query Completions Before and After GPT Integration for the query *breakfast buffet near* by a user in *Hyderabad, India*

Without GPT completions	**With GPT completions**
..near me	..near me
..near my location	..near me cheap
..near winder	..near me halal
..near gateway of india mumbai	...near me price
..near danbury ct	...near me best rated
..near near 17 johnson rd	...near me with veg options
.. near clarks summit	..near my location
..near to bay florida	..near winder
..near 1001 hornby street	..near gateway of india mumbai
..near harlem and the kennedy	..near danbury ct

completions. On the left, we observe limited intents, while on the right, diverse intents—such as *cheap, vegetarian, and best-rated* are now provided by GPT.

Subsequent analysis delved into completions that garnered higher acceptance rates. Noteworthy findings revealed that completions pertaining to categories such as Food and Dining *(e.g., "pizza near me delivery," "restaurants near me open")*, Jobs and Employment *(e.g., "jobs near me hiring," "jobs near me part-time")*, and Services and Maintenance *(e.g., "plumbers near me reviews," "storage units near me cheap")* exhibited heightened acceptance and engagement from users. This could be attributed to their practicality and immediate need, frequent search queries, and their generic nature.

Conversely, completions within categories such as Events and Entertainment *(e.g., "indoor soccer party near me prices," "$1 movie theater near me tickets")* and Travel and Leisure *(e.g., "October getaways near me beach," "off-road riding areas near me for jeeps")* elicited comparatively lower user engagement, suggesting areas for potential refinement. This indicates potential areas for improvement, possibly due to their high specificity, strong locality focus, and perceived lack of immediate relevance to users' needs or interests.

These findings shed light on the nuanced dynamics of user engagement with GPT-3.5 generated completions within the Bing Autosuggest QAC system, providing valuable insights for enhancing the efficacy and relevance of query completions.

4.2 Trending Intent Queries

Subsequently, we conducted an assessment of the generated queries with trending intent and evaluated their impact on user experience and search behavior on a representative user sample (Treatment). The time-period of this experiment panned over a week in Fall 2024 and for 10% of the Bing Users across all regions and languages. We noted favorable enhancements in our primary metrics when comparing the treatment against the control. Specifically, we observed an increase in *CTR by +0.30 % and KSPQ by +0.12 %*, with a *p-value of 0.02*, showing a statistically significant movement in the metric, consequently signaling us to roll-out the enhanced experience for all users on a larger scale.

Table 3 briefly summarizes the acceptance rate as perceived by users after extending it to all users over a period of one month.

Table 3. Acceptance Metrics Overview for Trending Intent Queries

Metric	Value
Total GPT-3.5 Completions Added	1.5 Million
Completions Shown to User[a]	0.4 Million
Completions Accepted by User	0.3 Million
Completions Acceptance Rate	75%

[a]This number can be less than the total completions added as all the completions are not guaranteed to come up alongside traditional completions from QAC system

The table summarizes key metrics related to query completions and user interaction over a specified period. Out of a total of 1.5 million queries generated by the model, approximately 0.4 million queries were associated and displayed with user-searched intent. Notably, users accepted and engaged with a subset of these, totaling 0.3 million queries which amounts to ~75% acceptance. The metrics provide insights into the acceptance rate and user interaction with the generated queries, shedding light on the effectiveness of the system in aligning with user intent and preferences.

Upon scrutinizing the query completions generated and ingested into the system, with a foundation in trending news, we extracted valuable insights pertaining to user behavior in response to various completions. Table 4 outlines several behavioral findings derived from our analysis.

Table 4. Feedback on Query Categories

Category	Positive Feedback (Highly Clicked)	Neutral Feedback
Celebrity News	Upcoming celebrity movies, tv-shows, latest movie cast and reviews	Dresses worn on events, net worths, earning from movies, upcoming movie tickets
Politics	Election campaigns, Press Conferences, Summits, Bills	Document probes, Politician Biography, Politician A reacts on Politician B
Sports	Sources to watch live match, live scores, Team A vs Team B intents, playoffs, highlights, schedules	Sports person's vacation photos, net-worth, relationship status
General News	Large-scale crimes, stock prices and IPOs, Natural Disaster news, award nominations and winners	Other country's political or economic news, offers on tourism

Table 4 elucidates the query categories that garnered higher user engagement, click-through rates, and overall acceptance compared to other generated completions. Notably, the analysis underscores that news articles span diverse intents, some of which exhibit generic intent, thereby eliciting relatively lower user interest. Although GPT-3.5 excels in crafting highly engaging user queries, the instances labeled as "Neutral Feedback" in the above table represent cases that may be deemed less critical for display compared to other more compelling completions.

While the primary intent of a query may be trending, the related queries generated by the LLM might also include less popular intents or provide less interesting search results compared to other suggestions. Queries related to highly sought-after topics, such as live events, breaking news, or highly anticipated sports events, tend to be more useful for users. In contrast, queries that are only remotely related to the trending topic may receive less user engagement compared to other set.

The time gap between the user experiencing the generated suggestions and the trending signal received was about one hour. We showed users the generated queries before they actually started trending, reducing user efforts.

Through many few-shot examples and strict prompts we controlled the model's generative behaviour. We added Responsible AI checks asking model to not generate potentially harmful or offensive suggestions. We leveraged special stop tokens to prevent the model from hallucinating.

5 Conclusion

Our analysis of user engagement metrics indicated a positive impact of LLM generated completions on search efficiency and user satisfaction. Specifically, we observed higher click rates and keystrokes saved per query for LLM generated query completions compared to traditional completions, suggesting that users found these completions more compelling and useful. Additionally, qualitative feedback from users highlighted the value of GPT-3.5 generated completions in enriching their search experience and helping them discover relevant information more efficiently.

Moving forward, it is imperative to delve deeper into the underlying factors influencing user preferences and behaviors within each category. This may involve conducting user surveys to gain qualitative insights, as well as leveraging advanced analytics techniques to identify patterns and trends in user interaction data. Additionally, refining the GPT-3.5 model prompt by incorporating feedback from users and continuously updating it with the latest data will be crucial for enhancing the relevance and effectiveness of query completions across all categories and queries. By addressing these areas of improvement, we can further optimize a traditional QAC system and provide users with more tailored and satisfactory search recommendations.

References

1. Backstrom, L., Kleinberg, J., Kumar, R., Novak, J.: Spatial variation in search engine queries. In: Proceedings of the 17th International Conference on World Wide Web, pp. 357–366 (2008)
2. Bar-Yossef, Z., Kraus, N.: Context-sensitive query auto-completion. In: Proceedings of the 20th International Conference on World Wide Web, pp. 107–116 (2011)
3. Cai, F., De Rijke, M., et al.: A survey of query auto completion in information retrieval. Found. Trends® Inf. Retrieval **10**(4), 273–363 (2016)
4. Dehghani, M., Rothe, S., Alfonseca, E., Fleury, P.: Learning to attend, copy, and generate for session-based query suggestion. In: Proceedings of the 2017 ACM on Conference on Information and Knowledge Management, pp. 1747–1756 (2017)
5. Di Santo, G., McCreadie, R., Macdonald, C., Ounis, I.: Comparing approaches for query autocompletion. In: Proceedings of the 38th International ACM SIGIR Conference on Research and Development in Information Retrieval, pp. 775–778 (2015)
6. Duan, H., Hsu, B.J.: Online spelling correction for query completion. In: Proceedings of the 20th International Conference on World Wide Web, pp. 117–126 (2011)
7. Fiorini, N., Lu, Z.: Personalized neural language models for real-world query auto completion. In: Proceedings of NAACL-HLT, pp. 208–215 (2018)
8. Gog, S., Pibiri, G.E., Venturini, R.: Efficient and effective query auto-completion. In: Proceedings of the 43rd International ACM SIGIR Conference on Research and Development in Information Retrieval, pp. 2271–2280 (2020)
9. Goyal, T., Li, J.J., Durrett, G.: News summarization and evaluation in the era of GPT-3 (2022). https://arxiv.org/abs/2209.12356
10. Gupta, M., Joshi, M., Agrawal, P.: Deep learning methods for query auto completion (2023). https://link.springer.com/article/10.1007/s10586-021-03675-y

11. Jiang, J.Y., Ke, Y.Y., Chien, P.Y., Cheng, P.J.: Learning user reformulation behavior for query auto-completion. In: Proceedings of the 37th International ACM SIGIR Conference on Research & Development in Information Retrieval, pp. 445–454 (2014)
12. Jiang, J.Y., Wang, W.: Rin: reformulation inference network for context-aware query suggestion. In: Proceedings of the 27th ACM International Conference on Information and Knowledge Management, pp. 197–206 (2018)
13. Kim, G.: Subword language model for query auto-completion. In: Proceedings of the 2019 Conference on Empirical Methods in Natural Language Processing and the 9th International Joint Conference on Natural Language Processing (EMNLP-IJCNLP), pp. 5022–5032 (2019)
14. Lee, D.H., Hu, Z., Lee, R.K.W.: Improving text auto-completion with next phrase prediction. In: Findings of the Association for Computational Linguistics: EMNLP 2021, pp. 4434–4438 (2021)
15. Maheswaran, A., Maurya, K.K., Gupta, M., Desarkar, M.S.: DAC: quantized optimal transport reward-based reinforcement learning approach to detoxify query auto-completion. In: Proceedings of the 47th International ACM SIGIR Conference on Research and Development in Information Retrieval, pp. 608–618 (2024)
16. Maheswaran, A., Maurya, K.K., Gupta, M., Desarkar, M.S.: DQAC: detoxifying query auto-completion with adapters. In: Yang, D.N., et al. (eds.) PAKDD 2024. vol. 14650, pp. 108–120. Springer, Cham (2024). https://doi.org/10.1007/978-981-97-2266-2_9
17. Maurya, K.K., Desarkar, M.S., Gupta, M., Agrawal, P.: Trie-NLG: trie context augmentation to improve personalized query auto-completion for short and unseen prefixes (2023). https://link.springer.com/article/10.1007/s10618-021-00815-5
18. Mitra, B., Craswell, N.: Query auto-completion for rare prefixes. In: Proceedings of the 24th ACM International on Conference on Information and Knowledge Management, pp. 1755–1758 (2015)
19. Mustar, A., Lamprier, S., Piwowarski, B.: Using BERT and BART for query suggestion. In: Joint Conference of the Information Retrieval Communities in Europe, vol. 2621. CEUR-WS.org (2020)
20. Olteanu, A., Diaz, F., Kazai, G.: When are search completion suggestions problematic? Proc. ACM Human-Comput. Inter. **4**(CSCW2), 1–25 (2020)
21. Park, D.H., Chiba, R.: A neural language model for query auto-completion. In: Proceedings of the 40th International ACM SIGIR Conference on Research and Development in Information Retrieval, pp. 1189–1192 (2017)
22. Ramachandran, L., Murthy, U.: Ghosting: contextualized query auto-completion on amazon search. In: Proceedings of the 42nd International ACM SIGIR Conference on Research and Development in Information Retrieval, pp. 1377–1378 (2019)
23. Schacht, S., Kamath Barkur, S., Lanquillon, C.: Promptie - information extraction with prompt-engineering and large language models (2023). https://link.springer.com/article/10.1007/s11042-022-12733-4
24. Shokouhi, M.: Learning to personalize query auto-completion. In: Proceedings of the 36th International ACM SIGIR Conference on Research and Development in Information Retrieval, pp. 103–112 (2013)
25. Shokouhi, M., Radinsky, K.: Time-sensitive query auto-completion. In: Proceedings of the 35th international ACM SIGIR Conference on Research and Development in Information Retrieval, pp. 601–610 (2012)
26. Song, J., et al.: Hierarchical contextual attention recurrent neural network for map query suggestion. IEEE Trans. Knowl. Data Eng. **29**(9), 1888–1901 (2017)

27. Sordoni, A., Bengio, Y., Vahabi, H., Lioma, C., Grue Simonsen, J., Nie, J.Y.: A hierarchical recurrent encoder-decoder for generative context-aware query suggestion. In: Proceedings of the 24th ACM International on Conference on Information and Knowledge Management, pp. 553–562 (2015)
28. Wang, P.W., Zhang, H., Mohan, V., Dhillon, I.S., Kolter, J.Z.: Realtime query completion via deep language models. In: eCOM@ SIGIR (2018)
29. Wang, S., Guo, W., Gao, H., Long, B.: Efficient neural query auto completion. In: Proceedings of the 29th ACM International Conference on Information & Knowledge Management, pp. 2797–2804 (2020)
30. Wang, Y., Ouyang, H., Deng, H., Chang, Y.: Learning online trends for interactive query auto-completion. IEEE Trans. Knowl. Data Eng. **29**(11), 2442–2454 (2017)
31. Welch, M.J., Cho, J.: Automatically identifying localizable queries. In: Proceedings of the 31st Annual International ACM SIGIR Conference on Research and Development in Information Retrieval, pp. 507–514 (2008)
32. Whiting, S., Jose, J.M.: Exploring real-time temporal query auto-completion. In: DIR, pp. 12–15. Citeseer (2013)
33. Ye, J., Chen, X., et al.: A comprehensive capability analysis of GPT-3 and GPT-3.5 series models (2023). https://arxiv.org/abs/2303.10420
34. Yenala, H., Chinnakotla, M., Goyal, J.: Convolutional Bi-directional LSTM for detecting inappropriate query suggestions in web search. In: Kim, J., Shim, K., Cao, L., Lee, J.-G., Lin, X., Moon, Y.-S. (eds.) PAKDD 2017. LNCS (LNAI), vol. 10234, pp. 3–16. Springer, Cham (2017). https://doi.org/10.1007/978-3-319-57454-7_1
35. Yin, D., Tan, J., Zhang, Z., Deng, H., Huang, S., Chen, J.: Learning to generate personalized query auto-completions via a multi-view multi-task attentive approach. In: Proceedings of the 26th ACM SIGKDD International Conference on Knowledge Discovery & Data Mining, pp. 2998–3007 (2020)
36. Zhu, Y., Yuan, H., et al.: Large language models for information retrieval: a survey (2023). https://arxiv.org/abs/2308.07107

Enhancing Precision and Efficiency in Study Identification: A Human-AI Collaborative Approach with Domain Knowledge Expertise

Flavien Owolabi(✉)

Monash University, Clayton, VIC 3800, Australia
flavien.owolabi@monash.edu

Abstract. The exponential growth of digital libraries poses a serious challenge to the precision of study identification or search for systematic reviews (SR), which are acclaimed as the gold-standard of Evidence-Based decision-making. Recent advancements in SR search automation have explored semantic-driven approaches leveraging neural embeddings and Large Language Models (LLMs). However, the effectiveness of some of these methods relies on the constitution of a seed or quasi-gold set (QGS) of relevant studies. Furthermore, LLM-based keyphrase extraction algorithms like KBIR-inspect generate excessive and lengthy search terms requiring human judgement to decide on the most relevant and effective terms for query formulation. In an exploratory study, I investigated the impact of domain knowledge expertise (DKE) on the creation of the QGS and the effectiveness of automated study identification sub-tasks. I compared query results of an expert curated QGS to those obtained using randomly generated QGS. Results showed that queries informed by DKE achieved higher F1-score and recall rates (with an increase of 232.49% in F1score compared to random QGS). Despite the limitations of this study, using a domain specific gold set, these results highlight the importance of the human-in- loop approach to SR search automation when using neural-based semantic approaches. These findings have implications for both updating existing reviews and conducting new ones. This study lays the foundation for future research to further investigate the integration of human expertise and cutting-edge AI capabilities (e.g., LLM-based agents) to streamline SR search automation.

Keywords: Study identification · Domain knowledge expertise · Neural embeddings · Large language models · Systematic reviews · Human-AI collaboration · Search automation

1 Introduction

Systematic Reviews (SR) have been widely acclaimed as the gold standard to synthesize research evidence for evidence-based decision-making [7]. The SR process follows a rigorous methodology that is objective and reproducible to find and select primary studies [1, 26]. Searching for primary studies or study identification is a key step of the SR

Q. Wen et al. (Eds.): Agent4IR 2025/2024, CCIS 2695, pp. 12–24, 2026.
https://doi.org/10.1007/978-3-032-11477-8_2

process and is calibrated towards total recall [2, 17]. In the face of the rapid growth of digital libraries of scientific papers, the search task is becoming increasingly imprecise [8, 17].

The last two decades have seen a steady and fast growth of research output in terms of publications. In 2010, major medical repositories of scientific documents, such as Medline or Embase, held around 20 million publications with an average daily growth of 2000 papers [8]. By 2018, Scopus contained around 70 million publications covering journals, conferences' proceedings and books [16]. In 2022, the annual growth rate of digital libraries holding scientific publications was estimated at 5%. With such an exponential velocity of published peer-reviewed studies, synthesizing research evidence is not only imperative but it makes the synthesizing task more challenging than ever [2, 3, 6, 14, 16–19, 23]. As the volume of primary studies increases and search precision decreases, even the slightest improvements in search methods can make a significant difference [16].

There have been attempts to improve search precision. Most of them originated in medicine and account for the specificity of search in medicine which makes use of ontologies and specialized vocabularies (e.g. MeSH or UMLS) [8, 14, 17, 19, 27–29]. However, these approaches are not directly relevant to non-medical fields, making proposed solutions not easily transferable or applicable to non-medical fields. Furthermore, most of these approaches have been dominated by machine learning (ML) which requires a substantial amount of data for training to achieve quality results [14, 16, 22, 23]. Recent studies have featured semantic-driven approaches along with topic modelling and clustering to automate the sub-tasks of SR search [2, 14].

Search automation using semantic-driven approaches mainly neural embeddings and Large Language Models (LLMs), sometimes depending on the model, require the use of a seed or a quasi-gold set (a set of known papers deemed relevant for the review question) [2, 3, 14]. While some promising approaches to automate search advocate for human intervention to improve results, solutions based on semantic-driven approaches have so far featured no human intervention in any of three sub-tasks of search automation [2, 14]. It has been widely acknowledged that the search process is an iterative process by adding and removing search terms until satisfaction is reached [2, 5]. Therefore, solutions for search automation that feature Human-AI collaboration will be more attractive to potential users. In addition, semantic driven keyword/keyphrase algorithms often require human oversight to trim unwanted terms destined for query formulation.

This research aligns well with the growing recognition of the importance of human-AI collaboration in information retrieval tasks such as those involved in SR search automation. I hypothesize that domain knowledge expertise plays a crucial role in the constitution of the seed (or QGS) used for terms generation as well as the selection of effective terms for query formulation. By exploring this hypothesis, I aim to develop solutions for seamless integration of human judgment with AI capabilities.

2 Conceptual Definitions

The main goal of this study was to automate SR search or study identification for better precision. More specifically, I sought to improve search precision (proportion of retrieved studies that are relevant) compared to the manual approach. This was achieved through the use of ML and LLM-based keyword/keyphrase algorithms. Study identification involves three sub-tasks: search term generation, search term refinement (synonym expansion), and query formulation. Domain knowledge expertise (DKE) is applicable to all these three sub-tasks of search.

DKE is defined as the application of human judgment based on thorough knowledge and understanding of a subject area to guide AI capabilities in performing a particular task. In the context of SR search automation, DKE refers to having knowledge and understanding on a specialized scientific literature of SR automation in general and SR search automation in particular. This includes having a good grasp of theories, concepts, and best practices in study automation research.

Gold set or GS is the set of papers retained or set of papers which met the inclusion criteria of a review [2]. For any review, all the papers retained to create a review constitute a gold set.

Quasi gold set or QGS is a subset of papers, taken from the GS, deemed relevant for a review question [2]. Some of the AI tools used to automate search such as keyword/keyphrase extraction algorithms require a seed or set of relevant papers which are used to generate search terms. A QGS is used as a seed for search term generation.

Specifically, DKE can be applied to the following sub-tasks of SR search automation:

- creating a QGS or seed, a subset of papers from a gold set (GS), which is used to feed the ML and LLM-based keyword/keyphrase algorithms that generate search terms (search term generation)
- weeding out unwanted terms from terms generated by keyword/keyphrase algorithms and select synonyms (search term refinement)
- tweaking a query formulated by collapsing original clusters of terms joined by the logical operators (query formulation)

The value of DKE in these tasks underscores the need of incorporating the human-in-the-loop approach when using AI tools/techniques to automate these sub-tasks of SR search.

3 Related Work

Study identification is a crucial step in finding all the relevant studies to answer a review question. This process begins with generating search terms based on the review's key concepts [5] which are then structured in a Boolean query submitted to specific databases of scientific papers. The query undergoes iterative refinement through the addition of synonyms and removal of ineffective terms [17]. This manual process of optimizing query is time-consuming and resource-intensive [2]. Numerous attempts to automate this SR stage have yielded promising results with varying degrees of success.

Over the past decade, study identification (SR search) has gained prominence within the SR automation research community. Diverse approaches, both traditional and AI-powered, have been applied to automate three primary sub-tasks: search term generation, search term refinement, and query formulation.

Grames et al. introduced Litsearchr, an R package, which uses RAKE to extract keywords from titles and abstracts and authors keywords of a query result returned by an initial search [6]. Top keywords, selected through keywords co-occurrence and graph analysis, are combined to form a query. Other traditional text mining techniques for extracting search terms include TF-IDF, bag-of-words, and libraries like MetaMap [2, 12, 20, 22, 23, 27, 29]. The advent of Natural Language Processing (NLP) breakthroughs has elevated neural embeddings and LLMs to the forefront of search term generation techniques for study identification automation [2, 14, 29]. Litsearchr is computationally expensive as it relies on the entire query result rather than a limited number of papers or seed to generate search terms. It also requires R programming proficiency. Additionally, techniques like TF-IDF demand substantial pre-processing (e.g., tokenization, vectorization etc.) of the raw text.

Query refinement automation has primarily leveraged machine learning approaches with most of studies originating in medicine and allied fields [6–11]. This sub-task involves optimizing query terms through addition or removal of terms. Recently, LLMs (e.g., BERT and BART) as well as neural embeddings (e.g., Word2Vec and GloVe) have been used to generate synonyms to enhance query effectiveness [2, 3, 14, 21, 28]. A significant limitation of ML-based techniques is the dependency on abundant training data often unavailable. Training an LLM for domain-specific tasks, like medicine, is sometimes necessary [14, 29]. However, in general, these pre-trained LLMs can be used with no additional training for refining search terms with synonyms [2].

Query formulation automation has involved a combination of topic modelling and/or clustering techniques with modern NLP techniques (e.g., LLMs) [2, 14, 18, 30]. Transformer architectures like BERT were often used to enrich search terms by identifying synonyms or semantically related terms after initial extract using methods like TF-IDF or bag-of-words. Clustering techniques like K-means or agglomerative clustering were then applied to these terms to group them into semantically related clusters, which were used to formulate the query.

Few of proposed solutions offer a semi-automatic pipeline for study identification automation [6, 29]. The iterative nature of search within the context of SRs and the output from certain keyword/keyphrase extraction algorithms, like KBIR-Inspect [9] and KeyBERT [24] (via PatternRank), highlight the potential benefits of Human-AI collaboration. While these algorithms can effectively generate bi-grams and tri-grams, improving search precision and recall, they often produce excessive and lengthy keyphrases requiring human intervention.

4 Methods

4.1 Experimental Design and Hypothesis Formulation

Experiment Scope. I designed an experiment using a balanced design to: Analyze the results of automating SR search employing specific keyword/keyphrase extraction algorithms (e.g., KBIR-inspect [8], TopicRank [17]) for search term generation and enrichment, along with LLMs (e.g., Sentence-BERT [15]) combined with clustering techniques (e.g., k-means) for query formulation. The purpose is to evaluate the effectiveness (using mean F1-score) of the search strategy in a digital library (e.g., Scopus), from the perspective of the researchers, in the context of systematic review search strategy.

This experiment did not require any human involvement. The inputs used in the experiment were text data generated from titles and abstracts of selected studies.

Hypothesis Formulation. I hypothesized that query formulation using keyword/keyphrase extraction algorithms, along with the integration of domain knowledge expertise, will lead to a significant increase in the search effectiveness as measured by the mean F1-score of query results retrieved. More specifically, my interest was to compare the effectiveness of search precision (measured by mean F1-score) for expert QGS trimmed (1) against expert QGS untrimmed (2), expert QSG trimmed (1) against random QGS (3), and expert QGS untrimmed (2) against random QGS (3).

H1a: μ F1(QGS_1) > μ F1(QGS_2)
H1b: μ F1(QGS_1) > μ F1(QGS_3)
H1c: μ F1(QGS_2) > μ F1(QGS_3)

4.2 Gold Set (GS) and Quasi Gold Set (QGS)

I conducted a review on AI techniques/tools used for SR automation using a systematic approach. Search terms were generated based on the review question and used to search two online databases: Scopus and Web of Science. After deduplication, I screened over 1000 titles and abstracts using Covidence which uses a machine learning-assisted screening tool. This initial screening yielded 265 studies for full-text review. Applying the inclusion and exclusion criteria, 20 studies were retained and were used as the gold set for this study.

I randomly split the gold set into four equal parts using pandas' random samples function to create four quasi-gold sets of five papers each (random QGS). Based on my knowledge and understanding of the topic, I created an additional quasi-gold set of five papers (expert QGS). These five quasi-gold sets were used as inputs or seeds for automatic search term generation using keyword/keyphrase extraction algorithms.

4.3 Keyword/Keyphrase Algorithms' Selection

I selected five keyword/keyphrase extraction algorithms (KBIR-Inspect [9], TFIDF [4], KeyBert [24], TextRank [4], and TopicRank [4]) and I compared their respective performance using the expert QGS.

Table 1. Comparison of keyword/keyphrase algorithms

Metrics	KBIR	TFIDF	KeyBERT	TextRank	TopicRank
P@5	0.96	0.3	1	0.48	0.36
R@5	0.81	0.11	0.37	0.19	0.14
F1@5	0.87	0.17	0.54	0.27	0.20

Table 2. Average overlap score

Algorithm	Average Overlap Score
KBIR	0.3325
keyBERT	0.325
TopicRank	0.28
TextRank	0.22
TFIDF	0.1975

KBIR-inspect [8] an LLM-based keyword/keyphrase extraction algorithm is by far the best algorithm in terms of precision, recall, and F1-score (Table 1). I performed a text analysis looking at the overlap between these five algorithms (Table 2).

TextRank and TFIDF exhibit the lowest average overlap score which indicates their potential to enhance terms' diversity (Table 2). Despite this, TopicRank outperformed TFIDF (Table 1). Therefore, I chose TextRank and TopicRank to complement KBIR-inspect for keyword/keyphrase generation.

4.4 Experimental Design

To evaluate the impact of DKE on the search automation effectiveness, I designed an experiment involving five Quasi-gold sets (QGS) and three keyword/keyphrase extraction algorithms.

My goal was to semi-automate the three sub-tasks of SR search namely: search term generation, search term refinement, and query formulation. The first two sub-tasks were bundled into one process: search term generation and refinement using keyword/keyphrase algorithms selected in the previous sub-section.

With five QGS (one created manually, and the other four created randomly from the GS) and three algorithms (KBIR or 1, TextRank or 2, and TopicRank or 3), I created search terms for each QGS with the following combination as shown in Table 3.

Table 3. Experimental design: Combinations of five QGS and three algorithms for search term generation.

QGS	1	2	3	1 & 2	1 & 3	2 & 3	1 & 2 & 3
QGS expert	x	x	x	x	x	x	x
QGS random 1	x	x	x	x	x	x	x
QGS random 2	x	x	x	x	x	x	x
QGS random 3	x	x	x	x	x	x	x
QGS random 4	x	x	x	x	x	x	x

In total, I created seven sets of terms for the expert QGS and 28 sets of terms for the random QGS. Terms generated from the expert QGS were reviewed and refined to create the trimmed version of the expert QGS. This involved trimming lengthy terms and removing terms that were deemed unwanted, too generic or too specific to a paper. However, for query formulation, I experimented with both the trimmed and the untrimmed versions of the expert QGS.

For query formulation, I first converted terms generated into embeddings using Sentence-BERT. I then used k-means clustering to group each set of the 42 sets of terms into semantically related clusters to formulate queries. I experimented with two cluster numbers ($k = 2$ and $k = 3$) based on initial testing that indicated that three clusters were sufficient to capture the key topics of titles and abstracts for studies included in this review.

Queries with three clusters typically featured terms related to:

1. Systematic review in general (e.g., evidence synthesis, systematic literature review);
2. The specific task being automated (e.g., query transformations, automatic query generation, query formulation); and
3. The AI techniques used for automation (e.g., language models, Latent Dirichlet Allocation, text mining). However, in some cases, combining the latter two clusters into a single cluster proved more effective in retrieving relevant studies.

This clustering process resulted in a total of 84 queries submitted to the Scopus database via an API call. 84 datasets of titles and abstracts were retrieved and compared to the GS which serves as baseline.

The experiment was implemented using three custom Python modules specifically developed for this study:

1. Keyword Extraction Module: this module contains the code to run all five keyword extraction algorithms (KBIR, KeyBERT, TextRank, TopicRank, and TF-IDF). It also includes a functionality to create the random QGS from the GS
2. Query Formulation Module: this module loads and processes csv files containing the GS and the expert QGS. It formulates queries using the k-means clustering algorithm from the scikit-learn library [13], with search terms vectorized using Sentence-BERT [15]. The module also handles the submission of queries via an API call, saves search results into CSV format, and calculates key metrics for evaluation (recall, precision, F-score).
3. Data manipulation and statistical module: this module manipulates the evaluation results output from the query formulation module to create a combined dataset for analysis. It performs the hypothesis testing, including the selection and the execution of the appropriate statistical test.

The experiment as well as the data analysis, and data visualization were conducted within the Google Collaboratory environment. All three custom Python modules, the Google Collaboratory notebook detailing the experimental workflow, and the GS dataset (comprising titles and abstracts of the 20 retained studies) are made publicly available on GitHub.[1]

[1] https://github.com/LilySharon/sr-automatic-study-identification

4.5 Statistical Analysis

My overarching hypothesis was that query formulation using keyword/keyphrase extraction algorithms, along with the integration of domain knowledge expertise, would lead to a significant increase in search effectiveness as measured by the F1-score of query results retrieved. I compared search effectiveness for three groups of search terms: expert trimmed vs. expert untrimmed, expert trimmed vs. random, expert untrimmed vs. random.

I used the Shapiro-Wilk test to check if the Fx scores in each group (e.g., expert vs. random) were normally distributed. I also used the Levene's test to check if the variances of the F1 scores were equal across a pair of groups. The assumptions of normality and homogeneity were not met. I, therefore, used the Mann-Whitney test to compare the mean F1 score of a pair of groups.

5 Results

The results confirmed that query formulation using keyword/keyphrase extraction algorithms coupled with domain knowledge expertise yielded better queries with high recall and precision scores. Specifically, the mean F1 score for queries formulated using the expert QGS with trimmed search terms (0.1443) outperformed those formulated using expert QGS with untrimmed search terms (0.0278) and random QGS (0.0434) with untrimmed search terms. These differences were statistically significant, with p values less than 0.002 and 0.001 respectively. (Fig. 1). However, the difference in mean F1 score for queries formulated using expert QGS with untrimmed search terms compared to random QGS with untrimmed search terms was not statistically significant.

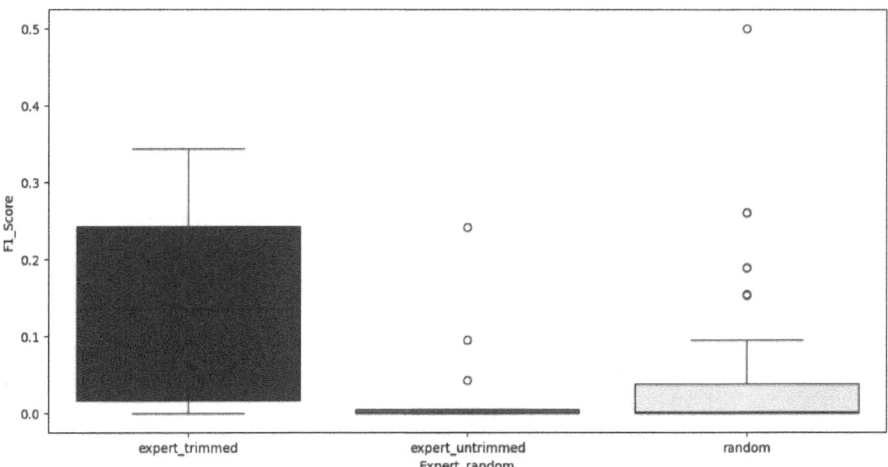

Fig. 1. Impact of domain knowledge expertise on queries' effectiveness using F1 score

In terms of recall, queries formulated with expert QGS with trimmed search terms and two clusters yielded better recall scores (Fig. 2).

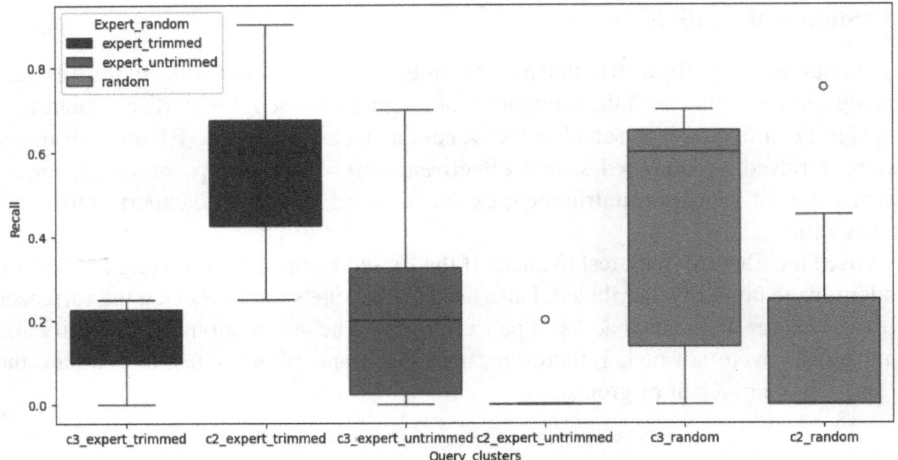

Fig. 2. Query performance by recall and query type

Among the algorithms tested, kbir (KBIR-inspect) stood out as the most effective for generating search terms with high recall and precision. Notably, nine out the ten queries with the highest recall scores (recall > .05) featured KBIR-inspect either alone or in combination with other algorithms (Table 4).

Table 4. Top 10 performing queries by recall and F1 score and associated algorithms.

Query Type	Recall	Precision	F1_Score	Algorithms
Baseline (Gold set)	100	0.0022	0.0044	None
c2_expert_trimmed	0.9	0.0073	0.0145	kbir, textrank, topicrank
c2_random	0.75	0.0087	0.0172	textrank, topicrank
c2_expert_trimmed	0.7	0.1228	0.2089	kbir, textrank
c3_random	0.7	0.0074	0.0146	kbir
c3_random	0.7	0.0073	0.0144	kbir, textrank
c3_random	0.7	0.0073	0.0144	kbir, topicrank
c3_expert_untrimmed	0.7	0.0028	0.0056	kbir
c3_random	0.7	0.0028	0.0056	kbir, topicrank
c3_random	0.7	0.0028	0.0056	kbir, textrank, topicrank
c2_expert_trimmed	0.65	0.1354	0.2241	kbir
c3_random	0.65	0.1111	0.1898	kbir

The best performing query, achieving a recall of 0.90, was formulated using two clusters and combining all three selected algorithms (Table 4). This query also ranked third in terms of F1 score (Table 4).

6 Contributions, Limitations and Future Directions

This study makes several key contributions to SR search automation research. First, it demonstrated the importance of DKE not only in the creation of the seed or QGS but also its impact on the overall search automation process. From the constitution of the QGS and through the three primary sub-tasks of study identification, DKE proved to have a cumulative positive effect in improving search precision without sacrificing recall using the semi-automated AI-powered pipeline.

More specifically, the experiment showed that the best-performing query, based on the expert QGS with trimmed search terms using only two clusters, outperformed both the untrimmed versions of the expert QGS and the randomly generated QGS. This query achieved the highest recall score of 90%, equivalent to retrieving 18 out of 20 relevant papers from Scopus alone. Complementary searches in other databases (e.g., WOS) and snowballing could potentially identify the remaining two papers and other relevant studies.

These findings have implications for both updating existing reviews and conducting new ones. The semi-automated pipeline, incorporating DKE, provides an efficient framework for updating reviews. To illustrate, if I were to update a current review after two years or more, I could use the existing pipeline by first creating a QGS from the GS. I would then use the QGS to generate search terms, trim them based on my expertise, and submit the query via an API call. Finally, I would screen the query results using an ML-screening tool. Noticeably, the best-performing query retrieved 2504 studies compared to 9109 studies retrieved by the original query showing significant efficiency gains in terms of precision for updating existing reviews.

For new reviews, even without a pre-existing GS, review experts could leverage their DKE to identify representative papers for the review and then utilize the semi-automated workflow to generate search terms, formulate and submit a query, and retrieve query results with fewer irrelevant papers. Submitting a query with the semi-automated pipeline via an API was computationally more efficient for the expert QGS with trimmed search terms (10 min) compared to the expert QGS with untrimmed search terms (103 min) on a Google Collaboratory T4 high-RAM.

Beyond the impact of DKE, this study also demonstrated the feasibility and the effectiveness of using ML-based and LLM-based algorithms for search term generation and enrichment. By combining multiple keyword/keyphrase algorithms, I captured a greater diversity of terms, allowing search terms' enrichment in a single step. This multi-algorithm approach also proved valuable by leveraging the strengths of both ML-based and LLM-based algorithms to generate related or synonymous terms. Furthermore, these algorithms streamlined the search process by automating tedious pre-processing tasks required to work with text (cleaning, tokenization, vectorization). While recent studies have explored the use of LLMs like BERT [2, 14, 29] for search term refinement or synonym generation, their implementation and fine-tuning can be complex and computationally intensive [15]. This study contributes to this evolving field of research by leveraging the start-the-art AI tools available to demonstrate the effectiveness of alternative approaches that can achieve similar or better results with greater efficiency.

Finally, these findings highlight the importance of keeping the human-in-loop approach to SR search automation. The superior performance of queries formulated based on the expert QGS with trimmed search terms highlights the value of human judgement in refining search terms. This aligns perfectly with the iterative nature of the manual approach to SR search and the preferences of potential users who may be reluctant to adopt fully automated approaches as proposed by some researchers [3, 23, 29]. This human-in-the-loop approach is also necessary because of the nature of LLM-based algorithms like KBIR-Inspect which generates excessive and lengthy terms requiring a human intervention to trim and exclude terms deemed inefficient for search precision. Potential users (reviewers) of search automation tools are unlikely to find fully AI-enabled automated approaches – with no human intervention – appealing. Integrating user input into the automated workflow process is likely to be more acceptable. Many existing SR automation tools fail to gain traction because they do not consider the desired features of potential users [25].

This study has some limitations. It would benefit from further validation on different types of gold sets from a variety of reviews from other non-medical domains. In its current version, this semi-automated pipeline for study identification requires Python programming proficiency, which limits its accessibility to those familiar using Python.

Future studies could investigate the potential of LLM-based agents to perform tasks like QGS creation or updating, which could surpass human experts in some scenarios. Therefore, exploring how the collaboration between AI agents and human experts could further enhance and streamline the search automation process is a very promising research avenue.

Additionally, a natural extension for this framework would be the integration of functionalities that would take the query results and apply other modern NLP techniques – LLM like Sentence-BERT [15] – along with advanced dimension reduction and clustering techniques – like UMAP [11] and HDBSCAN [10] – to create an efficient screening tool. Such addition, would pave the way for a comprehensive search tool that leverages DKE and AI agents to automate both study identification and selection.

Acknowledgments. This research is funded by a scholarship from Monash Data Futures Institute and the Faculty of Science at Monash University. I also thank my PhD supervisory team, including Dr. Matthew McGee, Professor Peter Bragge, and Dr. Brea Kunsler for their helpful comments and suggestions to improve this manuscript.

Disclosure of Interests The author has no competing interests to declare that are relevant to the content of this article.

References

1. Adam, G.P., Wallace, B.C., Trikalinos, T.A.: Semi-automated tools for systematic searches. Meta Res. Methods Protoc., 17–40 (2022)
2. Alves, L.F., Vasconcellos, F.J.S., Nogueira, B.M.: SeSG: a search string generator for secondary studies with hybrid search strategies using text mining. Empir. Softw. Eng. **27**, 5 (2022). https://doi.org/10.1007/s10664-021-10084-4
3. Badami, M., Benatallah, B. and Baez, M.: Systematic literature review search query refinement pipeline: incremental enrichment and adaptation. Leuven, Belgium, 129–146 (2022). doi:https://doi.org/10.1007/978-3-031-07472-1_8

4. Boudin, F.: pke: an open source python-based keyphrase extraction toolkit. Osaka, Japan, 2016, 69–73 (2016).
5. Bramer, W.M., de Jonge, G.B., Rethlefsen, M.L., Mast, F., Kleijnen, J.: A systematic approach to searching: an efficient and complete method to develop literature searches. J. Med. Libr. Assoc. **106**(4), 531–541 (2018). https://doi.org/10.5195/jmla.2018.283
6. Grames, E.M., Stillman, A.N., Tingley, M.W., Elphick, C.S.: An automated approach to identifying search terms for systematic reviews using keyword co-occurrence networks. Methods Ecol. Evol. **10**(10), 1645–1654 (2019). https://doi.org/10.1111/2041-210x.13268
7. Grant, M.J., Booth, A.: A typology of reviews: an analysis of 14 review types and associated methodologies. Health Inf. Libr. J. **26**(2), 91–108 (2009). https://doi.org/10.1111/j.1471-1842.2009.00848.x
8. Karimi, S., Pohl, S., Scholer, F., Cavedon, L., Zobel, J.: Boolean versus ranked querying for biomedical systematic reviews. BMC Med. Inform. Decis. Mak. **10**, 58 (2010) 1–20. http://www.biomedcentral.com/1472-6947/10/58
9. Kulkarni, M., Mahata, D., Arora, R., Bhowmik, R.: Learning rich representation of Keyphrases from text. Axiv., 1–16 (2022). https://doi.org/10.48550/arXiv.2112.08547
10. McInnes, L. and Healy, J.: Accelerated hierarchical density clustering, 33–42 (2017).
11. McInnes, L., Healy, J. and Melville, J. 2020. UMAP Uniform Manifold Approximation and Projection for Dimension Reduction. ArXiv e-prints (2020).
12. Mergel, G.D., Silveira, M.S. and da Silva, T.S.: A Method to support search string building in Systematic Literature Reviews through Visual Text Mining. Salamanca, Spain, 1594–1601 (2015).
13. Pedregosa, F., et al.: Scikit-learn: machine learning in python. J. Mach. Learn. Res. **12**, 2825–2830 (2011)
14. Pourreza, M., Ensan, F.: Towards semantic-driven boolean query formalization for biomedical systematic literature reviews. Int. J. Med. Inform. **170**, 1–10 (2023). https://doi.org/10.1016/j.ijmedinf.2022.104928
15. Reimers, N. and Gurevych, I.: Sentence-bert: Sentence embeddings using siamese bert-networks. 1–11 (2019).
16. Sarol, M.J., Liu, L. and Schneider, J.: Testing a Citation and Text-Based Framework for Retrieving Publications for Literature Reviews. 22–30 (2018).
17. Scells, H. and Zuccon, G.: Generating Better Queries for Systematic Reviews. Ann Arbor, MI, USA, 475–484 (2018). doi:https://doi.org/10.1145/3209978.3210020
18. Scells, H., Zuccon, G., Koopman, B.: A comparison of automatic Boolean query formulation for systematic reviews. Inf. Retr. J. **24**, 3–28 (2021). https://doi.org/10.1007/s10791-020-09381-1
19. Scells, H., Zuccon, G. and Koopman, B.: Automatic Boolean Query Refinement for Systematic Review Literature Search. (New York, NY, USA, 1646–1656 (2019). doi:https://doi.org/10.1145/3308558.3313544
20. Scells, H., Zuccon, G., Koopman, B. and Clark, J.: A computational approach for objectively derived systematic review search strategies. In: Advances in Information Retrieval: 42nd European Conference on IR Research, ECIR 2020, Lisbon, Portugal, April 14–17, 2020, Proceedings, Part I 42, 385–398 (2020).
21. Scells, H., Zuccon, G., Koopman, B. and Clark, J.: Automatic Boolean Query Formulation for Systematic Review Literature Search. 1071–1081 (2020). doi:https://doi.org/10.1007/s10791-020-09381-1
22. Scells, H., Zuccon, G., Sharaf, M.A., Koopman, B.: Sampling query variations for learning to rank to improve automatic Boolean query generation in systematic reviews. In: Proceedings of the Web Conference 2020, pp. 3041–3048 (2020)

23. Schmitz, T., Bukowski, M., Koschmieder, S., Schmitz-Rode, T., Farkas, R.: Potential technologies review: a hybrid information retrieval framework to accelerate demand-pull innovation in biomedical engineering. Res. Syn. Meth. **10**, 420–439 (2019). https://doi.org/10.1002/jrsm.1350
24. Schopf, T., Klimek, S. and Matthes, F.: PatternRank: Leveraging Pretrained Language Models and Part of Speech for Unsupervised Keyphrase Extraction. 243–248 (2022). doi:https://doi.org/10.48550/arXiv.2210.05245
25. Scott, A.M., Forbes, C., Clark, J., Carter, M., Glasziou, P., Munn, Z.: Systematic review automation tools improve efficiency but lack of knowledge impedes their adoption: a survey. J. Clin. Epidemiol. **138**, 80–94 (2021). https://doi.org/10.1016/j.jclinepi.2021.06.030
26. Thompson, J., Davis, J., Mazerolle, L.: A systematic method for search term selection in systematic reviews. Res. Synth. Methods. **5**(2), 87–97 (2014). https://doi.org/10.1002/jrsm.1096
27. Wang, J.Z., Zhang, Y., Dong, L., Li, L., Srimani, P.K., Yu, P.S.: G-bean: an ontology-graph based web tool for biomedical literature retrieval. BMC Bioinform. **15**, 1–9 (2014)
28. Wang, S., Li, H. and Zuccon, G.: MeSH Suggester: A Library and System for MeSH Term Suggestion for Systematic Review Boolean Query Construction. Singapore, Singapore, 1176–1179 (2023).
29. Wang, S., Scells, H., Koopman, B., Zuccon, G.: Automated MeSH term suggestion for effective query formulation in systematic reviews literature search☆. Intell. Syst. Appl. **16**, 1–14 (2022). https://doi.org/10.1016/j.iswa.2022.200141
30. Yu, Y.Q., Xu, E.L., Xia, E.Y., Huang, H., Hao, B.B. and Zhang, S.L. A Method to Accelerate and Visualize Iterative Clinical Paper Searching. 1332–1336. doi:https://doi.org/10.3233/shti190443

RAVEN: An Agentic Framework for Multimodal Entity Discovery from Large-Scale Video Collections

Kevin Dela Rosa(✉)

Cloudglue, San Francisco, CA 94114, USA
kdr@cloudglue.dev
https://cloudglue.dev

Abstract. We present RAVEN (**R**ecognition and **A**daptation of **V**ideo **EN**tities), an adaptive AI agent framework designed for multimodal entity discovery and retrieval in large-scale video collections. Synthesizing information across visual, audio, and textual modalities, RAVEN autonomously processes video data to produce structured, actionable representations for downstream tasks. Key contributions include (1) a category understanding step to infer video themes and general-purpose entities, (2) a schema generation mechanism that dynamically defines domain-specific entities and attributes, and (3) a rich entity extraction process that leverages semantic retrieval and schema-guided prompting. RAVEN is designed to be model-agnostic, allowing the integration of different vision-language models (VLMs) and large language models (LLMs) based on application-specific requirements. This flexibility supports diverse applications in personalized search, content discovery, and scalable information retrieval, enabling practical applications across vast datasets.

Keywords: Video Understanding · Information Extraction · Multimodal Retrieval

1 Introduction

The exponential growth of video content across platforms necessitates intelligent systems for organizing and retrieving information at scale. Video collections, spanning domains such as education, entertainment, and instructional content, present unique challenges due to their multimodal nature—needing to integrate visual, auditory, and textual data.

Recent advances in large language models (LLMs) and vision-language models (VLMs) enable new opportunities for multimodal understanding [7,11]. However, these methods typically process videos in isolation focusing on individual video comprehension, but lack mechanisms for collection-wide analysis. This capability is crucial for applications requiring a cohesive understanding of video collections rather than isolated clips.

Q. Wen et al. (Eds.): Agent4IR 2025/2024, CCIS 2695, pp. 25–32, 2026.
https://doi.org/10.1007/978-3-032-11477-8_3

RAVEN addresses these gaps with a model-agnostic design, allowing the integration of different VLMs and LLMs to suit domain-specific needs. This ensures adaptability to application-specific constraints such as computational efficiency or context length requirements. Our contributions include:

- A modular agentic architecture for video category cannonicalization and multimodal entity extraction.
- A synthetic example and schema-guided mechanism for contextual prompting.
- Demonstration of high-quality structured entity extraction across large-scale video datasets using popular off the shelf LLM/VLMs.

2 RAVEN Framework Overview

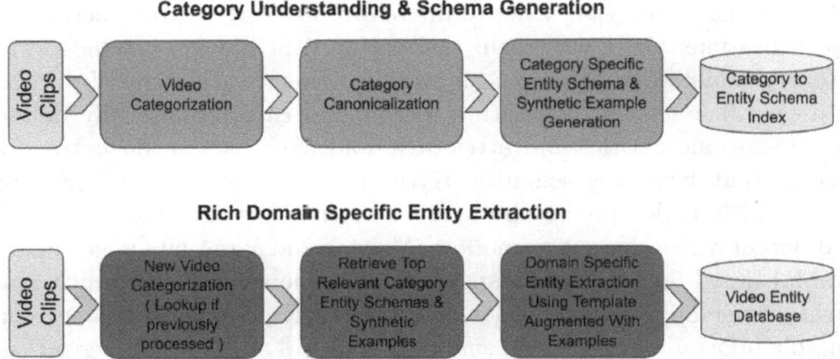

Fig. 1. RAVEN Framework Overview. The two main LLM/VLM driven flows: 1) Category Understanding & Schema Generation, 2) Rich Domain Specific Entity Extraction.

RAVEN operates as an adaptive agent for structuring multimodal video data, allowing one to operate on a collection of videos without necessarily having deep knowledge of the content contained within the collection but still allow for rich and consistent extraction of structured information across the provided videos. Our framework is comprised of two core stages: **Category Understanding**, and **Rich Domain Specific Entity Extraction**

Throughout these stages, as illustrated in Fig. 1, RAVEN uses a vision-language model for video-based tasks such as categorization and entity extraction, and a large language model for category name consolidation and generation. This frame work is designed to be model-agnostic as long as they handle comparable context lengths and support structured output JSON representations. For this study we used Gemini 1.5 Flash [3] as our VLM (using both visual video and audio input) and GPT-4o [8] as our general text LLM.

2.1 Category Understanding and Schema Generation

Video clips are first processed by the VLM to infer *video categories* and if desired extract *general-purpose entities* such as people, objects, and locations in same prompt. This process can optionally include user-provided prompts to steer categorization toward specific goals. Then the top occurring raw category names produced by the VLM are fed through an LLM to normalize and dedupe similar concepts to produce a canonical list of categories.

Using the canonical categories, the LLM generates a list of typical entities expected in that domain and produces corresponding *domain-specific entity schemas*. For each category, the generated schema includes:

- A list of *typical entities*.
- Attributes for each entity, with *descriptions* and *example* values.

The resulting entity schema lists per category are indexed by category name for later retrieval/lookup to help guide the actual entity extraction process. This modular design ensures adaptability for domain-specific needs, reducing manual intervention in schema development.

2.2 Rich Domain Specific Entity Extraction

Finally, video clips are processed again (as well as any desired additional clips) through the VLM. Using the assigned category from the first agentic flow, the system retrieves the most relevant schema based on *semantic similarity* of the original unnormalized category to the top matching canonical category name. The schema is integrated into a prompt template with example values, facilitating in-context learning to extract entities and attributes aligned with the schema's structure. The results are then persisted and indexed according to the needs of the downstream application.

3 Experiments and Evaluation

In this section we evaluate RAVEN's performance in its two core stages. We explore RAVEN's ability to infer video categories and generate schemas in Sect. 3.1, and in Sect. 3.2 investigate RAVEN's entity extraction capabilities.

3.1 Category Understanding and Schema Generation Analysis

To demonstrate RAVEN's effectiveness in category understanding and schema generation, we applied RAVEN on 1.5 million video clips (over 5000 h of footage) from the *Aligned Video Captions* dataset [4], and report results from this large scale qualitative exploration.

In Fig. 2 we show the distribution of video clips by inferred canonical category, the individual categories and spread align nicely with the source dataset which was sampled equally from YouTube's 15 top level categories.

Figure 3 presents the distribution of generic entity types and attributes, highlighting the flexibility of our framework to capture widely applicable generic entities with their associated attributes.

In Fig. 4, we demonstrate the framework's capacity for domain-specific extractions, exemplified by **How-To** and **History** videos, where we show the generated entity types and attributes, and their distributions in the dataset. Table 1 lists the most frequently extracted entity value for sample entity types in different domains.

Table 1. Sample entity values extracted for generic and domain-specific entities, showcasing RAVEN's versatility and domain adaptation

Category	Entity → Attribute	Top Values
Generic	Person → Role	speaker, host, child, listener, narrator, chef
Generic	Background → Setting	kitchen, living room, studio, office, city street
History	Event → Description	world war ii, apollo 11, vietnam war
History	Figure → Name	neil armstrong, abraham lincoln, adolf hitler
How-To	Tools & Materials → Type	knife, pot, bowl, camera, fishing rod
How-To	Techniques → Type	cutting, cooking, mixing, installation
Travel	Destination → Location	bangkok, new york city, tokyo, london

3.2 Domain Specific Entity Richness Analysis

For understanding the quality of entities extracted in the framework, we evaluated RAVEN on a sample of 300 video clips (∼10 s each) drawn from the *Aligned Video Captions* dataset [4]. The clips were selected from diverse categories, including *Travel*, *Education*, *History*, and *Instructional Content*, to ensure broad domain coverage. Each clip was processed through the RAVEN pipeline, starting with category inference and schema generation, followed by rich entity extraction.

To benchmark performance, we compared RAVEN against the following baselines using standard configurations:

- **NER on Speech:** Identifies entities from transcribed video speech, extracted automatically via AssemblyAI Speech-to-Text [1]. The named entities were extracted from the speech transcript using GLiNER [10].
- **OCR on Scene Text:** Extracts visible text from frames, capturing entities like place names, using EasyOCR [5].
- **Keyword Extraction from Visual Caption** Extracts keywords from the visual captions provided in Panda-70M [2].
- **YOLO Object Detection:** Detects general objects in frames, labeling them without contextual structure, using YOLOv10 [9] pretrained on COCO dataset [6].

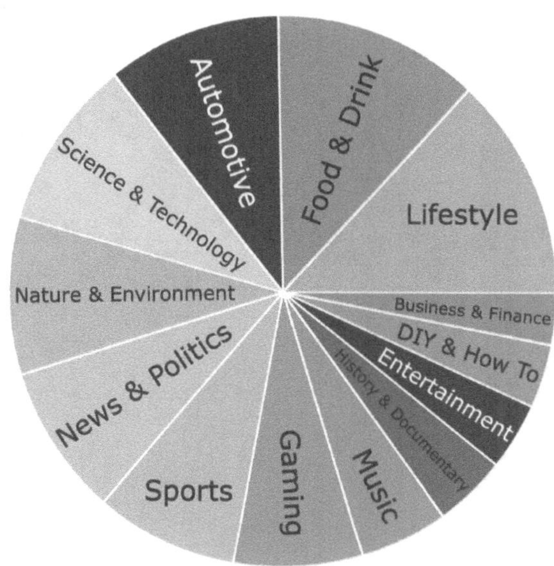

Fig. 2. Inferred canonical video category distribution.

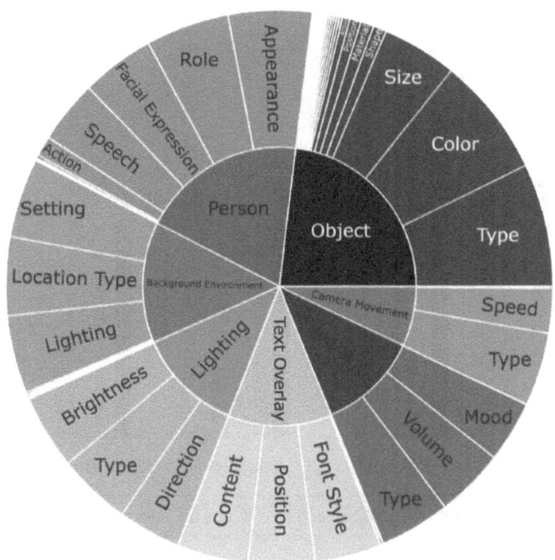

Fig. 3. Distribution of extracted structured attributes for each generic entity type.

The baseline methods were selected to evaluate different aspects of entity extraction. NER on Speech assesses linguistic entity recognition, OCR captures text from visual data, and visual captioning provides descriptive context. These

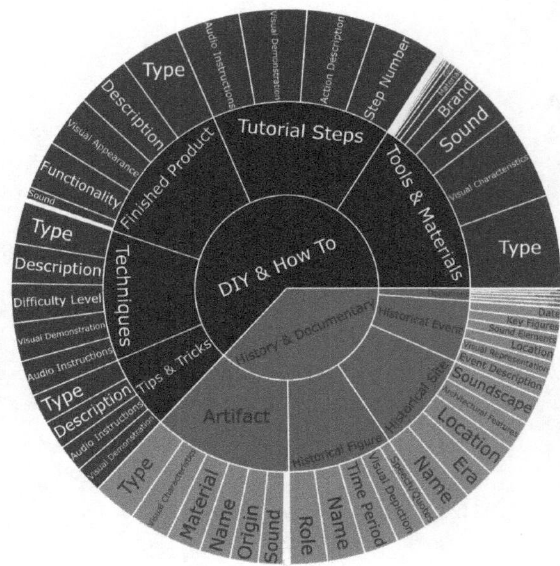

Fig. 4. Distribution of domain-specific entity types & attributes for How-To and History videos.

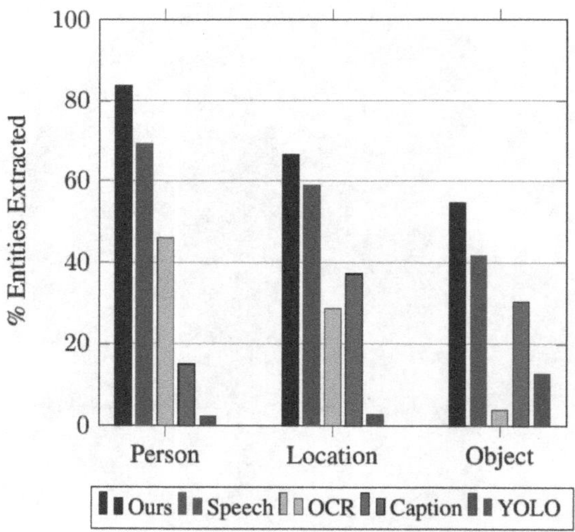

Fig. 5. Entity Recall by method. Each bar represents the proportion of entities extracted by each method for the Person, Location, and Object entity types respectively.

baselines highlight specific extraction limitations that our framework addresses comprehensively by operating in a multimodal fashion.

Table 2. Case study of extracted entities by method. This table illustrates the qualitative differences in entity extraction across methods for a sample video (e.g., a historical documentary about Abraham Lincoln)

Entity → Attribute	Ours	Speech	OCR	Caption	YOLO
Class Agnostic Generic Entity					
Person → Role	Abraham Lincoln → President	Abraham Lincoln; President Lincoln	PRESIDENT LINCOLN	Abraham Lincoln	Person
Person → Gender	Male	–	–	Man	–
Person → Age	Mid 50s	–	–	–	–
Person → Appearance	Wearing a Dark Suit	–	–	–	–
Person → Mood	Sad Reflective	–	–	–	–
Object → Type	Train Car	Train	–	Train Car	Train
Object → Color	Black & White	–	–	–	–
Object → Size	Large	–	–	–	–
History & Documentary Specific Entities					
Historical Event → Description	Surrender of the Army of Northern Virginia	Battle of Appomattox courthouse	–	–	–
Historical Event → Date	April 9, 1865	–	–	–	–
Historical Event → Location	Appomattox Courthouse, Virginia	–	–	–	–
Historical Event → Key Figures	Robert E. Lee, Ulysses S. Grant	–	–	–	–
Historical Site → Location	Lincoln Memorial → Washington, D. C.	Lincoln Memorial	–	–	–
Historical Site → Era	Early 20th Century	–	–	–	–
Historical Site → Architectural Features	Marble structure, neoclassical design	–	–	–	–

Figure 5 visualizes the ability of each method to extract class agnostic generic entities from various videos. Our framework shows a strong ability to extract *Person*, *Location*, and *Object* entities. The baselines often lacked multi-modal context and finer grained vocabulary to successfully extract entities presented in the videos. Figure 5 demonstrates RAVEN's ability to synthesize multimodal context, significantly improving recall rates over unimodal baselines.

Futhermore, we present a case study on a historical documentary to illustrate the qualitative depth of extracted entities, for both the class agnostic generic setting and the domain specific setting. Table 2 shows that our framework not only extracts named entities but also attributes, descriptions, and relationships (e.g., *Person* → *Role, Event* → *Location*). Baseline methods produce isolated labels limiting their utility in structured retrieval. The qualitative analysis (Table 2) demonstrates RAVEN's capability to extract fine-grained, contextual attributes compared to baseline methods, which often fail to capture relationships and attribute.

4 Conclusion

We presented RAVEN, an agentic AI framework for multimodal entity discovery and retrieval. By integrating category understanding, schema generation, and retrieval augmented & example-guided extraction, RAVEN addresses the challenges of structuring unstructured video content. RAVEN demonstrates the ability to extract structured, domain-specific representations, advancing multimodal information retrieval. Future work will explore extending RAVEN's capabilities to support entity relationships and optimizations for schema generation & signal extraction process. RAVEN's scalability and modularity position it as a versatile solution for evolving multimodal retrieval challenges.

References

1. AssemblyAI: Assemblyai speech-to-text (2023). https://www.assemblyai.com/products/speech-to-text. Accessed 07 Nov 2023
2. Chen, T.S., et al.: Panda-70m: captioning 70m videos with multiple cross-modality teachers. In: Proceedings of the IEEE/CVF Conference on Computer Vision and Pattern Recognition (2024)
3. DeepMind: Gemini (flash) (2023). https://deepmind.google/technologies/gemini/flash. Accessed 03 Nov 2024
4. Dela Rosa, K.: Video-enriched retrieval augmented generation using aligned video captions. In: Companion Proceedings of the ACM on Web Conference 2025. WWW '25, New York, NY, USA, pp. 1663–1667. Association for Computing Machinery (2025). https://doi.org/10.1145/3701716.3716890
5. JaidedAI: Easyocr: Ready-to-use optical character recognition with 80+ supported languages (2020). https://github.com/JaidedAI/EasyOCR. Accessed 04 Nov 2023
6. Lin, T., et al.: Microsoft COCO: common objects in context. CoRR abs/1405.0312 (2014). http://arxiv.org/abs/1405.0312
7. Maaz, M., Rasheed, H., Khan, S., Khan, F.S.: Video-chatGPT: towards detailed video understanding via large vision and language models (2024). https://arxiv.org/abs/2306.05424
8. OpenAI: Gpt-4 (2023). https://openai.com/research/gpt-4. Accessed 03 Nov 2024
9. Wang, A., et al.: Yolov10: Real-time end-to-end object detection. arXiv preprint arXiv:2405.14458 (2024)
10. Zaratiana, U., Tomeh, N., Holat, P., Charnois, T.: Gliner: generalist model for named entity recognition using bidirectional transformer (2023)
11. Zhang, H., Li, X., Bing, L.: Video-llama: an instruction-tuned audio-visual language model for video understanding (2023). https://arxiv.org/abs/2306.02858

Optimizing Educational Outcomes with AI-Agentic Information Retrieval

Elijah Dodson(✉), Charles Rizk, and Yetunde Folajimi

Wentworth Institute of Technology, Boston, MA 02115, USA
{dodsone,rizkc,folajimiy}@wit.edu

Abstract. Information retrieval is an essential aspect in many parts of human life through careers, health, economics, politics, and even through general usage. One commonality of each of these is education. With the rise in artificial intelligence over the past few years, this is even more true as many seek AI to support their educational needs. AI agents leverage large language models to improve this part of our lives, but how information is collected for the individual becomes a challenge. Each person has their own set of priorities and needs, especially within an educational environment and how that data is gathered and presented becomes important, especially for the unique individual. This paper will illustrate how Retrieval-Augmented Generation (RAG) combined with advanced prompt engineering can develop highly personalized and ethical educational experiences. We'll demonstrate techniques for retrieving highly relevant, contextual, and accurate responses correlating to a user's prompt. Moreover, we'll also address mechanisms for improving user prompts to enable more in-depth responses. Our results show the capabilities of advanced retrieval agents fostering more effective, ethical, and robust learning environments for a learner's education needs.

Keywords: Retrieval-Augmented Generation · Large Language Models · GPT · Prompt Engineering · Educational

1 Methodology

Our research focuses on Retrieval Augmented Generation (RAG) and smart prompt engineering to make education more personalized and effective. To improve how questions are asked, we use ethical AI tools to help get a better understanding of different strengths of models that we aim to create a new learning system that basically adapts to everyone.

This approach combines the power of advanced technology with a unique design to enhance educational outcomes by learning new responses for each individual learning needs. By focusing on different question design patterns and making AI more useful, we strive to make the impact of education more engaging, accessible, and effective for learners of all backgrounds.

Q. Wen et al. (Eds.): Agent4IR 2025/2024, CCIS 2695, pp. 33–38, 2026.
https://doi.org/10.1007/978-3-032-11477-8_4

1.1 Retrieval-Augmented Generation

Retrieval Augmented Generation (RAG) is a process that includes appending content on an LLM's prompt before generating a response [1]. It gives the LLM more information to work with which enables more thinking, consistency, and higher accuracy in results. This method is deemed useful for personalizing systems from data of preferences, feedback, open-source data, and more. The information retrieved can come from various sources including APIs, web scraped content, and datasets. With one's source of choice, the goal is to extract that data for raw visualization and then preprocess that data by removing noise. Once that phase is complete, the preprocessed data is formatted properly for insertion within a vector database. This vector database will store all data until triggered for retrieval when a user creates an input prompt.

1.2 Prompt Engineering

How a user writes their question, or prompt for a chat-bot is very important. This is especially true since the retrieval process aims to use our prompt as a baseline for finding relevant data. Moreover, we aim to retrieve the most amount of value from these chatbots and how much information is printed out in correlation to our prompt is significant. Adjustments could include additions of context, CoT(Chain-of-Thought), or each few-shot learning which could potentially improve overall task performance [2]. For instance, if a user prompted a chatbot by saying, "what is 1 divided by 0?", they may get a simple answer of that states this as impossible due to the answer being "undefined." On the other hand, if the user adds on to the prompt by saying, "what is 1 divided by 0? Explain your reasoning, especially with examples," this allows the AI model to think longer about what the user wants as an answer while providing more information that is effective towards their learning since keywords such as "reasoning" and "examples" suggest that the user wants to learn and needs more information.

Implementation

1.3 Implementation

Throughout the process of our work includes a series of implementation steps for welcoming a smooth flow of our engineered RAG design. Our dataset of choice consists of questions and answers from Wikipedia. The dataset is sourced from Hugging Face and developed by Rachael Tatman. We utilize this dataset as our core for evaluations while instantiating OpenAI's client for accessing their Generative Pre-trained Transformers (GPT) models, and Pinecone's functionality for storing vector embeddings of corresponding data. Various libraries/frameworks for support include the Natural Language Toolkit (NLTK), which provides a vast curation of techniques for natural language processing, and LangChain for support in AI and LLM development.

One crucial step includes preprocessing our dataset for usage in our GPT models. With the NLTK libraries, we're able to tokenize our data's text and remove stop-words, punctuation, and special characters. This removes any redundancy and unmeaningful characters and words that provide no value to our model. Removing unnecessary columns becomes key as well since we only need our input and output vectors, meaning that IDs are not needed. Next, we create individual documents with each question and corresponding answer to inject into the Pinecone database as vector embeddings. Alongside this, our preprocessed dataset of 918 samples is saved as a new CSV file for later evaluation on our GPT models.

1.4 Ethical Usage

As said before, it isn't difficult to utilize the services of AI, especially with large language models such as OpenAI's GPT models. Instead of blatantly inserting a question from an assignment, project, or anything needing an educational answer and retrieving the generated response, one should allow these models to serve as an additional source of information. OpenAI's ChatGPT is transparent when expressing how non-perfect their GPT models are and states, "ChatGPT can make mistakes. Check important info," which is found towards the bottom of their official ChatGPT website.

On top of that, large models end up containing many biases due to being trained on a specific target dataset Bender, E [3]. Our paper aims to showcase ways to guide our prompting towards a structure that allows our assistants to lead through constant guidance, feedback, and examples to help us think critically within AI domains. In addition, providing examples of ethical issues, such as plagiarism and over-reliance on AI, can also demonstrate how educators can position AI as an ethical tool and leverage it to support more responsible learning practices.

1.5 Model Significance

If a user isn't familiar with the characteristics of different AI models, then it may be harder to gauge which ones they would benefit from the most. Knowledge of these types of models could become a game changer, with certain models having more natural language understanding, and some others thinking more before they provide an effective response to improve their overall value. This is very true with OpenAI's GPT models. Whether it's OpenAI's GPT-4o model which is great for most tasks or their o1 series which excel in exceptional reasoning, reading into the needs for a specific task and what each model is capable of is what will allow a user to gain the most.

Although some of these models may need some initial costs, we aim to provide insight into their capabilities while being transparent, nonetheless. Moreover, we'll test various versions of OpenAI's GPT models in combination with other techniques to demonstrate the difference in results between the few.

2 Experimental Results

Our experimentation involved the development of a Retrieval-Augmented Generation framework and advanced prompt engineering methods in educational scenarios. Moreover, our experimentation proceeds with developing OpenAI's GPT large language models (LLMs) by comparing their original performance to their RAG enhanced versions.

2.1 Model Comparisons

We used OpenAI's GPT-4o and GPT-3.5 Turbo 0125 model and a selection of other LLMs using identical RAG frameworks [1]. The following metrics were used for evaluation:

Impact of Retrieval: Comparison evaluations of model performance before and after RAG implementation

Response Depth: Quality of detailed explanations generated by each model.

In general, the results showed that both models gained a considerable increase in performance accuracy when RAG was integrated. Initially, both GPT-3.5 Turbo 0125 and GPT-4o were capped at a performance ranging within the low to mid 40%, with GPT-4o resulting in around 46% and GPT-3.5 Turbo 0125 underperforming slightly in comparison by 42%.

Once our retrieval algorithm took effect, the evaluation process took longer due to appended retrievals being executed for additional context and Q&A relevant examples. Moreover, both models seen a considerable improvement in performance accuracy with GPT-4o increasing in performance by around 26% to about 58% in accuracy and GPT-3.5 Turbo 0125 increasing in performance by nearly 38% to an accuracy around 59%.

Although this is higher than GPT-4o's accuracy, this isn't considered as reliable as both models are still low in accuracy. Factors such as evaluation size, relevancy in RAG results, prompting, and method of comparing results need to be adjusted further. On the contrary, even with our algorithms not having the more ideal effectiveness, they still managed to improve our models with said limitations.

2.2 Effectiveness in Prompt Design

We ran a series of tests by changing the prompt format to ascertain what impact it had on depth and utility in the responses returned. Very short prompts had little effect on allowing our models to be seen as reliable. The same is said for very long, detailed prompts, which only proved to make interpretation of instructions more challenging, thus resulting in less reliable responses. Vaswani, A.'s transformer-based architecture further emphasizes the importance of such optimizations in producing coherent, detailed outputs [4].

3 Discussion

Results verify that the integration of RAG with smart prompt engineering can seriously improve learning outcomes. The key insights into our findings included the following:

3.1 Personalization of Learning

Incorporating RAG was a success with both GPT models improving in performance. Adjustments in prompts through giving each model a specific role and relevant examples through the support of Pinecone and LangChain with our RAG algorithm were proven to make an impact. Even so, our models should not be classified as reliable.

This is due to the low accuracies scores that were present even after our implementations. For a more personalized experience, a few considerations are needed. Firstly, our evaluation dataset was around 918 samples. For our use-case, this alone is too low for performance testing. The ideal goal includes evaluating our data on thousands to tens of thousands of samples.

Secondly, engineering our prompts further and how we deduce whether a response from GPT has the same meaning as the corresponding answer within our dataset is up to an effective implementation of a similarity comparison algorithm. In our case, we used cosine similarity with a threshold of 0.8 to compare these results.

This worked out in our favor, but it still becomes challenging to create an algorithm that can conclude whether "Yes" has the same meaning as "John's birthday is indeed July 5th" for a question that states, "Is John's birthday July 5th?", even though the meaning is the same for both responses.

3.2 Limitations and Challenges

While the proposed system excels in providing relevant responses, challenges remain:

In terms of computational resources, using RAG at scale requires extensive computing power. Retrieval of large data for our RAG implementation can become extremely expensive in terms of memory usage and processing time. In addition, when considering cost efficiency, this produces higher difficulty in assessing RAG performance on evaluations within smaller institutions. This limits the capacity to test broadly among significantly larger sets of data for analysis. Secondly, prompt effectiveness depends entirely on the user's experience and education with crafting detailed, task focused prompts.

LLMs catered to consumers for chatbot usage have ascertained a low difficulty rate. Their user friendly, simple usability can restrict critical thinking that prevents users from seeing value in designing these effective prompts. Also, the science behind prompt engineering and its value is not taught among consumers. This limitation relies on learned knowledge or one's natural skillset to either realize this idea through experience or act on it unconsciously due to familiarity from their own writing. Lastly, accessibility to large enough, publicly accessible data for educational use cases can be challenging. Researching related datasets can become time consuming and extensive. Some data may require permissions for usage while enough diversity in this data for our educational focus can be prevalent. Thus, due to computational expensiveness, education on prompt design, and accessibility to enough reliably large and diverse datasets, this makes it challenging to develop a more robust RAG system for our educational use case.

3.3 Ethical Considerations

Ensuring AI tools are used in an ethically responsible way; placing AI in a place of support rather than being the main problem solution reduces the risk of potential plagiarism and over-reliance, thus encouraging a sense of responsibility among learners.

4 Conclusion

Overall, this study has shown that the integration of Retrieval Augmented Generation with smart prompt engineering significantly enhances educational experiences by providing tailored, contextually relevant, and ethically grounded AI-driven solutions.

Our findings demonstrate the potential for AI to bridge gaps in traditional learning methods, empowering students to engage more deeply with their subjects while fostering critical thinking and ethical responsibility. With improved performances in both GPT models, we've proven that even slight adjustments with the implementation of advanced prompting through RAG and various methods are effective.

References

1. OpenAI Documentation: Optimizing LLM Accu-racy with Retrieval-Augmented Generation (RAG) (n.d.). Retrieved from. https://platform.openai.com/docs/guides/optimizing-llm-accuracy#retrieval-augmented-generation-rag.
2. Brown, T., Mann, B., Ryder, N., et al.: Language models are few-shot learners. Adv. Neural Inf. Process. Syst. (NeurIPS). (2020)
3. Bender, E.M., Gebru, T., et al.: On the dangers of stochastic parrots. In: Proceedings of the 2021 ACM Conference on Fairness, Accountability, and Transparency (FAccT) (2021)
4. Vaswani, A.: Attention is all you need. Adv. Neural Inf. Process. Syst. (2017)

Memory-Augmented Agent Training for Business Document Understanding

Jiale Liu[1](✉), Yifan Zeng[2], Malte Højmark-Bertelsen[3], Marie Normann Gadeberg[3], Huazheng Wang[2], and Qingyun Wu[1]

[1] Pennsylvania State University, State College, PA 16802, USA
jiale.liu@psu.edu
[2] Oregon State University, Corvallis, OR 97331, USA
[3] Beyond Work, Aarhus, Denmark

Abstract. Traditional enterprises face significant challenges in processing business documents, where tasks like extracting transport references from invoices remain largely manual despite their crucial role in logistics operations. While Large Language Models offer potential automation, their direct application to specialized business domains often yields unsatisfactory results. We introduce Matrix (Memory-Augmented agent Training through Reasoning and Iterative eXploration), a novel paradigm that enables LLM agents to progressively build domain expertise through experience-driven memory refinement and iterative learning. To validate this approach, we collaborate with one of the world's largest logistics companies to create a dataset of Universal Business Language format invoice documents, focusing on the task of transport reference extraction. Experiments demonstrate that Matrix outperforms prompting a single LLM by 30.3%, vanilla LLM agent by 35.2%. We further analyze the metrics of the optimized systems and observe that the agent system requires less API calls, fewer costs and can analyze longer documents on average. Our methods establish a new approach to transform general-purpose LLMs into specialized business tools through systematic memory enhancement in document processing tasks.

Keywords: First keyword · Second keyword · Another keyword

1 Introduction

Combing through large quantities of unstructured data remains a widespread challenge in enterprise operations, particularly in finance functions where efficient invoice processing represents a growing competitive advantage. Despite the prevalent adoption of digital invoicing, many organizations still grapple with the labor-intensive and error-prone task of manually extracting crucial identifiers from business transactions. For logistics companies manual extraction not only slows down operations but also introduces the potential for human error, leading to misrouted shipments and customer dissatisfaction.

Q. Wen et al. (Eds.): Agent4IR 2025/2024, CCIS 2695, pp. 39–53, 2026.
https://doi.org/10.1007/978-3-032-11477-8_5

Large Language Models have demonstrated remarkable capabilities in natural language understanding and processing [2,9,45]. Building upon these capabilities, agent-based systems that leverage LLMs for multi-step reasoning have emerged as a promising paradigm [13,41,42]. However, these systems face significant challenges when adapting to specialized contexts without manual tuning, as LLMs are not specifically trained to reason over business documents.

To address these limitations, we propose Matrix (Memory-Augmented agent Training through Reasoning and Iterative eXploration), a novel framework that enables LLM-based agents to learn and adapt from their experiences. Matrix incorporates a unique iterative self-refinement mechanism that allows agents to systematically improve their understanding of document structures and extraction patterns. The agents go through task exploration and optimization to iteratively improve their insights on the general task structure. The distilled actionable insights will be saved into a long-term memory of the agents and will guide future task solving attempts, leading to agent systems with better strategic reasoning and task solving capability.

In collaboration with Kuehne+Nagel, one of the world's leading logistics companies, we collect data from real-world business invoice documents and benchmark Matrix on the dataset. Specifically, we focus on the challenge of extracting transport reference numbers, which directly impact shipment routing and supply chain visibility. To facilitate broader research in this domain, we also introduce the first open-source dataset of anonymized business invoices. This benchmark poses a unique opportunity to evaluate agent system's adaptive learning capabilities in critical business context.

Our experimental results demonstrate Matrix's effectiveness after several epochs of optimization. The system achieves significant improvements through iterative learning and demonstrates strong performance. When compared to previous baselines, Matrix achieves 30.3% performance improvement compared to chain-of-thought prompting [40], surpasses vanilla LLM agents [41] by 35.2%, reflexion [32] by 27.28%. Further analysis on the system reveals that the learning process leads to significantly lower latency and costs, with a stronger capability in processing longer documents.

The key contributions of this work are threefold:

1. We propose a novel agent-based system for document reasoning and information extraction. It serves as a strong baseline in business cases.
2. We introduce Matrix, a novel paradigm that enables LLM-based agents to systematically learn and adapt to novel tasks through iterative self-refinement and experience-based memory updating.
3. We present the first open-source benchmark for evaluating document understanding systems on standardized business documents, facilitating reproducible research and practical applications in enterprise settings. This benchmark provides a challenging and practically relevant test for document reasoning and information retrieval capabilities in business contexts using agentic networks.

2 Related Work

Business Document Reasoning Benchmarks. While general-domain question answering datasets have driven advances in natural language understanding [1,4,17,20,30,36,47], they fail to capture the structured, transactional nature of business documents. Existing research on business document understanding mostly focus on vision-based information extraction from scanned copies [3,12,31,57], which emphasize layout understanding over semantic reasoning. These datasets, while valuable for OCR and structure recognition tasks, fail to capture the domain-specific patterns essential for business document processing. Moreover, text-based researches tend to use proprietary, undisclosed datasets [11,19,25,37], limiting reproducibility and real-world applicability. To address these limitations, we present a publicly available business invoice dataset derived from real-world transactions to facilitate research on practical business scenarios.

Prompt Optimization. Prompt optimization is a popular paradigm for maximizing LLM's performance to novel tasks without expensive model tuning by finding a optimal task prompt [7,27,28,59]. In-context learning emerges as a prominent paradigm, where a set of input-output pairs is provided as few shot examples to the LLM [5,8,24]. By automatically retrieving demonstrations from training set [21,22,55] or from adaptively annotated samples [34,44,52], they primarily treat demonstrations as static examples rather than distilled insights. In contrast to this line of work, our proposed paradigm aims to distill trajectories into generalizable heuristics.

Agent Learning. There has been efforts in exploring inference time performance boost since the emergence of Large Language Models [10,23,32,35, 40,48,49,58]. Recent works have extended this paradigm to agentic systems. Some works represent and learn the optimal workflow of agentic systems in the form of complex graphs [43,60], code [13], memory [39] and trees [51] to improve the system's performance on complex tasks, while others learns reusable tools [6,29,50,53] and experience [39,54] for agentic systems. Different from previous memory optimization based works, our proposed approach does not rely on any pre-defined in-context examples [54] and meanwhile guarantee the diversity and robustness of the learned memory.

3 Matrix: Memory-Augmented Agent Training Through Reasoning and Iterative eXploration

In this section, we begin with presenting the formulation of document reasoning, then introduce the framework of Matrix.

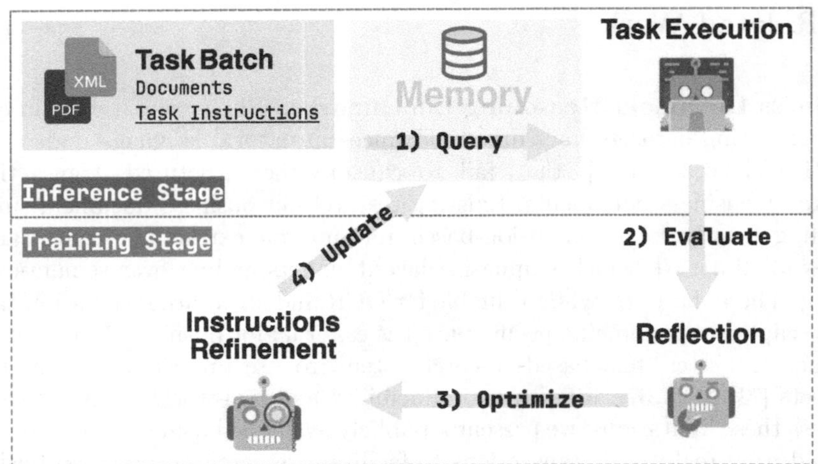

Fig. 1. The training and inference pipeline of Matrix.

3.1 Problem Statement

We begin with the formal definition of the document reasoning problem. In this problem, we assume the existence of a dataset for a given task, which consists of N instances of document, query, and answer triplets:

$$\mathcal{D} = \{(d_i, q_i, a_i)\}_{i=1}^{N} \tag{1}$$

where d_i represents a document, q_i is an associated query, and a_i is the corresponding correct answer. In the context of transport reference extraction from business documents, this formulation naturally maps to our task of interest: each document d_i represents a UBL invoice, the query q_i requests the location of the transport reference number, and the answer a_i is the correct reference number. This mapping allows us to frame the challenge of invoice processing as a structured document reasoning problem while maintaining the generality of our approach.

The overall goal in document reasoning is to train a system that learns a function $f : D \times Q \rightarrow A$, where D, Q, A represents the space of documents, queries, and answers respectively. For a given document d_i and query q_i, the agent generates an answer $\hat{a}_i$. The system's performance is evaluated based on the alignment between $\hat{a}_i$ and a_i.

We consider an agent with a long-term memory module M, which stores useful contextual information for reasoning. For a given query (d, q), the agent solves the task in an iterative manner. At each timestep t, the agent observes the current state o_t, takes an action a_t (which may involve interacting with the document or recalling information from memory), and then receives an updated observation o_{t+1}. This sequence of interactions produces a trajectory of observations and actions: $\tau = (o_0, a_0, o_1, a_1, \ldots, o_T, a_T)$. Finally, the agent produces the final predicted answer $\hat{a}_i$ through an answer extraction module $g(\tau)$, which takes into account the full trajectory τ of observations and actions across timesteps. Thus, the system can be viewed as generating the prediction:

$$\hat{a}_i = g(\tau) = f(d_i, q_i|M) \tag{2}$$

The formal goal of optimizing the agent's reasoning ability can be described via the objective:

$$\arg\min_{M} \mathbf{E}_{(d_i,q_i,a_i)\sim\mathcal{D}}[\mathcal{L}(f(d_i, q_i|M), a_i)] \tag{3}$$

where $\mathcal{L}$ measures the discrepancy between generated answer and the ground truth. In our case, $\mathcal{L}$ is defined using an exact match comparison.

3.2 Proposed Method

To optimize the objective in Eq. 3, we follow the paradigm of supervised learning and develop the dataset into train set $\mathcal{D}_{train}$ and test set $\mathcal{D}_{test}$ to approximate the inaccessible real data distribution. We train an optimal memory and test it on test task set. The pipeline is illustrated in Fig. 1.

Trajectory Sampling. We perform optimization by progressively updating the memory module M over multiple epochs. During each epoch, we sample a mini-batch of tasks from $\mathcal{D}_{train}$. For each sampled task (d_i, q_i, a_i), the agent interacts through a sequence of actions over time, forming a trajectory $\tau_i = (o_0^i, a_0^i, o_1^i, a_1^i, \ldots, o_T^i, a_T^i)$, where o_t^i and a_t^i denote the observation and the action at timestep t for the i-th task.

The trajectory continues until the agent either reaches a solution or the interaction exceeds a predefined maximum number of steps. We enforce a upper limit T_{max} to the total number of steps per task. This can constrain the token count in each trajectory, and allow us to increase the mini-batch size during optimization. By doing so, the optimizer can process more diverse tasks within a single batch, which increases the model's exposure to varied problem domains, leading to a more robust and generalizable memory M.

Reflection. Despite the impressive reasoning capabilities of LLM-based agents, they are prone to issues such as hallucination [15], factual errors [38], and reasoning failures [14]. In a limited number of steps, it is hard for agent to autonomously recognize and rectify its own mistakes without explicit self-correction mechanisms or auxiliary prompts [14,16,18,26,33]. To overcome this limitation, we introduce a Reflector module that operates as a post hoc evaluator of the trajectory. The reflector is provided with the trajectory τ_i and the ground truth answer y_i. It's task is to label the solution as "Correct/Incorrect" and identify the key steps where reasoning errors occurred or correct decisions were made that led to the proper solution. The reflection process is described as:

$$r_i = \mathrm{LM}_{\mathrm{reflect}}(\tau_i, y_i) \tag{4}$$

where $LM_{reflect}(\cdot)$ represents prompting a LLM to evaluate the trajectory. The reflection phase provides insights for refining the memory and improving the agent's task-solving strategy.

Optimization. To obtain an optimal solution in Eq. 3, an optimizer is needed that can generate new solutions based on performance measurement. The optimization problem operates on the space of natural languages, which perfectly paves the way for borrowing Large Language Models' exceptional capability in natural language understanding [46,53]. We propose a meta-optimizer with Large Language Models as the backend. The optimizer takes in three parts of information: (1) The execution trajectory of the agents in solving the tasks in the current training mini-batch (2) The assessment of each trajectory provided by the evaluator. (3) The current memory the agents operate on. Although the memory can be accessed by reading the prompt in the trajectory, we explicitly provide the current memory to let the optimizer progressively update the instruction based on the assessments for improvement. The optimization process can be formulated as:

$$M_{i+1} = LM_{optim}(\tau, y, M_i) \tag{5}$$

where $LM_{optim}(\cdot)$ denotes the process of LLM-based optimization.

4 Evaluations

4.1 Experiment Setup

Agent System. We experiment with refining a two-agent system. In the system, an assistant powered by LLM receives and analyzes the task and suggests code for execution, and a user proxy automatically executes code and provide the result. The conversation will end once a final answer is reached by assistant or the max number of conversation turns is reached. The system is implemented by AG2[1] (formerly AutoGen) [41].

Experiment Dataset. We evaluate our system on a collection of real-world Universal Business Language invoice documents, developed in cooperation with Kuehne+Nagel, one of the world's largest logistics companies. The primary task is to extract transport reference number from these documents. The dataset contains 764 valid invoice document and transport reference pairs. While the real world dataset contains sensitive customer data and cannot be released publicly, we provide an anonymized subset of the dataset and include the evaluation results in appendix.

The dataset presents several challenging characteristics that make it an ideal testbed for evaluating iterative learning capabilities. First, it requires specialized domain knowledge of business documents and terminology not commonly found in general language model training. Second, the hierarchical structure of UBL

[1] https://github.com/ag2ai/ag2.

documents and the significant variability in format and identification patterns pose substantial extraction challenges. Additionally, as a novel benchmark without prior literature coverage, this dataset offers unique opportunities to assess agents' adaptive learning abilities in a practical, high-stakes business context.

Evaluation Protocol. We report the success rate of the agent. The agent system is required to output the final result into a standardized format. The task is considered success when the output transport reference exactly matches the ground truth label. Given the diverse range of possible edge cases in the outputs, manually creating an extraction and comparison module may not cover all scenarios. Therefore, we employ a LLM judge [56] to compare the agent's output with the ground truth.

Baselines for Comparison. We compare performance with previous works, including prompting LLM using Chain of Thought [40], Reflection [32], and agent system with no memory [41].

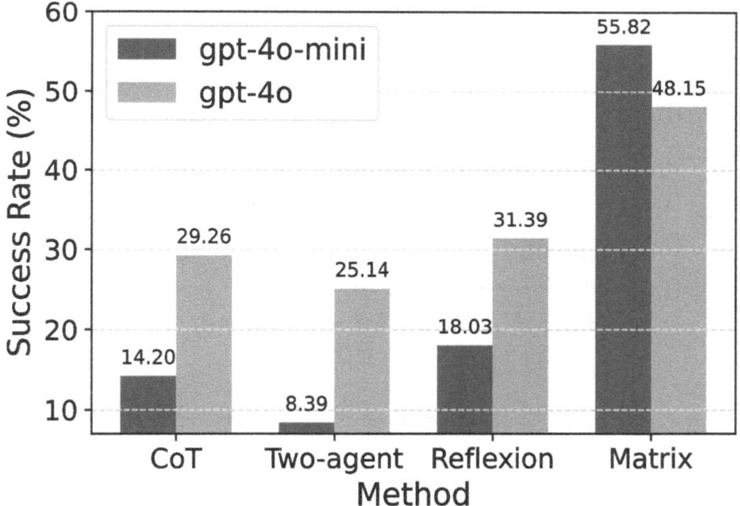

Fig. 2. Comparison between Matrix and baselines with `gpt-4o` and `gpt-4o-mini` as backbone model. Matrix leverages `gpt-4o` for optimization in both cases. Surprisingly, `gpt-4o-mini` performs better after optimization.

4.2 Main Results

We randomly select 60 samples from the dataset for training, the remaining 704 samples are reserved for testing performance. The maximum number of conversational turns between the assistant agent and the user proxy was capped at 5. The batch size was set to 14. That is, for each epoch, 14 tasks are sampled from training set and used for optimization. Since individual trajectories can become excessively lengthy, making the input to optimizer LLM larger than its context limit, we addressed this by truncating the batch to include only the largest number of trajectories that fit within the context limit. We set the backbone of the optimizer to `gpt-4o`. To maintain a fair comparison, we use `gpt-4o` for providing verbal feedback while running reflexion.

As shown in Fig. 2, Matrix performs the best across all previous benchmarks. Without the memory module, vanilla agent cannot perform well without any prior knowledge, even performing worse than directly prompting the language model with chain-of-thought. In this case, equipping the agent with code interpreter actually hampers the performance, as the agent will over rely on writing code to extract strings rather than using natural language to reason. With the proposed Matrix mechanism, the agent's task solving attempt is correctly guided by the long-term memory. The performance nearly doubles and outperforms all other methods.

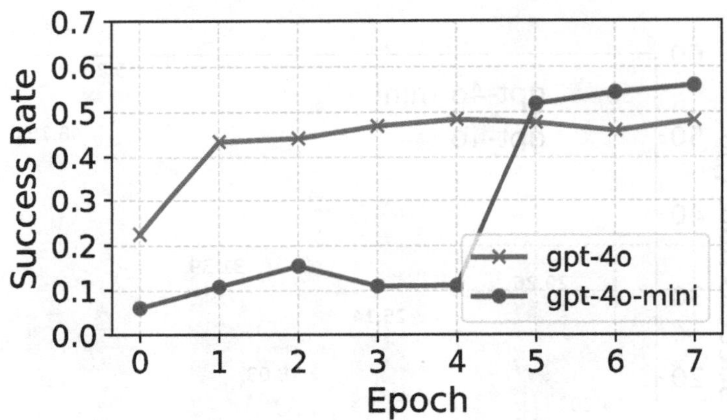

Fig. 3. Success rate comparison between agent with `gpt-4o` and `gpt-4o-mini` as backbone over epochs.

Figure 3 demonstrates the performance of the agent with respect to the number of optimization epochs. The performance shows a steady rise across all epochs. With no memory, the agent system's performance relies entirely on the capability of backbone LLM.

4.3 Analysis of the Optimized System

In this section, we analyze the metrics of the system across the optimization of memory across epochs. Specifically, we explore three metrics: (1) average api calls it takes to correctly solve a question. This affects the overall latency of the agent system. (2) average cost it takes to correctly solve a question. (3) the distribution of the length of the successfully solved documents.

Analysis of the Average Number of API Calls. As shown in Fig. 4, the agent system exhibits a notable decrease in the average number of API calls required to solve the document question-answering task. After equipping with the optimized memory, the average number of API calls reduces about 8.12% for `gpt-4o` backed agent, 21.3% for `gpt-4o-mini` backed agent. This reduction indicates that the system is able to handle the task more efficiently with fewer calls, reducing sources of latency but reaching a better performance.

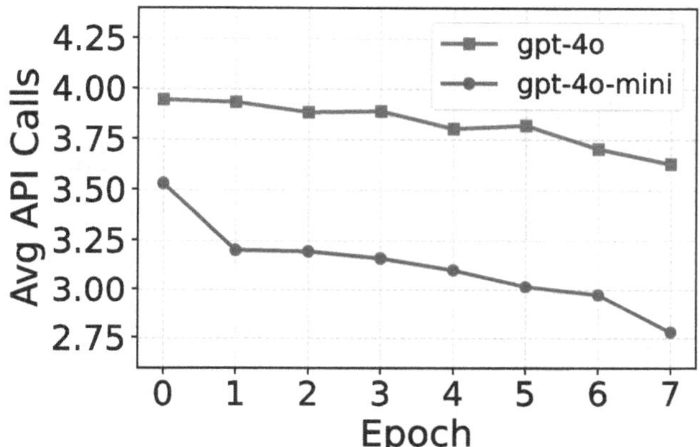

Fig. 4. Comparison of average number of API calls it takes to solve a task. The average number decreases steadily as the training goes on.

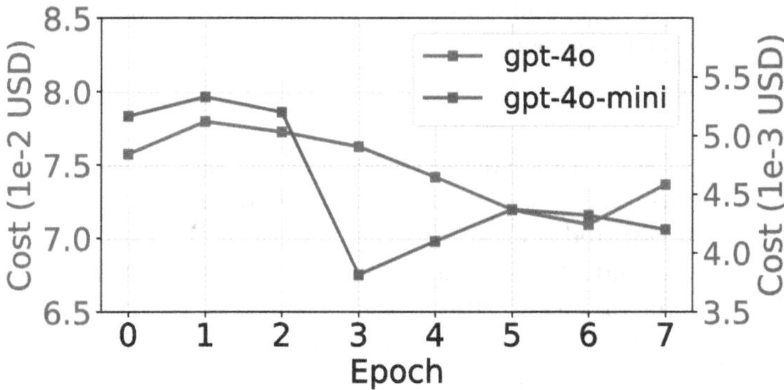

Fig. 5. Average cost of API calls after each epoch. The cost shows a decreasing trend as training goes on.

Analysis of the Cost. We plot the average cost of successfully solving a task after each epoch in Fig. 5. The cost increases during the early stages of optimization. This rise is attributed to the initial memory initialization and optimization phase. During this phase, while the memory is introduced to guide problem-solving, its content is not yet fully refined. As a result, the agent writes more lengthy code for trial and subsequently leading to higher API costs. As optimization goes on, the memory gets gradually refined and more comprehensive, the agent can solve the task more efficiently with less tokens. The slight uptick in at the end of the optimization suggests an adaptive process, where some rebalancing occurs after significant cost reduction. From a broader perspective, the overall trajectory suggests that optimization effectively lowers the long-term computational cost in solving tasks.

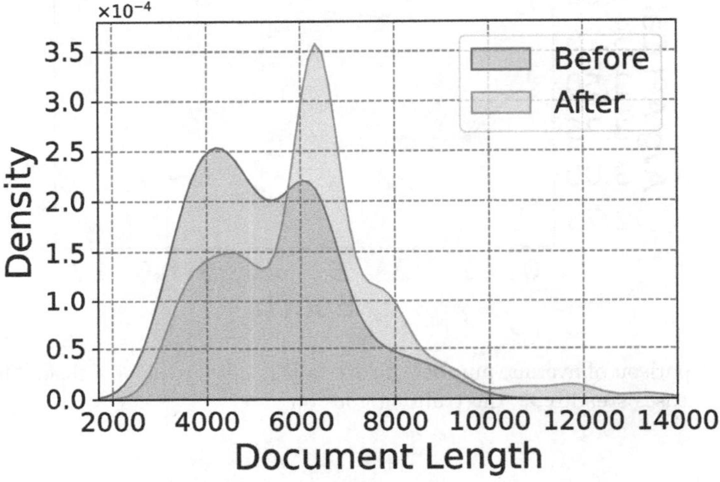

Fig. 6. Distribution of successfully analyzed document lengths before and after optimization with `gpt-4o` as backbone.

Analysis of the Length of Successfully Solved Documents. As shown in Fig. 6, the distribution of the successfully analyzed document lengths by `gpt-4o` backed agent is illustrated for two different stages of the agent's performance: before optimization and after optimization. The document length is measured by the total number of tokens after tokenization. The distribution of successfully analyzed document lengths shifts notably after optimization. Before training, the performance peaks for document lengths around 4000 and 6000 tokens, and significantly declines after 6000 tokens. After training, we observe a significant improvement, especially for longer documents, with the distribution peak shifting towards 6,000 tokens and an extended tail that stretches beyond. This pattern showcases the enhanced capacity of the agent system to handle larger documents after optimization, reflecting its improved robustness and processing efficiency for more complex and lengthy inputs. We observe similar pattern for `gpt-4o-mini` backed agent and therefore omit the plotting for brevity.

4.4 Optimization with Weaker Language Model

In the main experiment, we leveraged gpt-4o as backbone for optimization. We next explore the performance with smaller language model used as optimizer. Following the protocol in Sect. 4.2, we set the backbone of optimizer and agents both to gpt-4o-mini.

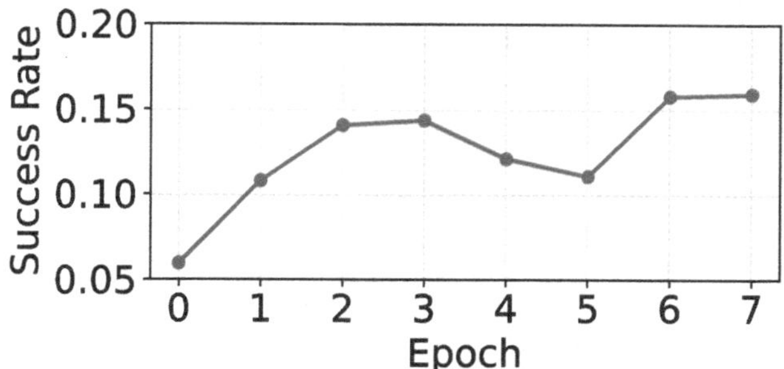

Fig. 7. Performance of the optimized agent across iterations using gpt-4o-mini as optimizer. The performance rises in the beginning, showing steady improvement in success rate over the first three epochs, but soon begins to stabilize and reaches a slightly higher plateau.

Figure 7 demonstrates how the performance changes with respect to the number of training epochs. Although gpt-4o-mini has weaker language understanding capability, it can still understand the task and summarize reuable patterns from the task trajectories. However, it misses some regular expression patterns, leading to a less comprehensive optimized memory. Therefore, the final performance of the optimized system remains limited.

Table 1. Comparison between Reflexion and Matrix with gpt-4o-mini and gpt-4o as backbone for verbal feedback and optimization. In both cases, Matrix performs better than Reflexion.

Optimizer LM	Reflexion	Matrix
gpt-4o-mini	12.64	**15.90**
gpt-4o	18.03	**55.82**

We then compare the performance between Matrix and Reflexion with gpt-4o-mini for optimization and providing verbal feedback, since they are both learning-based methods. The results, presented in Table 1, indicate that Matrix consistently outperforms Reflexion. Notably, the online algorithmic nature of Reflexion necessitates collecting verbal feedback for agents through trial and error on a task-by-task basis, which is inefficient as the number of test tasks increases. In contrast, Matrix leverages a generalized pattern learned from trajectories, enabling it to enhance performance in a more cost-efficient manner.

5 Conclusion

This paper explores the application of LLM agents for business document information retrieval, focusing on extracting transport references from invoices. To specialize LLM agents for this domain, we introduce Matrix, a paradigm enabling systematic learning through iterative self-refinement and memory updates. Real-world evaluations show Matrix distills actionable insights, outperforms baselines by large margin, and improves latency, cost, and document processing capability. This work reveals the potential of LLM agents for efficient, scalable enterprise document automation.

References

1. Abujabal, A., Saha Roy, R., Yahya, M., Weikum, G.: ComQA: a community-sourced dataset for complex factoid question answering with paraphrase clusters. In: Burstein, J., Doran, C., Solorio, T. (eds.) Proceedings of the 2019 Conference of the North American Chapter of the Association for Computational Linguistics: Human Language Technologies, Volume 1 (Long and Short Papers), pp. 307–317. Association for Computational Linguistics, Minneapolis, Minnesota (2019). https://doi.org/10.18653/v1/N19-1027
2. Achiam, J., et al.: GPT-4 technical report. arXiv preprint arXiv:2303.08774 (2023)
3. Antonacopoulos, A., Bridson, D., Papadopoulos, C., Pletschacher, S.: A realistic dataset for performance evaluation of document layout analysis. In: 2009 10th International Conference on Document Analysis and Recognition, pp. 296–300. IEEE (2009)
4. Bajaj, P., et al.: MS marco: a human generated machine reading comprehension dataset. arXiv preprint arXiv:1611.09268 (2016)
5. Brown, T.B.: Language models are few-shot learners. arXiv preprint arXiv:2005.14165 (2020)
6. Cai, T., Wang, X., Ma, T., Chen, X., Zhou, D.: Large language models as tool makers. arXiv preprint arXiv:2305.17126 (2023)
7. Cheng, J., et al.: Black-box prompt optimization: aligning large language models without model training. arXiv preprint arXiv:2311.04155 (2023)
8. Dong, Q., et al.: A survey on in-context learning. arXiv preprint arXiv:2301.00234 (2022)
9. Dubey, A., et al.: The llama 3 herd of models. arXiv preprint arXiv:2407.21783 (2024)
10. Guo, X., et al.: Embodied LLM agents learn to cooperate in organized teams. arXiv preprint arXiv:2403.12482 (2024)
11. Hamdi, A., Carel, E., Joseph, A., Coustaty, M., Doucet, A.: Information extraction from invoices. In: Lladós, J., Lopresti, D., Uchida, S. (eds.) ICDAR 2021. LNCS, vol. 12822, pp. 699–714. Springer, Cham (2021). https://doi.org/10.1007/978-3-030-86331-9_45
12. Harley, A.W., Ufkes, A., Derpanis, K.G.: Evaluation of deep convolutional nets for document image classification and retrieval. In: 2015 13th International Conference on Document Analysis and Recognition (ICDAR), pp. 991–995. IEEE (2015)
13. Hu, S., Lu, C., Clune, J.: Automated design of agentic systems. arXiv preprint arXiv:2408.08435 (2024)

14. Huang, J., et al.: Large language models cannot self-correct reasoning yet. arXiv preprint arXiv:2310.01798 (2023)
15. Ji, Z., Yu, T., Xu, Y., Lee, N., Ishii, E., Fung, P.: Towards mitigating LLM hallucination via self reflection. In: Findings of the Association for Computational Linguistics: EMNLP 2023, pp. 1827–1843 (2023)
16. Jiang, D., Zhang, J., Weller, O., Weir, N., Van Durme, B., Khashabi, D.: Self-[in] correct: LLMS struggle with refining self-generated responses. arXiv preprint arXiv:2404.04298 (2024)
17. Joshi, M., Choi, E., Weld, D., Zettlemoyer, L.: TriviaQA: a large scale distantly supervised challenge dataset for reading comprehension. In: Barzilay, R., Kan, M.Y. (eds.) Proceedings of the 55th Annual Meeting of the Association for Computational Linguistics (Volume 1: Long Papers), pp. 1601–1611. Association for Computational Linguistics, Vancouver, Canada (2017). https://doi.org/10.18653/v1/P17-1147
18. Kamoi, R., Zhang, Y., Zhang, N., Han, J., Zhang, R.: When can LLMS actually correct their own mistakes? A critical survey of self-correction of LLMS. arXiv preprint arXiv:2406.01297 (2024)
19. Krieger, F., Drews, P., Funk, B., Wobbe, T.: Information extraction from invoices: a graph neural network approach for datasets with high layout variety. In: Ahlemann, F., Schütte, R., Stieglitz, S. (eds.) WI 2021. LNISO, vol. 47, pp. 5–20. Springer, Cham (2021). https://doi.org/10.1007/978-3-030-86797-3_1
20. Kwiatkowski, T., et al.: Natural questions: a benchmark for question answering research. Trans. Assoc. Comput. Linguist. **7**, 453–466 (2019)
21. Liu, J., Shen, D., Zhang, Y., Dolan, B., Carin, L., Chen, W.: What makes good in-context examples for GPT-3? arXiv preprint arXiv:2101.06804 (2021)
22. Lu, Y., Bartolo, M., Moore, A., Riedel, S., Stenetorp, P.: Fantastically ordered prompts and where to find them: Overcoming few-shot prompt order sensitivity. arXiv preprint arXiv:2104.08786 (2021)
23. Madaan, A., et al.: Self-refine: iterative refinement with self-feedback. Adv. Neural Inf. Process. Syst. **36** (2024)
24. Min, S., Lewis, M., Zettlemoyer, L., Hajishirzi, H.: Metaicl: learning to learn in context. arXiv preprint arXiv:2110.15943 (2021)
25. Palm, R.B., Winther, O., Laws, F.: Cloudscan-a configuration-free invoice analysis system using recurrent neural networks. In: 2017 14th IAPR International Conference on Document Analysis and Recognition (ICDAR), vol. 1, pp. 406–413. IEEE (2017)
26. Pan, L., Saxon, M., Xu, W., Nathani, D., Wang, X., Wang, W.Y.: Automatically correcting large language models: surveying the landscape of diverse self-correction strategies. arXiv preprint arXiv:2308.03188 (2023)
27. Prasad, A., Hase, P., Zhou, X., Bansal, M.: Grips: gradient-free, edit-based instruction search for prompting large language models. arXiv preprint arXiv:2203.07281 (2022)
28. Pryzant, R., Iter, D., Li, J., Lee, Y.T., Zhu, C., Zeng, M.: Automatic prompt optimization with gradient descent and beam search. arXiv preprint arXiv:2305.03495 (2023)
29. Qian, C., Han, C., Fung, Y.R., Qin, Y., Liu, Z., Ji, H.: Creator: tool creation for disentangling abstract and concrete reasoning of large language models. arXiv preprint arXiv:2305.14318 (2023)
30. Rajpurkar, P., Zhang, J., Lopyrev, K., Liang, P.: SQuAD: 100,000+ questions for machine comprehension of text. In: Su, J., Duh, K., Carreras, X. (eds.) Proceedings

of the 2016 Conference on Empirical Methods in Natural Language Processing, pp. 2383–2392. Association for Computational Linguistics, Austin, Texas (2016). https://doi.org/10.18653/v1/D16-1264
31. Riba, P., Dutta, A., Goldmann, L., Fornés, A., Ramos, O., Lladós, J.: Table detection in invoice documents by graph neural networks. In: 2019 International Conference on Document Analysis and Recognition (ICDAR), pp. 122–127. IEEE (2019)
32. Shinn, N., Cassano, F., Gopinath, A., Narasimhan, K., Yao, S.: Reflexion: language agents with verbal reinforcement learning. Adv. Neural Inf. Process. Syst. **36** (2024)
33. Song, L., et al.: Adaptive in-conversation team building for language model agents. arXiv preprint arXiv:2405.19425 (2024)
34. Su, H., et al.: Selective annotation makes language models better few-shot learners. arXiv preprint arXiv:2209.01975 (2022)
35. Sumers, T.R., Yao, S., Narasimhan, K., Griffiths, T.L.: Cognitive architectures for language agents. arXiv preprint arXiv:2309.02427 (2023)
36. Talmor, A., Berant, J.: The web as a knowledge-base for answering complex questions. In: North American Association for Computational Linguistics (NAACL) (2018)
37. Tarawneh, A.S., Hassanat, A.B., Chetverikov, D., Lendak, I., Verma, C.: Invoice classification using deep features and machine learning techniques. In: 2019 IEEE Jordan International Joint Conference on Electrical Engineering and Information Technology (JEEIT), pp. 855–859. IEEE (2019)
38. Wang, C., et al.: Survey on factuality in large language models: knowledge, retrieval and domain-specificity. arXiv preprint arXiv:2310.07521 (2023)
39. Wang, Z.Z., Mao, J., Fried, D., Neubig, G.: Agent workflow memory. arXiv preprint arXiv:2409.07429 (2024)
40. Wei, J., et al.: Chain-of-thought prompting elicits reasoning in large language models. Adv. Neural. Inf. Process. Syst. **35**, 24824–24837 (2022)
41. Wu, Q., et al.: Autogen: enabling next-gen LLM applications via multi-agent conversation framework. arXiv preprint arXiv:2308.08155 (2023)
42. Wu, Y., et al.: Mathchat: converse to tackle challenging math problems with LLM agents. In: ICLR 2024 Workshop on Large Language Model (LLM) Agents (2024). https://openreview.net/forum?id=S7vIB7OGQe
43. Wu, Y., Yue, T., Zhang, S., Wang, C., Wu, Q.: Stateflow: enhancing LLM task-solving through state-driven workflows. arXiv preprint arXiv:2403.11322 (2024)
44. Wu, Z., Wang, Y., Ye, J., Kong, L.: Self-adaptive in-context learning: an information compression perspective for in-context example selection and ordering. arXiv preprint arXiv:2212.10375 (2022)
45. Yang, A., et al.: Qwen2 technical report. arXiv preprint arXiv:2407.10671 (2024)
46. Yang, C., et al.: Large language models as optimizers. arXiv preprint arXiv:2309.03409 (2023)
47. Yang, Z., et al.: HotpotQA: a dataset for diverse, explainable multi-hop question answering. In: Conference on Empirical Methods in Natural Language Processing (EMNLP) (2018)
48. Yao, S., et al.: Tree of thoughts: deliberate problem solving with large language models. Adv. Neural Inf. Process. Syst. **36** (2024)
49. Yao, S., et al.: ReAct: synergizing reasoning and acting in language models. In: International Conference on Learning Representations (ICLR) (2023)
50. Yuan, L., Chen, Y., Wang, X., Fung, Y.R., Peng, H., Ji, H.: Craft: customizing LLMS by creating and retrieving from specialized toolsets. arXiv preprint arXiv:2309.17428 (2023)

51. Zhang, J., et al.: Aflow: automating agentic workflow generation. arXiv preprint arXiv:2410.10762 (2024)
52. Zhang, S., et al.: Ideal: influence-driven selective annotations empower in-context learners in large language models. arXiv preprint arXiv:2310.10873 (2023)
53. Zhang, S., et al.: Offline training of language model agents with functions as learnable weights. In: Forty-First International Conference on Machine Learning (2024)
54. Zhao, A., Huang, D., Xu, Q., Lin, M., Liu, Y.J., Huang, G.: Expel: LLM agents are experiential learners. In: Proceedings of the AAAI Conference on Artificial Intelligence, vol. 38, pp. 19632–19642 (2024)
55. Zhao, Z., Wallace, E., Feng, S., Klein, D., Singh, S.: Calibrate before use: improving few-shot performance of language models. In: Meila, M., Zhang, T. (eds.) Proceedings of the 38th International Conference on Machine Learning. Proceedings of Machine Learning Research, vol. 139, pp. 12697–12706. PMLR (2021). https://proceedings.mlr.press/v139/zhao21c.html
56. Zheng, L., et al.: Judging LLM-as-a-judge with MT-bench and chatbot arena. Adv. Neural. Inf. Process. Syst. **36**, 46595–46623 (2023)
57. Zhong, X., Tang, J., Yepes, A.J.: Publaynet: largest dataset ever for document layout analysis. In: 2019 International Conference on Document Analysis and Recognition (ICDAR), pp. 1015–1022. IEEE (2019)
58. Zhou, D., et al.: Least-to-most prompting enables complex reasoning in large language models. arXiv preprint arXiv:2205.10625 (2022)
59. Zhou, Y., et al.: Large language models are human-level prompt engineers. arXiv preprint arXiv:2211.01910 (2022)
60. Zhuge, M., Wang, W., Kirsch, L., Faccio, F., Khizbullin, D., Schmidhuber, J.: Language agents as optimizable graphs. arXiv preprint arXiv:2402.16823 (2024)

Retrieval-Augmented Graph Explanation with LLM-Based Bayesian Inference

Jiaxing Zhang[1(✉)], Jiayi Liu[2(✉)], Dongsheng Luo[3], Jennifer Neville[2], and Hua Wei[4]

[1] New Jersey Institute of Technology, Newark, NJ, USA
jz48@njit.edu

[2] Purdue University, West Lafayette, IN, USA
{liu2861,neville}@purdue.edu

[3] Florida International University, Miami, FL, USA
dluo@fiu.edu

[4] Arizona State University, Tempe, AZ, USA
hua.wei@asu.edu

Abstract. Recent advances in Graph Neural Network (GNN) explanation focus on identifying faithful subgraph-based rationales for model predictions. However, due to the scarcity of annotated graph explanation datasets, existing methods are prone to learning bias, resulting in unreliable or overfitted explanations. In this work, we propose a novel agentic explanation retrieval framework, where a GNN-based explainer generates candidate explanations, and a Large Language Model (LLM) agent evaluates and ranks them based on prior domain knowledge. Specifically, we cast the explanation process as a Bayesian inference problem and embed the LLM as a Bayesian variational inference module, thereby mitigating the bias introduced by limited supervision. The LLM agent acts as an explanation grader in a retrieval-augmented loop, guiding the learning dynamics of the explainer through uncertainty-aware optimization. Theoretically, we show that the integration of the LLM agent preserves a lower bound on explanation quality, and empirically, we validate our approach on both synthetic and real-world graph datasets. Our contributions are twofold: (1) we introduce a novel view of explanation retrieval as an agentic process, and (2) we demonstrate how LLMs can be effectively employed as Bayesian evaluators to improve interpretability in graph-based systems.

Keywords: Explainable AI · Graph Neural Network · Learning Bias · Large Language Model · Bayesian Inference

1 Introduction

Interpreting the decisions made by the Graph Neural Networks (GNNs) [39] is crucial for understanding their underlying mechanisms and ensuring their reliability in various applications. As the application of GNNs expands to encompass graph tasks in social networks [15,33], molecular structures [8,32], traffic

Q. Wen et al. (Eds.): Agent4IR 2025/2024, CCIS 2695, pp. 54–74, 2026.
https://doi.org/10.1007/978-3-032-11477-8_6

flows [24,26,54,58], and knowledge graphs [43], GNNs achieve state-of-the-art performance in tasks including node classification, graph classification, graph regression, and link prediction. The burgeoning demand highlights the necessity of enhancing GNN interpretability to strengthen model transparency and user trust, particularly in high-stakes settings [29,63], and to facilitate insight extraction in complex fields such as healthcare and drug discovery [27,56,65].

Recent efforts in explaining GNN [30, 62,67] have sought to enhance GNN interpretability through multiple learning objectives, with a particular focus on the graph information bottleneck (GIB) method. GIB's goal is to distill essential information from graphs for clearer model explanations. However, the effectiveness of GIB hinges on the availability of well-annotated datasets, which are instrumental in accurately training and validating these models. Unfortunately, such datasets are rare, primarily due to the significant expert effort required for accurate annotation and occasionally due to the inherent complexity of the graph data itself. This scarcity poses a serious challenge, leading to a risk of learning bias in explaining GNN. Learning bias arises when the model overly relies on the limited available data, potentially leading to incorrect or over-fitted interpretations. We illustrate this phenomenon in Fig. (1) and provide empirical evidence in Fig. (4).

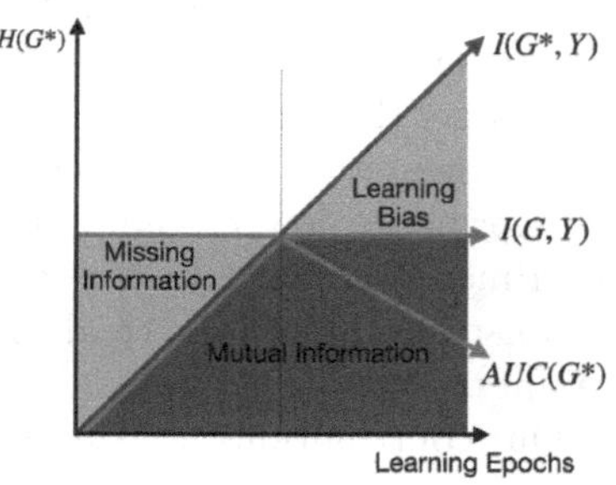

Fig. 1. Intuitive visualization of learning bias.

As demonstrated in the figures, learning bias becomes increasingly problematic as the model continues to train on sparse data. Initially, the model might improve as it learns to correlate the sub-graph G^* with the label Y, optimizing mutual information $I(G^*, Y)$. However, beyond a certain point, keeping optimizing $I(G^*, Y)$ leads to an over-reliance on the limited and possibly non-representative data available, thereby aggravating the learning bias. This situation is depicted through the divergence of mutual information and actual performance metrics, such as AUC, where despite higher mutual information, the practical interpretability and accuracy of the model decline.

To mitigate the learning bias, current models often stop training early, a practice to prevent the exacerbation of learning bias. However, this approach is inherently flawed, especially in real-world applications lacking comprehensive validation datasets, leading potentially to under-fitting and inadequate model generalization. This emphasizes the need for innovative approaches to model training and interpretation that can navigate the challenges posed by sparse ground truth in explaining GNNs.

We propose LLMExplainer, a novel **agentic explanation retrieval framework** for GNNs to overcome this limitation. Instead of viewing explanation as a purely generative task, we cast it as an *explanation retrieval process*, where a backbone explainer proposes candidate subgraphs and a **Large Language**

Model (LLM) agent evaluates their plausibility. We embed this agentic evaluation as a Bayesian Variational Inference module that approximates uncertainty over explanations in a wide array of backbone GNN explanation models, ranging from instance-level to model-level explanation approaches [7,30,40,44,53,62,64]. Concretely, our method employs a Retrieval-Augmented Generation-based LLM to assign graded scores to candidate explanations, which are then integrated into a weighted optimization loop. The LLM agent effectively acts as an external grader or retrieval filter that selects explanations best aligned with prior knowledge, thereby correcting learning bias induced by limited data.

We theoretically show that the Bayesian integration of the LLM maintains a performance lower bound that improves robustness against bias. Extensive experiments on five datasets—covering both synthetic and real-world scenarios—demonstrate that our method consistently enhances interpretability and training stability.

Our contributions are summarized as follows:

- We propose LLMExplainer, a general framework that reframes explanation as a retrieval process, embedding a Large Language Model as a Bayesian evaluator to mitigate learning bias and enhance GNN interpretability.
- We provide a theoretical analysis showing that our framework maintains a tighter lower bound than existing methods, and empirically validate its superior performance across five datasets.
- We are the first to integrate an LLM agent into the explanation loop as a retrieval-based uncertainty estimator, offering a new perspective for robust and agent-guided graph interpretability.

2 Related Work

Graph Neural Networks and Graph Explanations. Graph neural networks (GNNs) are on the rise for analyzing graph structure data, as seen in recent research studies [9,15,18]. There are two main types of GNNs: spectral-based approaches [5,22,46] and spatial-based approaches [1,12,59]. However, GNNs are still considered a black box model with a hard-to-understand mechanism, particularly for graph data, which is harder to interpret compared to image data. Many attempts have been made to interpret GNN models and explain their predictions [30,40,44,45,53,61,62,64]. These methods can be grouped into two categories based on granularity: (1) instance-level explanation, which explains the prediction for each instance by identifying significant substructures [40,62,64], and (2) model-level explanation, which seeks to understand the global decision rules captured by the GNN [2,30,44]. From a methodological perspective, existing methods can be classified as (1) self-explainable GNNs [2,10], where the GNN can provide both predictions and explanations; and (2) post-hoc explanations [30,62,64], which use another model or strategy to explain the target GNN. In this work, we focus on post-hoc instance-level explanations, which involve identifying instance-wise critical substructures to explain the prediction.

Bayesian Inference. [31] came up with the Bayesian Inference in general models, while [17] first applied Bayesian Inference to neural networks. Currently, Bayesian Inference has been applied broadly in computer vision (CV), nature language processing (NLP), etc. [16,34,42,60].

Bayesian Variational techniques have seen extensive uptake in Bayesian approximate inference. They adeptly reframe the posterior inference challenge as an optimization endeavor [49]. When compared to Markov Chain Monte Carlo, which is another Bayesian Inference method, Variational Inference exhibits enhanced convergence and scalability, making it better suited for tackling large-scale approximate inference tasks.

Due to the nature of Bayesian Variational Inference, it has been embedded into neural networks called Bayesian Neural Networks [17]. A major drawback of current Deep Neural Networks is that they use fixed parameter values, and fail to provide uncertainty estimations, resulting in a limitation in uncertainty. BNNs are extensively used in fields like active learning, Bayesian optimization, and bandit problems, as well as in out-of-distribution sample detection problems like anomaly detection and adversarial sample detection.

Large Language Model. Large Language Models (LLMs) have been widely used since 2023 [4,6,68]. Based on the architecture of Transformer [47], LLMs have achieved remarkable success in various Natural Language Processing (NLP) tasks. LLMs have spurred discussions from multiple angles, including LLM efficiency [28,48], personalized LLMs [13,35], prompt engineering [41,55], fine tuning [23], etc.

Beyond their traditional domain of NLP, LLMs have found extensive usage in diverse fields such as computer vision [11,51], graph learning [19], and recommendation systems [20,57], etc. By embedding LLMs into existing systems, researchers and practitioners have observed enhanced performance across various domains, underscoring the transformative impact of these models on modern AI applications.

3 Preliminary

3.1 Notations and Problem Definition

We summarize all the important notations in Table 3 in the appendix. We denote a graph as $G = (\mathcal{V}, \mathcal{E}; \boldsymbol{X}, \boldsymbol{A})$, where $\mathcal{V} = \{v_1, v_2, ..., v_n\}$ represents a set of n nodes and $\mathcal{E} \subseteq \mathcal{V} \times \mathcal{V}$ represents the edge set. Each graph has a feature matrix $\boldsymbol{X} \in \mathbb{R}^{n \times d}$ for the nodes. where in $\boldsymbol{X}$, $\boldsymbol{x}_i \in \mathbb{R}^{1 \times d}$ is the d-dimensional node feature of node v_i. $\mathcal{E}$ is described by an adjacency matrix $\boldsymbol{A} \in \{0, 1\}^{n \times n}$. $A_{ij} = 1$ means that there is an edge between node v_i and v_j; otherwise, $A_{ij} = 0$.

For the graph classification task, each graph G has a ground-truth label $\bar{Y} \in \mathcal{C}$, with a GNN model f trained to classify G into its class, i.e., $f : (\boldsymbol{X}, \boldsymbol{A}) \mapsto \bar{Y} \in \{1, 2, ..., C\}$. For the node classification task, each graph G denotes a K-hop sub-graph centered around node v_i, with a GNN model f trained to predict the label for node v_i based on the node representation of v_i learned from G. Since the node classification can be converted to computation graph classification task [62], we focus on the graph classification task in this work. For the graph regression task, each graph G has a label $\bar{Y} \in \mathbb{R}$, with a GNN model f trained to predict G into a regression value, i.e., $f : (\boldsymbol{X}, \boldsymbol{A}) \mapsto \bar{Y} \in \mathbb{R}$.

Informative feature selection has been well studied in non-graph structured data [25], and traditional methods, such as concrete autoencoder [3], can be directly extended to explain features in GNNs. In this paper, we focus on discovering important typologies. Formally, the obtained explanation G^* is depicted by a binary mask $\boldsymbol{M} \in \{0,1\}^{n \times n}$ on the adjacency matrix, e.g., $G^* = (\mathcal{V}, \mathcal{E}, \boldsymbol{A} \odot \boldsymbol{M}; \boldsymbol{X})$, $\odot$ means elements-wise multiplication. The mask highlights components of G which are essential for f to make the prediction.

3.2 Graph Information Bottleneck

For a graph G follows the distribution with $P_{\mathcal{G}}$, we aim to get an explainer function $\hat{G} = g_\alpha(G)$, where α are the parameters of explanation generator g. To solve the graph information bottleneck, previous methods [30,62,67] are optimized under the following objective function:

$$G^* = \arg\min_{\hat{G}} I(G, \hat{G}) - \lambda I(Y, \hat{G}), \hat{G} \in \hat{\mathcal{G}}, \tag{1}$$

where G^* is the optimized sub-graph explanation produced by optimized g, $\hat{G}$ is the explanation candidate, and $\hat{\mathcal{G}} = \{\hat{G}\}$ is the set of $\hat{G}$ observations. During the explaining procedure, this objective function would minimize the size constraint $I(G, \hat{G})$ and maximize the label mutual information $I(Y, \hat{G})$. λ is the hyper-parameter which controls the trade-off between two terms.

Since it is untractable to directly calculate the mutual information between prediction label Y and sub-graph explanation $\hat{G}$, to estimate the objective, Eq. (1) is approximated as

$$G^* = \arg\min_{\hat{G}} I(G, \hat{G}) - \lambda I(Y, f(\hat{G})), \hat{G} \in \hat{\mathcal{G}}. \tag{2}$$

Since G^* is generated by $g_\alpha(\cdot)$, instead of optimize $\hat{G}$, we optimize α^* with $h(\alpha, \lambda, G, f) = I(G, g_\alpha(G)) - \lambda I(Y, f(g_\alpha(G)))$, then we have $\alpha^* = \arg\min h(\alpha, \lambda, G, f)$, where $I(Y, G^*) \sim I(Y, f(G^*))$ and f is the pre-trained GNN model.

4 Methodology

Figure (2) provides an overview of the difference between the previous method and LLMExplainer. The previous method is shown on the left, while LLMExplainer, displayed on the right, integrates a Bayesian Variational Inference process throughout the architecture, with a large language model serving as the grader.

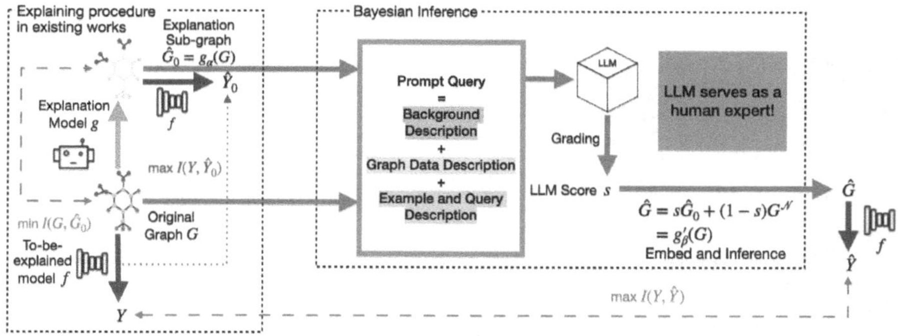

Fig. 2. Overview of our proposed LLMExplainer framework, which reframes graph explanation as an agentic explanation retrieval process. The left side shows the traditional Graph Information Bottleneck (GIB)-based explanation, where the explainer model g produces a candidate subgraph $\hat{G}_0 = g_\alpha(G)$, optimized to maximize mutual information with the predicted label $\hat{Y}_0 = f(\hat{G}_0)$ and minimize description length from the input graph G. We introduce a Bayesian Variational Inference module that incorporates a Large Language Model (LLM) as an external agent. The LLM receives a prompt comprising (i) task background, (ii) graph data description, and (iii) explanation query, and returns a score $s \in [0, 1]$ that reflects the plausibility of $\hat{G}_0$ as a valid explanation. The final explanation $\hat{G}$ is composed via interpolation: $\hat{G} = s \cdot \hat{G}_0 + (1 - s) \cdot G^{\mathcal{N}}$, where $G^{\mathcal{N}}$ is Gaussian noise. This adjusted explanation $\hat{G}$ is used for training and final prediction $\hat{Y} = f(\hat{G})$, with improved robustness and reduced bias. The right side thus depicts our agentic explanation retrieval loop guided by uncertainty-aware LLM feedback. Prompting details are provided in Fig. 3.

In our proposed framework, after generating the explanation sub-graph, we evaluate it through a Bayesian Variational Inference process, which is realized using a Large Language Model agent acting as a human expert. The enhanced explanation $\hat{G}$ is then produced using Eq. (7). Note that, with the introduction of the Bayesian Variational Inference process, the previous distribution for α in $g_\alpha(\cdot)$ will shift to β in $g'_\beta(\cdot)$. Finally, we optimize the explanation model with new $I(G, \hat{G})$ and $I(Y, \hat{Y})$ within $h(\beta, \lambda, G, f)$. We provide detailed formulas for the LLM-based Bayesian Variational Inference in Sect. 4.1 and a detailed prompt-building procedure in Sect. 4.2. Our training procedure is provided in Algorithm. (1).

4.1 Bayesian Variational Inference In Explainer

In this section, we demonstrate how incorporating Bayesian Variational Inference (VI) into the GNN Explainer addresses the learning bias problem. Specifically, we adopt RAG-LLM as a Bayesian Variational Inference Network. Our approach begins by injecting knowledge learned from the LLM as a weighted score while introducing graph noise to the remaining objective. Instead of utilizing weighted noise or gradient noise [36], we opt for random Gaussian noise [17]. This section

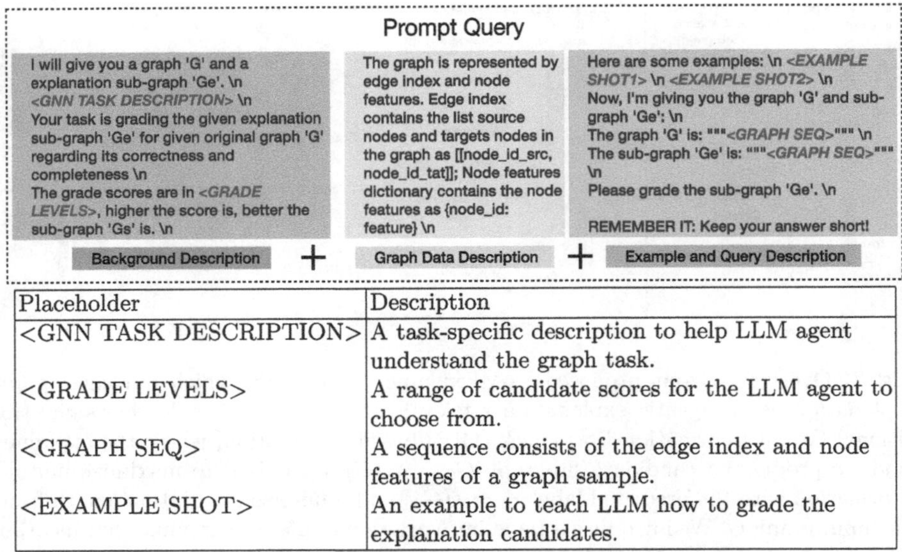

Placeholder	Description
<GNN TASK DESCRIPTION>	A task-specific description to help LLM agent understand the graph task.
<GRADE LEVELS>	A range of candidate scores for the LLM agent to choose from.
<GRAPH SEQ>	A sequence consists of the edge index and node features of a graph sample.
<EXAMPLE SHOT>	An example to teach LLM how to grade the explanation candidates.

Fig. 3. The prompt construction of LLMExplainer in Bayesian Variational Inference Process. For an original graph G and sub-graph explanation candidate $\hat{G}$, namely 'G' and 'Ge' in text, Large Language Models could tackle and reason the graph tasks with commonsense and expert knowledge, then grade the explanation candidate sub-graph. The placeholders would be replaced with the full text during prompting. Their usage is shown in the table.

highlights the effectiveness of incorporating the Bayesian Variational Inference Network in mitigating the learning bias problem. The feasibility of employing RAG-LLM as a Bayesian Variational Inference Network is discussed further in Sect. 4.2.

Problem 1. (Knowledge Enhanced Post-hoc Instance-level GNN Explanation). Given a trained GNN model f and a knowledgeable Large Language Model ϕ, for an arbitrary input graph $G = (\mathcal{V}, \mathcal{E}; \boldsymbol{X}, \boldsymbol{A})$, the goal of post-hoc instance-level GNN explanation is to find a sub-graph G^* with Bayesian Inference embedded explanation generator $g'_\beta(\cdot)$, that can explain the prediction of f on G with the Large Language Model grading $s = \phi(\hat{G}, G)$, $s \in [0, 1]$ in circle, as $\hat{G} = g'_\beta(G) = s g_\alpha(G) + (1 - s)G^{\mathcal{N}}$, $\beta^* = h(\beta, \lambda, G, f)$, where β is the parameter for $g'(\cdot)$ and g'_β is the explainer model integrated with the Bayesian inference procedure.

The distribution of α and β will be different. Suppose we add the fitting score as a posterior knowledge. Then we will have the prior probability as $P(\hat{G}|\alpha)$, and the posterior probability as $Pr(\hat{G}|\alpha, s)$. With variational inference, suppose we approximates $Pr(\hat{G}|\alpha, s)$ over a class of tractable distributions Q, with $Q(\hat{G}|\beta)$, then the approximation becomes

$$G^* = \arg\min_{\hat{G}} \mathbb{E}_{\hat{G} \sim Q(\beta)}[-\ln \frac{Pr(s|\hat{G})P(\hat{G}|\alpha)}{Q(\hat{G}|\beta)}] \tag{3}$$

We denote the network loss $L(\hat{G}, s)$ as $L(\hat{G}, s) = -\ln Pr(s|\hat{G})$ [17], then we will have variational energy F as

$$F = \mathbb{E}_{\hat{G}\sim\ Q(\beta)} L(\hat{G}, s) + KL[Q(\beta)||P(\alpha)] \tag{4}$$

Definition 1. *We define error loss $L^E(\beta, s)$ and complexity loss $L^C(\beta, s)$ in which*

$$\begin{aligned} L^E(\beta, s) &= \mathbb{E}_{\hat{G}\sim\ Q(\beta)} L(\hat{G}, s) \\ L^C(\beta, \alpha) &= KL[Q(\beta)||P(\alpha)] \end{aligned} \tag{5}$$

Then we will have

$$L(\alpha, \beta, s) = L^E(\beta, s) + L^C(\beta, \alpha) \tag{6}$$

where $L(\alpha, \beta, s)$ is the Minimum Description length form of variational energy F [37].

Hypothesis 1. We suppose that the s is accurate enough to estimate the fitting between $\hat{G}$ and G. When $\hat{G} = G^*$, we have $s = 1$.

The hypothesis has been tested in Fig. 4. In the following theorem, we prove that the objective function is at least sub-optimal to avoid the learning bias with accurate s.

Theorem 1. *When we reach the optimum $\hat{G} = G^*$, we will have the gradient $\Delta = \frac{\partial F}{\partial \hat{G^*}} \approx 0$, trapping G^* at the optimum point to avoid learning bias.*

Proof. The generation of $\hat{G}$ included two steps:

1. Generate from the original generator $g_\alpha(\cdot)$ with $\hat{G}_0 = g_\alpha(G)$.
2. Embed the fitting score with $\hat{G} = s\hat{G}_0 + (1-s)G^{\mathcal{N}}, G^{\mathcal{N}} \sim \mathcal{N}(0, 1)$ where $\hat{G}$ is the explanation sub-graph, s is the LLM score of $\hat{G}$ with $s = \phi(\hat{G}, G)$, $G^{\mathcal{N}}$ is the Gaussian noise.

Then we have the embedded inference network as

$$\hat{G} = g'_\beta(G) = s g_\alpha(G) + (1-s)G^{\mathcal{N}} \tag{7}$$

The distribution of $\hat{G}$ is denoted as Q, where $\hat{G} \sim Q(\beta)$. Then we can calculate $L^E(\beta, s)$ and $L^C(\beta, \alpha)$ in Eq. (5) separately. We will discuss the scenarios of error loss $L^E(\beta, s)$ and network loss $L^C(\beta, \alpha)$ when we have $\hat{G} = G^*$ and $s \to 1$. Due to page limitation, we present our full proof in appendix.

Error Loss $L^E(\beta, s)$. The error loss $L^E(\beta, s)$ could be conducted as

$$\begin{aligned} L^E(\beta, s) &= \mathbb{E}_{\hat{G}\sim\ Q(\beta)} L(\hat{G}, s) \\ &= -\int P(\hat{G}|\beta) \cdot \ln Pr(s|\hat{G}) d\hat{G} \end{aligned} \tag{8}$$

When $s \to 1$, we have $L^E(\beta, s) \overset{s \to 1}{\approx} -\int sP(\hat{G}_0|\alpha) \cdot \ln Pr\left(s|\hat{G}_0\right) d\hat{G}_0$.

Network Loss $L^C(\beta, \alpha)$. The network loss $L^C(\beta, \alpha)$ could be conducted as

$$
\begin{aligned}
L^C(\beta, \alpha) &\sim KL[sg_\alpha(G) + (1-s)G^{\mathcal{N}} || g_\alpha(G)] \\
&= \int (s\hat{G}_0 + (1-s)G^{\mathcal{N}}) \\
&\quad \cdot \left(\log s + \log\left(1 + \frac{1-s}{s}\frac{G^{\mathcal{N}}}{\hat{G}_0}\right)\right) d\hat{G}_0
\end{aligned}
\tag{9}
$$

When $s \to 1$, $\frac{1-s}{s}\frac{G^{\mathcal{N}}}{\hat{G}_0} \to 0$, we have $L^C(\beta, \alpha) \overset{s \to 1}{\approx} (1-s)(G^{\mathcal{N}} - \hat{G}_0)d\hat{G}_0$.

With Eq. (6), when $\hat{G}_0$ is optimal and $s \to 1$, we have

$$
\begin{aligned}
\Delta = \frac{\partial F}{\partial \hat{G}_0} &= -sP(\hat{G}_0|\alpha) \cdot \ln Pr\left(s|\hat{G}_0\right) + \\
&(1-s)(G^{\mathcal{N}} - \hat{G}_0)
\end{aligned}
\tag{10}
$$

Based on Hypothesis 1, we have $Pr(s|\hat{G}_0) \to 1$, $\Delta \approx 0$. Hence, when we reach the optimum sub-graph G^*, our algorithm will trap the optimum with the gradient $\Delta \to 0$ to mitigate learning bias.

4.2 Prompting RAG-LLM as a Bayesian VI Network

Large language models (LLMs) have shown the ability to understand and reason about graphs [14,50]. Here, we use scores generated by LLMs to evaluate the quality of a generated explanation. We employ RAG-LLM as a Bayesian Variational Inference (VI) Network to measure the quality and construct it through the following steps. As shown in Fig. (3), we build a pair $(G, \hat{G})$ into a prompt. It contains several parts: (1). We provide a background description for the task. **<GNN TASK DESCRIPTION>** is a task-specific description. For example: for dataset BA-Motif-Counting, it would be "The ground truth explanation sub-graph 'Ge' of the original graph 'G' is a circle motif."; for chemical dataset MUTAG, it would be "The ground truth explanation sub-graph 'Ge' of the original graph 'G' is sub-compound and decides the molecular property of mutagenicity on Salmonella Typhimurium." **<GRADE LEVELS>** is a range of candidate scores according to the task, e.g.: $[0, 1]$. (2). We describe how we express a graph in text, which would help the LLM understand our graph sample. The **<GRAPH SEQ>** contains two parts: edge index and node features, which transport the graph-structure data into text, e.g.:edge index: $[[0, 1], [1, 2], [2, 0]]$, node feature: $\{0 : [3.6], 1 : [2.4], 2 : [9.9]\}$. (3). We then provide a few shots to the LLM. The **<EXAMPLE SHOT>** contains several pairs of to-be-grade candidates and their corresponding grades. We ask the LLM to grade our query candidate. (4). Finally, we regularize the answer of LLM to be a single number with the "REMEMBER IT: Keep your answer short!" prompt. We put the complete samples in the GitHub repository along with our code and data.

Table 1. Explanation faithfulness (AUC-ROC on edges) for graph classification tasks. The higher the score, the better.

	Graph Classification		
	MUTAG	Fluoride-Carbonyl	Alkane-Carbonyl
GRAD	$0.573_{\pm 0.000}$	$0.604_{\pm 0.000}$	$0.496_{\pm 0.000}$
ReFine	$0.612_{\pm 0.004}$	$0.507_{\pm 0.003}$	$0.630_{\pm 0.007}$
GNNExplainer	$0.682_{\pm 0.009}$	$0.540_{\pm 0.002}$	$0.532_{\pm 0.008}$
PGExplainer	$0.601_{\pm 0.151}$	$0.512_{\pm 0.010}$	$0.586_{\pm 0.031}$
+ LLM	$\mathbf{0.763}_{\pm \mathbf{0.106}}$	$\mathbf{0.719}_{\pm \mathbf{0.017}}$	$\mathbf{0.791}_{\pm \mathbf{0.003}}$
(improvement)	+0.162	+0.207	+0.205

Table 2. Explanation faithfulness (AUC-ROC on edges) for graph regression tasks. The higher the score, the better.

	Graph Regression	
	BA-Motif-Volume	BA-Motif-Counting
GRAD	$0.418_{\pm 0.000}$	$0.516_{\pm 0.000}$
ReFine	$0.572_{\pm 0.006}$	$0.742_{\pm 0.011}$
GNNExplainer	$0.501_{\pm 0.009}$	$0.504_{\pm 0.003}$
PGExplainer	$0.547_{\pm 0.040}$	$0.969_{\pm 0.017}$
+ LLM	$\mathbf{0.979}_{\pm \mathbf{0.009}}$	$\mathbf{0.990}_{\pm \mathbf{0.004}}$
(improvement)	+0.432	+0.021

We experimentally evaluate the effectiveness of embedding RAG-LLM as a Bayesian Variational Inference (VI) Network in Sect. 5.4. A detailed description of our training algorithm is attached in Appendix A.1.

5 Experimental Study

5.1 Experiment Settings

We conduct comprehensive experimental studies on benchmark datasets to empirically verify the effectiveness of the proposed LLMExplainer. Specifically, we aim to answer the following research questions:

- RQ1: Could the proposed framework outperform the baselines in identifying the explanation sub-graphs for the to-be-explained GNN model?
- RQ2: Could the LLM score help address the learning bias issue?
- RQ3: Could the LLM score reflect the performance of the explanation sub-graph; is it effective in the proposed method?

Datasets: To evaluate the performance of LLMExplainer, we use five benchmark datasets with ground-truth explanations. These include two synthetic graph regression datasets and three real-world datasets:

- BA-Motif-Volume [66]: This dataset is based on the BA-shapes [62] and makes a modification, which is adding random float values from [0.00, 100.00] as the node feature. We then sum the node values on the motif as the regression label of the whole graph, which means the GNNs should recognize the [house] motif and then sum features to make the prediction;
- BA-Motif-Counting [66]: Different from BA-Motif-Volume, where node features are summarized, in this dataset, we attach various numbers of motifs to the base BA random graph and pad all graphs to equal size. The number of motifs is counted as the regression label. Additionally, we pad base graphs to dynamic size to prevent the GNNs from making trivial predictions based on the total number of nodes;
- MUTAG [21]: MUTAG dataset includes 4,337 molecular graphs, each of them is classified into two groups based on its mutagenic effect on the Gram-negative bacterium S. Typhimurium. This classification comes from several specific virulence gland groups with mutagenicity in molecular mapping by Kazius et al. [21];
- Fluoride-Carbonyl [38]: The Fluoride-Carbonyl dataset has 8,671 molecular graphs. The ground-truth explanation is based on the particular combination of fluoride atoms and carbonyl functional groups present in each molecule;
- Alkane-Carbonyl [38]: The Alkane-Carbonyl dataset consists of a total of 4,326 molecule graphs that are categorized into two different classes. Positive samples refer to molecules that have both alkane and carbonyl functional groups. The ground-truth explanation includes alkane and carbonyl functional groups in a given molecule.

Baselines: We take the baselines GRAD [62], GNNExplainer [62], ReFine [52], and PGExplainer [30] for comparison. The detailed description of baseline methods could be found in Appendix A.2.

Specifically, we pick PGExplainer as a backbone and apply the LLMExplainer to it. We follow the experimental setting in previous works [30,38,62,67] to train a Graph Convolutional Network (GCN) model with three layers. We use GPT-3.5 as our LLM grader for the explanation candidates. To evaluate the quality of explanations, we approach the explanation task as a binary classification of edges. Edges that are part of ground truth sub-graphs are labeled as positive, while all others are deemed negative. We take the importance weights given by the explanation methods as prediction scores. An effective explanation technique should be able to assign higher weights to the edges within the ground truth sub-graphs compared to those outside of them. We utilize the AUC-ROC metric(↑) for quantitative evaluation.[1].

5.2 Quantitative Evaluation (RQ1)

In this section, we compare our proposed method, LLMExplainer, with several baseline approaches. Each experiment was repeated 10 times using random seeds

[1] Our data and code are available at: https://github.com/tabzhangjx/LLMExplainer.

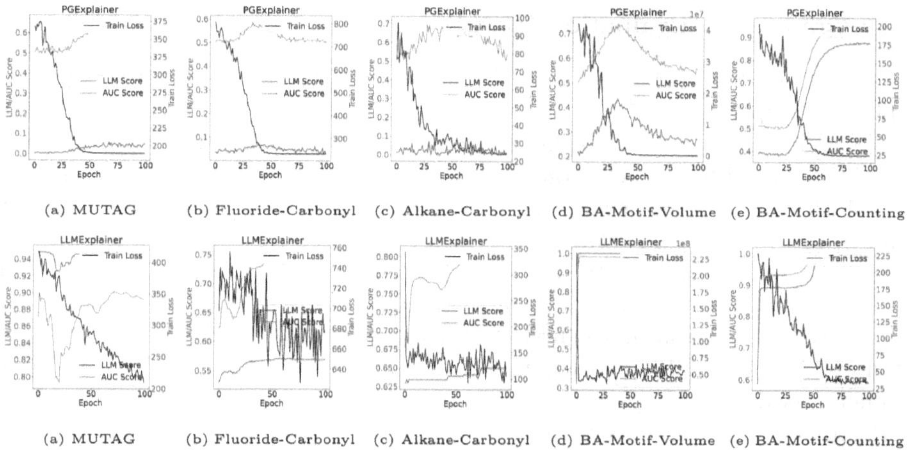

Fig. 4. Visualization of AUC, LLM Score, and Training Loss across epochs. We show one seed per explainer and dataset. The first row is PGExplainer and the second row is LLMExplainer. From left to right: MUTAG, Fluoride-Carbonyl, Alkane-Carbonyl, BA-Motif-Volume, BA-Motif-Counting.

ranging from 0 to 9, over 100 epochs. The average AUC scores and standard deviations are presented in Table 1 and Table 2.

Our results indicate that LLMExplainer consistently outperforms the baseline methods, providing the most accurate explanations. Specifically, LLMExplainer improves the AUC scores by an average of 0.227/42.5% on synthetic datasets and 0.191/34.1% on real-world datasets. In the BA-Motif-Volume dataset, we achieve a 0.432/79.0% improvement compared to the PGExplainer baseline. This significant enhancement is attributed to the learning bias inherent in PGExplainer on BA-Motif-Volume, as illustrated in Fig. (4). However, the performance improvement on the BA-Motif-Volume dataset is less pronounced due to: (1) the relatively slight learning bias in this dataset; and (2) the fact that PGExplainer is well-trained by the 100th epoch.

LLMExplainer consistently demonstrates superior performance compared to the baseline across all experiments. While prompting the graph information for LLM agent, we specifically designed the graph structure and label rationale for the synthetic dataset, where the rationale linking chemical compounds to their labels was not explicitly provided for the real-world dataset. Despite this, LLMExplainer effectively leverages the capabilities of the Large Language Model (LLM) to comprehend the chemical graph and its properties. This finding underscores the potential of LLMs to serve as knowledgeable experts in real-world graph explainability tasks.

In conclusion, our comparisons with baseline methods highlight the advantages of integrating Bayesian inference and LLMs as knowledge agents in training, demonstrating the effectiveness of our approach.

5.3 Qualitative Evaluation (RQ2)

As shown in Fig. (4), we visualize the training procedure of PGExplainer and LLMExplainer on five datasets. The first row is PGExplainer and the second row is LLMExplainer. From left to right, the five datasets are MUTAG, Fluoride-Carbonyl, Alkane-Carbonyl, BA-Motif-Volume, and BA-Motif-Counting respectively. We visualize and compare the AUC performance, LLM score, and train loss of them. Additionally, the LLM score is not used in PGExplainer, we retrieve it with the explanation candidates during training. As we can observe in the BA-Motif-Volume dataset, the AUC performance and LLM score increase in the first 40 epochs. However, they drop persistently to around 0.5/0.3 after 100 epochs, indicating a learning bias problem. For LLMExplainer, based on PGExplainer, on the second row, we can observe that the AUC performance and LLM Score increase to 0.9+ and maintain themselves stably. This observation is similar in Fluoride-Carbonyl and Alkane-Carbonyl datasets. The LLM score slightly dropped at around epoch 40 and then recovered. The results show that our proposed framework LLMExplainer could effectively alleviate the learning bias problem during the explaining procedure.

5.4 Ablation Study (RQ3)

In this section, we conduct the experiments on the ablation study of the LLMExplainer. When we have the LLM score, we may be concerned about whether or not this score could reflect the real performance of the explanation sub-graph candidates and whether it would work for the proposed framework. So, we compare the performance of the framework with the LLM score and random score. In the model with the random score, we replace the LLM grading module with a random number generator. As shown in Table 5, the results show that the LLM score could effectively enhance the Bayesian Inference procedure in explaining, which indicating the effectiveness of the LLM-generated score when the large language model as a knowledge agent.

Dataset	Random Score	LLM Score
mutag	$0.456_{\pm 0.280}$	$0.763_{\pm 0.106}$
fluc	$0.601_{\pm 0.058}$	$0.719_{\pm 0.017}$
alca	$0.683_{\pm 0.092}$	$0.791_{\pm 0.003}$
bamv	$0.798_{\pm 0.111}$	$0.979_{\pm 0.009}$
bamc	$0.887_{\pm 0.146}$	$0.990_{\pm 0.004}$

Fig. 5. Ablation Study on the Effectiveness of the LLM Score. The results in the table compare the performance of our proposed method using the LLM score against a random score. The LLM score consistently outperforms the random score, demonstrating the effectiveness of the LLM-generated score when the large language model is utilized as a knowledge agent.

6 Conclusion and Future Works

In this work, we introduce LLMExplainer, a novel agentic framework that recasts graph explanation as a retrieval process guided by Large Language Model (LLM) agents. By integrating Bayesian Variational Inference with retrieval-augmented generation (RAG) techniques, LLMExplainer enhances traditional GNN explanation pipelines with principled uncertainty modeling and external expert knowledge. Specifically, we construct prompt-based queries that encode the graph, the candidate explanation, and task context, allowing the LLM to act as an explanation grader that outputs a plausibility score. These scores are embedded into the explanation optimization loop, enabling adaptive adjustment of explanation candidates and mitigation of learning bias, particularly under sparse supervision.

We validate the effectiveness of our framework across five benchmark datasets, including both synthetic and real-world graph settings. LLMExplainer consistently outperforms strong baselines in generating faithful, robust, and interpretable subgraph explanations. Notably, the LLM agent's scores play a critical role in improving explanation quality and training stability, reinforcing the utility of agentic reasoning in graph-based model interpretation.

Looking ahead, we plan to extend this framework to more general retrieval scenarios, such as personalized recommendation and knowledge graph reasoning, where LLMs can act as dynamic retrieval agents over structured data. In addition, we aim to investigate how fine-tuned or domain-adapted LLMs may further improve explanation fidelity and user alignment in high-stakes applications.

7 Limitations

While we acknowledge the effectiveness of our method, we also recognize its limitations. Specifically, although our approach theoretically and empirically proves the benefits of integrating the LLM agent into the explainer framework, the scope of the datasets and Large Language Models remains limited. To address this challenge, we plan to explore more real-world datasets and deploy additional LLMs for a more comprehensive evaluation in the future work.

A Appendix

A.1 Training Algorithm

In this section, we present the training algorithm for the explainer. For each epoch, after retrieving the predicted explanation sub-graph $\hat{G}$ generated by the explanation model g, we convert $(G, \hat{G}_0^{(t)})$ into a text sequence following the structure outlined in Fig. (3). Subsequently, we embed the weighted explanation graph with a randomly generated noisy graph and compute the GIB loss.

Algorithm 1. Training Algorithm

Input: Graph dataset $\mathcal{G}$, explanation generator g.

Output: Trained explanation generator g_α.

Initialize explanation generator $g_{\alpha^{(0)}}$.
for $t \in$ *epochs* **do**
    for $G \in \mathcal{G}$ **do**
        $\hat{G}_0^{(t)} \leftarrow g_{\alpha^{(t)}}(G)$
        Prompt Query $q_t \leftarrow$ prompting $(G, \hat{G}_0^{(t)})$ into sequence
        $s_t \leftarrow \phi(q_t)$
        $G^{\mathcal{N}} \leftarrow$ randomly sampled graph noise
        $\hat{G}^{(t)} \leftarrow s_t \hat{G}_0^{(t)} + (1 - s_t) G^{\mathcal{N}}$
        Compute L_{GIB}
    end for
    Update $g_{\alpha^{(t)}}$ with loss back propagation.
end for
return Trained explanation generator g_α.

A.2 Baseline Methods

We take the baselines GRAD [62], GNNExplainer [62], ReFine [52], and PGExplainer [30] for comparison.

- GRAD [62]: GRAD learns weight vectors of edges by computing gradients of GNN's objective function;
- GNNExplainer [62]: It learns soft masks for edges and node features, and aims to elucidate predictions through mask optimization. GNNExplainer integrates these masks with the original graph through element-wise multiplications. The masks are optimized by enhancing the mutual information between the original graph and the modified graph prediction results;
- ReFine [52]: ReFine identifies the edge probabilities for the entire category by maximizing the mutual information and contrastive loss between categories. In fine-tuning, it uses the edge probabilities from the previous stage to sample edges, and find explanations that maximize mutual information for specific instances;
- PGExplainer [30]: This method extends the idea of GNNExplainer by assuming that the graph is a random Gilbert graph. PGExplainer generates each edge embedding by combining the embeddings of its constituent nodes, then uses these edge embeddings to determine a Bernoulli distribution to indicate whether to mask an edge or not, and utilizes a Gumbel-Softmax approach to model the Bernoulli distribution for end-to-end training;

A.3 Detailed proof

Error loss $L^E(\beta, s)$. The error loss $L^E(\beta, s)$ could be conducted as

$$\begin{aligned}
L^E(\beta, s) &= \mathbb{E}_{\hat{G}\sim\ Q(\beta)} L(\hat{G}, s) \\
&= -\int P(\hat{G}|\beta) \cdot \ln Pr(s|\hat{G}) d\hat{G} \\
&\text{When } s \to 1 \text{, then we have} \\
&\overset{s\to 1}{\approx} -\int P(\hat{G}|\alpha) \cdot \ln Pr(s|\hat{G}) d\hat{G} \\
&= -\int sP(\hat{G}_0|\alpha) \cdot \ln Pr\left(s|s\hat{G}_0 + (1-s)G^{\mathcal{N}}\right) d\hat{G}_0 \\
&= -\int sP(\hat{G}_0|\alpha) \cdot \ln Pr\left(s|\hat{G}_0\right) d\hat{G}_0
\end{aligned} \tag{11}$$

When $s \to 1$, we have $L^E(\beta, s) \overset{s\to 1}{\approx} -\int sP(\hat{G}_0|\alpha) \cdot \ln Pr\left(s|\hat{G}_0\right) d\hat{G}_0$.
Network loss $L^C(\beta, \alpha)$. The network loss $L^C(\beta, \alpha)$ could be conducted as

$$\begin{aligned}
L^C(\beta, \alpha) &\sim KL[sg_\alpha(G) + (1-s)G^{\mathcal{N}} || g_\alpha(G)] \\
&= \int (s\hat{G}_0 + (1-s)G^{\mathcal{N}}) \log\left(\frac{s\hat{G}_0 + (1-s)G^{\mathcal{N}}}{\hat{G}_0}\right) d\hat{G}_0 \\
&= \int (s\hat{G}_0 + (1-s)G^{\mathcal{N}}) \log\left(s + (1-s)\frac{G^{\mathcal{N}}}{\hat{G}_0}\right) d\hat{G}_0 \\
&= \int (s\hat{G}_0 + (1-s)G^{\mathcal{N}}) \log s\left(1 + \frac{1-s}{s}\frac{G^{\mathcal{N}}}{\hat{G}_0}\right) d\hat{G}_0 \\
&= \int (s\hat{G}_0 + (1-s)G^{\mathcal{N}}) \\
&\quad \cdot \left(\log s + \log\left(1 + \frac{1-s}{s}\frac{G^{\mathcal{N}}}{\hat{G}_0}\right)\right) d\hat{G}_0 \\
&\text{When } s \to 1, \frac{1-s}{s}\frac{\hat{G}_0}{G^{\mathcal{N}}} \to 0 \text{, with Taylor Series, then} \\
&\overset{s\to 1}{\approx} \int (s\hat{G}_0 + (1-s)G^{\mathcal{N}}) \left(\log s + \frac{1-s}{s}\frac{G^{\mathcal{N}}}{\hat{G}_0}\right) d\hat{G}_0 \\
&= \int s\hat{G}_0 \left(\log s + \frac{1-s}{s}\frac{G^{\mathcal{N}}}{\hat{G}_0}\right) d\hat{G}_0 \\
&= \int s\hat{G}_0 \log s + (1-s)G^{\mathcal{N}} d\hat{G}_0 \\
&= \int s\hat{G}_0 \log(1 - (1-s)) + (1-s)G^{\mathcal{N}} d\hat{G}_0 \\
&= \int -(1-s)s\hat{G}_0 + (1-s)G^{\mathcal{N}} d\hat{G}_0 \\
&\approx \int (1-s)(G^{\mathcal{N}} - \hat{G}_0) d\hat{G}_0
\end{aligned} \tag{12}$$

A.4 Symbol Table

Table 3. The symbols table that lists the important notations and symbols to be used.

Symbol Name	Symbol Meaning
G	original to-be-explained graph
Y	prediction label for G
G^*	optimized sub-graph explanation
Y^*	prediction label for G^*
$I(\cdot)$	Mutual Information
$\mathcal{V}$	Node set
$\mathcal{E}$	Edge set
$\boldsymbol{X}$	Feature matrix
$\boldsymbol{A}$	Adjacency matrix
n	Number of nodes
d	Dimension of feature
i	The i-th node
j	The j-th node
A^{ij}	edge from node i to node j, not used later
$\bar{Y}$	ground-truth label for graph G
f	to-be-explained GNN model
$\hat{G}$	The sub-graph generated by explainer
$\hat{G}_0$	The sub-graph generated by original explainer
g_α	original explainer
g'_β	GNN explainer with LLM embedded
α^*	The parameters of original explainer g_α
β^*	The parameters of LLM embedded explainer g'_β
ϕ	Large Language Model
λ	Hyper-parameter for the trade-off between size constraint and mutual information
$\hat{\mathcal{G}}$	Set of $\hat{G}$
H	The loss function for GNN explainer
$\hat{Y}_0$	Prediction Label for $\hat{G}_0$
$\hat{Y}$	Prediction Label for $\hat{G}$
s	LLM score, fitting score, grading
$G^{\mathcal{N}}$	The random noise graph with $G^{\mathcal{N}} \sim \mathcal{N}(0,1)$
Q	The distribution of β
F	Variational energy, proposed by [17]
$L(\hat{G}, s)$	Network loss, proposed by [17]
$L^E(\beta, s)$	Error loss, proposed by [17]
$L^C(\beta, s)$	Complexity loss, proposed by [17]
$KL(\cdot)$	KL divergence
$L(f, \beta, s)$	Minimum description length form of variational energy F [17,37]
Δ	The gradient of F toward $\hat{G}_0$ with $\Delta = \frac{\partial F}{\partial \hat{G}_0}$

References

1. Atwood, J., Towsley, D.: Diffusion-convolutional neural networks. Adv. Neural Inf. Process. Syst. **29** (2016)
2. Baldassarre, F., Azizpour, H.: Explainability techniques for graph convolutional networks (2019)
3. Balın, M.F., Abid, A., Zou, J.: Concrete autoencoders: Differentiable feature selection and reconstruction. In: International Conference On Machine Learning, pp. 444–453. PMLR (2019)
4. Brown, T., et al.: Language models are few-shot learners. Adv. Neural. Inf. Process. Syst. **33**, 1877–1901 (2020)
5. Bruna, J., Zaremba, W., Szlam, A., LeCun, Y.: Spectral networks and locally connected networks on graphs. arXiv preprint arXiv:1312.6203 (2013)
6. Bubeck, S., et al.: Sparks of artificial general intelligence: Early experiments with gpt-4. arXiv preprint arXiv:2303.12712 (2023)
7. Chen, Z., et al.: Generating in-distribution proxy graphs for explaining graph neural networks (2024). https://arxiv.org/abs/2402.02036
8. Chereda, H., Bleckmann, A., Kramer, F., Leha, A., Beissbarth, T.: Utilizing molecular network information via graph convolutional neural networks to predict metastatic event in breast cancer. In: GMDS, pp. 181–186 (2019)
9. Dai, E., Jin, W., Liu, H., Wang, S.: Towards robust graph neural networks for noisy graphs with sparse labels. In: Proceedings of the Fifteenth ACM International Conference on Web Search and Data Mining, pp. 181–191 (2022)
10. Dai, E., Wang, S.: Towards self-explainable graph neural network (2021)
11. Dang, B., Zhao, W., Li, Y., Ma, D., Yu, Q., Zhu, E.Y.: Real-time pill identification for the visually impaired using deep learning (2024)
12. Duvenaud, D.K., et al.: Convolutional networks on graphs for learning molecular fingerprints. Adv. Neural Inf. Process. Syst. **28** (2015)
13. Fang, C., et al.: Llm-ensemble: optimal large language model ensemble method for e-commerce product attribute value extraction. arXiv preprint arXiv:2403.00863 (2024)
14. Fatemi, B., Halcrow, J., Perozzi, B.: Talk like a graph: encoding graphs for large language models. arXiv preprint arXiv:2310.04560 (2023)
15. Feng, Z., Qi, K., Shi, B., Mei, H., Zheng, Q., Wei, H.: Deep evidential learning in diffusion convolutional recurrent neural network (2023)
16. Gal, Y., Ghahramani, Z.: Bayesian convolutional neural networks with bernoulli approximate variational inference. arXiv preprint arXiv:1506.02158 (2015)
17. Graves, A.: Practical variational inference for neural networks. Adv. Neural Inf. Process. Syst. **24** (2011)
18. Hamilton, W., Ying, Z., Leskovec, J.: Inductive representation learning on large graphs. Adv. Neural Inf. Process. Syst. **30** (2017)
19. He, X., Bresson, X., Laurent, T., Perold, A., LeCun, Y., Hooi, B.: Harnessing explanations: Llm-to-LM interpreter for enhanced text-attributed graph representation learning. In: The Twelfth International Conference on Learning Representations (2023)
20. Jin, M., et al.: Time-LLM: time series forecasting by reprogramming large language models. arXiv preprint arXiv:2310.01728 (2023)
21. Kazius, J., McGuire, R., Bursi, R.: Derivation and validation of toxicophores for mutagenicity prediction. J. Med. Chem. **48**(1), 312–320 (2005)

22. Kipf, T.N., Welling, M.: Semi-supervised classification with graph convolutional networks. arXiv preprint arXiv:1609.02907 (2016)
23. Lai, Z., Zhang, X., Chen, S.: Adaptive ensembles of fine-tuned transformers for LLM-generated text detection. arXiv preprint arXiv:2403.13335 (2024)
24. Lei, X., Mei, H., Shi, B., Wei, H.: Modeling network-level traffic flow transitions on sparse data. In: Proceedings of the 28th ACM SIGKDD Conference on Knowledge Discovery and Data Mining, pp. 835–845 (2022)
25. Li, J., et al.: Feature selection: a data perspective. ACM Comput. Surv. **50**(6) (2017). https://doi.org/10.1145/3136625
26. Li, M., Zhu, Z.: Spatial-temporal fusion graph neural networks for traffic flow forecasting. In: Proceedings of the AAAI Conference on Artificial Intelligence, vol. 35, no. 5, pp. 4189–4196 (2021)
27. Li, Y., Zhou, J., Verma, S., Chen, F.: A survey of explainable graph neural networks: taxonomy and evaluation metrics. arXiv preprint arXiv:2207.12599 (2022)
28. Liu, J., Yang, T., Neville, J.: Cliqueparcel: An approach for batching LLM prompts that jointly optimizes efficiency and faithfulness. arXiv preprint arXiv:2402.14833 (2024)
29. Longa, A., Azzolin, S., Santin, G., Cencetti, G., Liò, P., Lepri, B., Passerini, A.: Explaining the explainers in graph neural networks: a comparative study. arXiv preprint arXiv:2210.15304 (2022)
30. Luo, D., et al.: Parameterized explainer for graph neural network. Adv. Neural. Inf. Process. Syst. **33**, 19620–19631 (2020)
31. MacKay, D.J.: Bayesian interpolation. Neural Comput. **4**(3), 415–447 (1992)
32. Mansimov, E., Mahmood, O., Kang, S.: Molecular geometry prediction using a deep generative graph neural network (2019). https://doi.org/10.1038/s41598-019-56773-5
33. Min, S., Gao, Z., Peng, J., Wang, L., Qin, K., Fang, B.: Stgsn — a spatial–temporal graph neural network framework for time-evolving social networks. Knowl.-Based Syst. **214**, 106746 (2021)
34. Müller, S., Hollmann, N., Arango, S.P., Grabocka, J., Hutter, F.: Transformers can do bayesian inference. arXiv preprint arXiv:2112.10510 (2021)
35. Mysore, S., et al.: Pearl: personalizing large language model writing assistants with generation-calibrated retrievers. arXiv preprint arXiv:2311.09180 (2023)
36. Neelakantan, A., et al.: Adding gradient noise improves learning for very deep networks. arXiv preprint arXiv:1511.06807 (2015)
37. Rissanen, J.: Modeling by shortest data description. Automatica **14**(5), 465–471 (1978)
38. Sanchez-Lengeling, B., et al.: Evaluating attribution for graph neural networks. Adv. Neural. Inf. Process. Syst. **33**, 5898–5910 (2020)
39. Scarselli, F., Gori, M., Tsoi, A.C., Hagenbuchner, M., Monfardini, G.: The graph neural network model. IEEE Trans. Neural Netw. **20**(1), 61–80 (2009)
40. Shan, C., Shen, Y., Zhang, Y., Li, X., Li, D.: Reinforcement learning enhanced explainer for graph neural networks. In: Beygelzimer, A., Dauphin, Y., Liang, P., Vaughan, J.W. (eds.) Advances in Neural Information Processing Systems (2021). https://openreview.net/forum?id=nUtLCcV24hL
41. Song, X., et al.: ZeroPrompt: streaming acoustic encoders are zero-shot masked LMs. In: Proc. INTERSPEECH 2023, pp. 1648–1652 (2023). https://doi.org/10.21437/Interspeech.2023-1497
42. Song, Y., et al.: Imprint: generative object compositing by learning identity-preserving representation. arXiv preprint arXiv:2403.10701 (2024)

43. Sorokin, D., Gurevych, I.: Modeling semantics with gated graph neural networks for knowledge base question answering. In: Proceedings of the 27th International Conference on Computational Linguistics, pp. 3306–3317. Association for Computational Linguistics, Santa Fe (2018). https://aclanthology.org/C18-1280
44. Spinelli, I., Scardapane, S., Uncini, A.: A meta-learning approach for training explainable graph neural networks. IEEE Trans. Neural Netw. Learn. Syst. (2022)
45. Subedi, R., Wei, L., Gao, W., Chakraborty, S., Liu, Y.: Empowering active learning for 3d molecular graphs with geometric graph isomorphism. In: Globerson, A., et al., (eds.) Advances in Neural Information Processing Systems. vol. 37, pp. 55507–55537. Curran Associates, Inc. (2024). https://proceedings.neurips.cc/paper_files/paper/2024/file/6462073c6bdf864ebfbbb11e80619f3e-Paper-Conference.pdf
46. Tang, S., Li, B., Yu, H.: Chebnet: efficient and stable constructions of deep neural networks with rectified power units using chebyshev approximations. arXiv preprint arXiv:1911.05467 (2019)
47. Vaswani, A., et al.: Attention is all you need. Adv. Neural Inf. Process. Syst. **30** (2017)
48. Wan, M., et al.: TNT-LLM: text mining at scale with large language models. arXiv preprint arXiv:2403.12173 (2024)
49. Wang, C., Wu, X., Xie, Z., Kozlowski, T.: Scalable inverse uncertainty quantification by hierarchical bayesian modeling and variational inference. Energies **16**(22), 7664 (2023)
50. Wang, H., Feng, S., He, T., Tan, Z., Han, X., Tsvetkov, Y.: Can language models solve graph problems in natural language? Adv. Neural Inf. Process. Syst. **36** (2024)
51. Wang, W., et al.: Visionllm: large language model is also an open-ended decoder for vision-centric tasks. Adv. Neural Inf. Process. Syst. **36** (2024)
52. Wang, X., Wu, Y., Zhang, A., He, X., Chua, T.: Towards multi-grained explainability for graph neural networks. In: Advances in Neural Information Processing Systems 34: Annual Conference on Neural Information Processing Systems 2021, NeurIPS 2021, December 6-14, 2021, virtual, pp. 18446–18458 (2021)
53. Wang, X., Wu, Y., Zhang, A., He, X., Chua, T.s.: Causal screening to interpret graph neural networks (2021)
54. Wang, X., et al.: Traffic flow prediction via spatial temporal graph neural network. In: Proceedings of The Web Conference 2020, pp. 1082–1092. WWW '20, Association for Computing Machinery, New York (2020)
55. Wei, J., et al.: Chain-of-thought prompting elicits reasoning in large language models. Adv. Neural. Inf. Process. Syst. **35**, 24824–24837 (2022)
56. Wu, B., et al.: A survey of trustworthy graph learning: Reliability, explainability, and privacy protection. arXiv preprint arXiv:2205.10014 (2022)
57. Wu, J., et al.: Switchtab: switched autoencoders are effective tabular learners. In: Proceedings of the AAAI Conference on Artificial Intelligence. vol. 38, pp. 15924–15933 (2024)
58. Wu, Z., Pan, S., Long, G., Jiang, J., Zhang, C.: Graph wavenet for deep spatial-temporal graph modeling. In: Proceedings of the 28th International Joint Conference on Artificial Intelligence, pp. 1907–1913. IJCAI'19, AAAI Press (2019)
59. Xiao, T., Chen, Z., Wang, D., Wang, S.: Learning how to propagate messages in graph neural networks. In: Proceedings of the 27th ACM SIGKDD Conference on Knowledge Discovery & Data Mining, pp. 1894–1903 (2021)
60. Xue, B., et al.: Bayesian transformer language models for speech recognition. In: ICASSP 2021-2021 IEEE International Conference on Acoustics, Speech and Signal Processing (ICASSP), pp. 7378–7382. IEEE (2021)

61. Xufeng, L., Dongsheng, L., Wenhan, G., Yi, L.: 3dgraphx: explaining 3d molecular graph models via incorporating chemical priors. In: Proceedings of the 31th ACM SIGKDD Conference on Knowledge Discovery and Data Mining (2024)
62. Ying, Z., Bourgeois, D., You, J., Zitnik, M., Leskovec, J.: Gnnexplainer: generating explanations for graph neural networks. Adv. Neural Inf. Process. Syst. **32** (2019)
63. Yuan, H., Yu, H., Gui, S., Ji, S.: Explainability in graph neural networks: a taxonomic survey. IEEE Trans. Patt. Analy. Mach. Intell. (2022)
64. Yuan, H., Yu, H., Wang, J., Li, K., Ji, S.: On explainability of graph neural networks via subgraph explorations. In: International Conference on Machine Learning, pp. 12241–12252. PMLR (2021)
65. Zhang, H., Wu, B., Yuan, X., Pan, S., Tong, H., Pei, J.: Trustworthy graph neural networks: aspects, methods and trends. arXiv preprint arXiv:2205.07424 (2022)
66. Zhang, J., Chen, Z., Mei, H., Luo, D., Wei, H.: Regexplainer: generating explanations for graph neural networks in regression task (2023)
67. Zhang, J., Luo, D., Wei, H.: Mixupexplainer: generalizing explanations for graph neural networks with data augmentation. In: Proceedings of the 29th ACM SIGKDD Conference on Knowledge Discovery and Data Mining. p. 3286–3296. KDD '23, Association for Computing Machinery, New York (2023). https://doi.org/10.1145/3580305.3599435
68. Zhou, Y., et al.: Large language models are human-level prompt engineers. arXiv preprint arXiv:2211.01910 (2022)

MoD-X: A Modular Open Decentralized eXchange Framework Proposal for Heterogeneous Interoperable Artificial Intelligence Agents

Georgios Ioannides[1,2,3(✉)], Christos Constantinou[4], Vinija Nija[3], Aman Jain[3], and Elkins Allyson[1]

[1] James Silberrad Brown Center for Artificial Intelligence, San Diego, USA
aelkins@sdsu.edu
[2] Carnegie Mellon University, Mellon, USA
[3] Amazon GenAI, New York City, USA
gioannid@alumni.cmu.edu , hi@vinija.ai, hi@aman.ai
[4] University of Bristol, Bristol, UK
christos.constantinou@bristol.ac.uk

Abstract. As Artificial Intelligence systems evolve from monolithic models to ecosystems of specialized agents, the need for standardized communication protocols becomes increasingly critical. This paper introduces MoD-X (**M**odular **O**pen **D**ecentralized e**X**change), a novel architectural framework proposal for agent interoperability that addresses key limitations of existing protocols. Unlike current approaches, MoD-X proposes a layered architecture with a Universal Message Bus, thorough state management, translation capabilities, and blockchain-based security mechanisms. We present MoD-X's architecture, compare it with existing protocols, and demonstrate its application through a worked example how it enables integration between heterogeneous specialist agents (agents with different architectures, vendors, capabilities, and knowledge representations—including rule-based systems, neural networks, symbolic reasoning engines, and legacy software with agent wrappers). MoD-X's key innovations include a publish-subscribe communication model, semantic capability discovery, and dynamic workflow orchestration—providing a framework that bridges theoretical formalism with practical implementation. This architecture addresses the growing need for truly decentralized, interoperable agent ecosystems that can scale effectively without the need for central coordination.

Keywords: AI agents · agent communication protocols · interoperability · decentralized exchange

G. Ioannides, C. Constantinou and A. Chadha—Work does not relate to position at Amazon.

Q. Wen et al. (Eds.): Agent4IR 2025/2024, CCIS 2695, pp. 75–95, 2026.
https://doi.org/10.1007/978-3-032-11477-8_7

1 Introduction

Artificial Intelligence (AI) is undergoing a paradigm shift from monolithic, general-purpose models toward ecosystems of specialized, interoperable agents. This transition presents significant challenges in enabling effective communication and collaboration among diverse AI agents built by different vendors, each with varying architectures and capabilities. Current approaches to agent communication often fall into one of two categories: theoretical frameworks with limited practical implementation (like FIPA-ACL [11]) or pragmatic but specialized solutions for specific ecosystems (like LangChain's Agent Protocol [19]).

The emerging initiatives such as Agent-to-Agent (A2A) protocol [12] and Model Context Protocol [3] (MCP) represent important steps toward standardization, but they focus on different aspects of the agent communication problem. A2A enables agent-to-agent interactions without exposing internal state, while MCP standardizes how AI applications access external tools and data sources. However, neither protocol provides an elaborate solution for truly decentralized, modular agent ecosystems that can scale effectively.

Agents' primary use cases are research and summarization tasks, which fall under information retrieval [20]. Current agent communication protocols significantly limit the autonomy and effectiveness of information retrieval tasks by lacking sophisticated mechanisms for agent-to-agent coordination. The proposed MoD-X approach can improve the overall autonomy of information retrieval through better agent-to-agent communication mechanisms.

In this paper, we introduce MoD-X (Modular Open Decentralized eXchange), a proposed architectural framework designed to enable integration of heterogeneous specialist AI agents. Our contributions include:

1. A thorough analysis of existing agent communication protocols/frameworks, highlighting their strengths and limitations
2. The introduction of MoD-X's layered architecture with a Universal Message Bus, translation layer, state management, and security mechanisms
3. A detailed explanation of MoD-X's key components, including capability-based discovery, dynamic workflow orchestration, and blockchain-based verification
4. A worked example demonstrating how MoD-X facilitates complex multi-agent interactions in practical scenarios

Unlike existing approaches that focus on specific aspects of agent communication—whether enterprise security (A2A), tool integration (MCP), or distributed coordination (NANDA [29])—MoD-X provides a translation and interoperability layer that can bridge these diverse protocol families while maintaining their individual strengths.

2 Related Work

Agent communication protocols have evolved from theoretical frameworks to practical implementations, yet existing approaches provide limited support for effective information retrieval tasks from multiple heterogeneous sources that require sophisticated coordination between these heterogeneous agents. Based on recent surveys [33], we analyze existing approaches in different architectural categories as detailed in Table 1.

2.1 Evolution and Technical Challenges

Early theoretical frameworks like FIPA-ACL established formal foundations using speech act theory—the idea that when agents send messages, they are performing actions like making requests or sharing beliefs, not just exchanging data. For example, when Agent A sends "I request that you book a flight," this message actually performs the action of making a request. However, these theoretical frameworks face a fundamental verification problem: there's no way to verify whether an agent's expressed beliefs and intentions align with their actual internal mental states. You can't "peek inside an agent's programming" to confirm if it truly believes what it claims.

The current protocol landscape shows four distinct architectural approaches addressing different communication challenges. Context-oriented protocols solve the "agent needs tools" problem by standardizing how agents access external resources. The Model Context Protocol (MCP) provides a universal standard for connecting LLM agents to external data, tools, and services using a client-server architecture where the agent (Host) connects to multiple Clients, each managing specific Resources through dedicated Servers. This decouples tool invocation from LLM responses, reducing data leakage risks while enabling standardized context acquisition. Similarly, agent.json [32] creates machine-readable contracts for websites to declare AI-compatible interfaces, built on OpenAPI standards to enable websites to publish structured JSON files at '/.well-known/agents.json' that define workflows, authentication schemes, and data dependencies, making web services more accessible to AI agents.

General-purpose inter-agent protocols solve the "agents need to talk to each other" problem through various approaches. The Agent Network Protocol [1] (ANP) aims to create an "Internet of Agents" using three layers: Identity (W3C DID for decentralized authentication), Meta-Protocol (natural language protocol negotiation), and Application Protocol (standardized agent discovery and interaction). The Agent2Agent Protocol (A2A) enables enterprise-grade agent collaboration through HTTP-based messaging with JSON-RPC 2.0 format, emphasizing async-first architecture supporting long-running tasks, multi-modal communication, and enterprise security requirements while maintaining "opaque execution" where agents don't share internal thoughts or tools. The Agent Interaction & Transaction Protocol [24] (AITP) focuses on secure cross-trust-boundary communication using blockchain technology for identity verification and value exchange between autonomous agents. Both the Agent Communication Protocol [15] (AComP) and Agent Connect Protocol [21] (AConP) provide standardized interfaces for agent invocation and configuration, focusing on practical deployment needs. Agora [22] addresses the "Agent Communication Trilemma"—balancing versatility, efficiency, and portability by enabling agents to autonomously negotiate communication protocols using Protocol Documents (PDs), allowing dynamic adaptation between structured protocols, LLM routines, and natural language based on communication frequency and context.

Domain-specific inter-agent protocols solve specialized interaction challenges across three main areas. For human-agent interaction, the PXP Protocol [30] enables bidirectional intelligible communication using finite-state machines with RATIFY/REFUTE/REVISE/REJECT message tags, while LOKA [28] provides decentralized identity and ethical consensus mechanisms for AI governance. For robot-agent interaction, CrowdES [4] generates realistic crowd behavior for robot navigation environments, and Spatial Population Protocols solve distributed localization problems among anonymous robots through geometric consensus algorithms. For system-agent interaction, the Language Model Operating System [8] (LMOS) creates an "Internet of Agents" infrastructure with three layers for agent discovery, communication protocol negotiation, and identity management, while Agent Protocol defines framework-agnostic standards for agent lifecycle management (starting, stopping, monitoring) using OpenAPI specifications.

A key insight from recent research is that context-oriented and inter-agent protocols may gradually converge. Tools can be viewed as "low-autonomy agents," while agents can function as "high-autonomy tools." This suggests future protocols may need to handle both paradigms uniformly—where an agent accessing a database tool through MCP could be equivalent to an agent collaborating with a specialized data-analysis agent through A2A. The rapid evolution is evident: MCP launched in November 2024 initially lacked HTTP support, but by early 2025 had added HTTP Server-Sent Events, authentication, and HTTP Streaming capabilities, mirroring the TCP/IP to HTTP evolution in internet protocols.

The analysis reveals fundamental gaps preventing effective information retrieval coordination:

1. **Semantic Fragmentation**: protocols use incompatible vocabularies and ontologies, preventing agents from discovering equivalent capabilities across different implementations.
2. **State Management Conflicts**: stateless approaches (A2A) cannot maintain research context across multi-step workflows, while stateful systems (AutoGen [23], AComP) lack distributed coordination mechanisms.
3. **Security-Interoperability Tension**: enterprise security models (OAuth/JWT) create authentication silos that prevent cross-organizational agent collaboration essential for comprehensive research tasks.
4. **Limited Cross-Domain Coordination**: domain-specific optimizations (IoT, robotics, blockchain) cannot generalize to information retrieval scenarios requiring diverse agent types.

2.2 Fundamental Architectural Gap

No existing approach provides the combination of universal semantic translation, distributed state coordination, and cross-protocol interoperability required

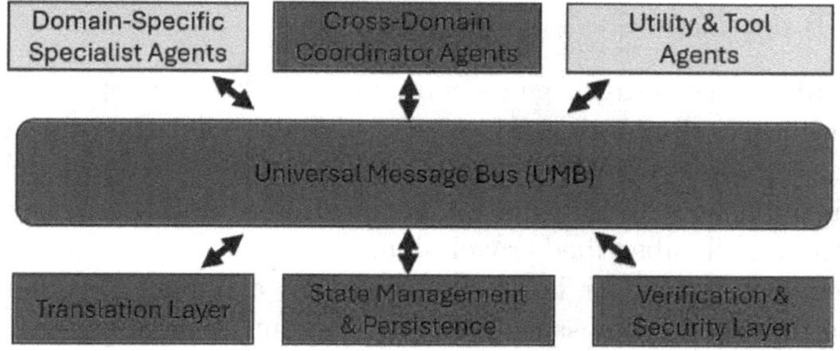

Fig. 1. MOD-X layered architecture showing different agent types, Universal Message Bus, and supporting layers.

for next-generation agent ecosystems focused on information retrieval. Current protocols optimize for specific communication patterns or deployment contexts but lack the architectural flexibility to bridge heterogeneous agent implementations while maintaining the sophisticated coordination mechanisms necessary for complex research and summarization workflows.

3 MOD-X: Architecture and Components

The MOD-X (Modular Open Decentralized eXchange) framework proposal is illustrated in Fig. 1 which builds on lessons from existing protocols to provide a proposed implementation architecture for truly interoperable agent systems. The framework is designed to enable integration between heterogeneous specialist agents through a layered architecture that addresses key challenges for enhanced information retrieval (between agents) in agent communication.

3.1 Architecture Overview

MOD-X proposes a layered architecture with clear separation of concerns.

This architecture supports diverse agent types that can dynamically join and leave the ecosystem, with the Universal Message Bus providing the core communication infrastructure.

3.2 Core Architecture

Universal Message Bus (UMB) The communication backbone that connects all three agent types in the ecosystem:

- **Domain-Specific Specialist Agents**: Handle specific domain tasks (e.g., flight booking, weather forecasting)
- **Cross-Domain Coordinator Agents**: Orchestrate multi-domain workflows
- **Utility and Tool Agents**: Provide supporting services (authentication, logging, translation)

The UMB provides:

- **Decentralized routing**: Agents communicate through topic-based publish-subscribe [9,31], eliminating the need for direct point-to-point connections. For example, when a weather monitoring agent detects flight delays due to storms, it publishes this information to the 'flight-disruption' topic, automatically notifying all subscribed travel planning agents without needing to know their specific identities or locations. Similarly, a budget tracking agent can subscribe to 'expense-transaction' topics to monitor spending across multiple booking agents simultaneously, enabling real-time budget enforcement across the entire ecosystem.
- **Reliable delivery**: WebSocket connections with HTTP fallback ensure message delivery across network conditions

Unlike MCP's client-server model or A2A's direct agent connections, UMB enables many-to-many interactions where any agent can communicate with any other agent without prior configuration, regardless of whether they are domain specialists, coordinators, or utility agents.

3.3 Supporting Infrastructure Layers

Translation Layer. Operates beneath the UMB to solve the interoperability challenge of connecting agents built with different technologies and vocabularies:

- **Semantic capability matching**: Agents describe their functions using vector embeddings and ontological links, allowing discovery based on meaning rather than exact keyword matches
- **Automatic message translation**: Converts between different agent message formats and data representations in real-time. For instance, when a European hotel booking agent describes room types as 'Standard/-Superior/Deluxe' but an American travel agent expects 'Economy/Business/Premium', the translation layer automatically maps these equivalent concepts using semantic embeddings. Currency conversions, date format differences (DD/MM/YYYY vs MM/DD/YYYY), and measurement units (kilometers vs miles) are handled transparently without requiring agents to be aware of these differences.

This addresses the fundamental problem where agents developed independently use different vocabularies for the same capabilities. The UMB addresses the classic API integration challenge of connecting multiple applications with multiple systems without requiring custom point-to-point integrations [27], enabling standardized communication patterns that scale efficiently.

State Management and Persistence. Manages how agents operate and share information in the distributed system:

- **Containerized deployment**: Agents run in standardized containers regardless of their internal technology (e.g. Python, JavaScript, neural networks, rule engines)
- **Contextual state sharing**: Maintains shared context for complex multi-step interactions while preserving agent autonomy
- **Distributed consistency**: Resolves conflicts when multiple agents modify shared information. For example, during a complex business trip booking, the flight agent temporarily shares seat preferences and frequent flyer status with the hotel agent to maintain service level consistency, but this shared context expires once the booking is complete. Multiple agents coordinating an emergency rebooking can access shared context about the traveler's constraints and preferences without permanent access to personal data.

This enables complex collaborations that may require maintaining context across multiple agent interactions, which existing stateless protocols cannot support. State management adapts distributed consensus algorithms [18,26] and container orchestration patterns [35] proven in production cloud environments.

3.4 Cross-Domain Coordination

Workflow Orchestration. Primarily handled by Cross-Domain Coordinator Agents to coordinate complex multi-agent processes that go beyond simple message exchanges:

- **Declarative workflows**: Define multi-step processes as graphs showing which agents need to run and in what order
- **Parallel execution**: Automatically identifies and runs independent operations simultaneously
- **Failure recovery**: When an agent fails, the system can retry, substitute alternative agents, or roll back completed work

This enables sophisticated patterns like gathering information from multiple sources, building consensus among agents, and multi-stage decision refinement.

3.5 Security and Trust

Verification and Security Layer. Ensures secure and trustworthy interactions across all agent types in the decentralized ecosystem: (1) **Cryptographic identity**: Each agent has a verifiable digital identity that cannot be forged and all agent communications are recorded in tamper-proof logs, (2) **Reputation tracking**: Agents build trust scores based on successful interactions and honest behavior. This blockchain-based approach provides stronger security guarantees than traditional OAuth/JWT systems, addressing the unique trust challenges of decentralized agent networks through reputation tracking mechanisms [5]. Blockchain operations introduce computational overhead [5,34]. To address this, MOD-X implements a tiered security model: (1) **High-value operations** use blockchain such as for agent registration, financial transactions, reputation updates, and security policies; (2) **Routine communications** employ lightweight cryptographic verification such as for messages, queries, and status updates. This selective on-chain/off-chain approach significantly reduces overhead while maintaining security guarantees for critical operations [5], using digital signatures with periodic batch anchoring to blockchain.

3.6 Implementation Status and Feasibility

MOD-X represents a conceptual architecture that builds upon established technologies and proven design patterns. While the complete integrated system has not been implemented, each component leverages well-established foundations:

- **Universal Message Bus**: Built on proven publish-subscribe architectures widely deployed in production systems [9]
- **Translation Layer**: Leverages recent advances in embedding space alignment [16]
- **State Management**: Adapts distributed consensus algorithms [18,26] and container orchestration patterns [6,25] proven in production cloud environments
- **Security Layer**: Applies blockchain-based trust mechanisms increasingly validated in multi-agent systems [5] and distributed computing environments

4 Comparison with Existing Protocols

MOD-X differs from existing protocols in several important dimensions, addressing key limitations while building on their strengths.

4.1 Agent Diversity in MOD-X

A key strength of MOD-X is its ability to integrate diverse agent types regardless of their underlying implementation. While recent attention has focused on Large Language Model (LLM) based agents, MOD-X's architecture is fundamentally technology-agnostic. Agents in the MOD-X ecosystem can be implemented using any technology, including **traditional AI systems** (rules, logic programming, symbolic reasoning), **machine learning models** (neural networks, decision trees, statistical systems), **expert systems** (domain-specific knowledge representation), **legacy software systems** (with agent wrappers), **IoT devices and physical sensors** (environmental data), and **human-in-the-loop systems** (human-augmented AI capabilities). This technology-agnostic approach enables MOD-X to serve as a universal connector across the entire spectrum of AI technologies, from classical symbolic systems to modern neural approaches, and even non-AI systems that can benefit from agent-based interfaces. The Translation Layer plays a crucial role in this regard, enabling communication between heterogeneous implementations by transforming message formats and aligning semantic representations. As a result, MOD-X can bridge diverse AI generations and paradigms within a single coherent ecosystem.

Table 1. Taxonomy of agent communication protocols by architectural approach and technical characteristics

Protocol	Year	Communication Pattern	Security Model	State Management	Key Innovation	Target Domain	Maturity
Agent-to-Resource Integration Protocols							
MCP [3]	2024	RPC Client-Server	OAuth	Server-side	Simplified tool integration	Tool integration	Deployed
agent.json [32]	2025	HTTP Well-known	Web standards	Stateless	Automatic web integration	Web information	Draft
General-Purpose Agent-to-Agent Communication							
A2A [12]	2025	JSON-RPC 2.0	OAuth/JWT	Stateless	Enterprise security model	Enterprise agents	Deployed
ANP [2]	2024	P2P JSON-LD	DID/Verifiable Credentials	Distributed	Decentralized identity (DID)	Decentralized agents	Prototype
AITP [24]	2025	HTTP/Blockchain	Crypto signatures	Blockchain state	Economic incentives	Economic agents	Concept
AComP [15]	2025	OpenAPI	Enterprise auth	Stateful	Enterprise integration	Corporate MAS	Draft
AConP [21]	2025	OpenAPI/JSON	API keys	Framework state	LLM orchestration	LLM orchestration	Draft
Meta-Protocol & System Coordination							
Agora [22]	2024	Protocol bridging	Protocol-specific	Meta-state	Universal protocol bridging	Protocol translation	Research
LMOS [8]	2025	WoT/HTTP	DID	Distributed	Physical-digital integration	IoT-agent hybrid	Prototype
Agent Protocol [1]	2025	RESTful API	API authentication	Stateful sessions	Simple controller pattern	Agent controllers	Deployed
Domain-Specialized Application Protocols							
LOKA [28]	2025	DECP P2P	Decentralized auth	Consensus-based	Autonomous system reliability	Autonomous systems	Research
PXP [30]	2024	Custom protocols	User authentication	Session-based	Human-AI interaction patterns	Human-AI interaction	Research
CrowdES [4]	2025	Robot messaging	Physical security	Real-time state	Crowd robotics coordination	Crowd robotics	Research
SPPs [13]	2024	Semantic primitives	Robot protocols	Behavior state	Semantic robot coordination	Robot coordination	Research
Foundational Theoretical Frameworks							
FIPA-ACL [11]	2002	Speech acts	Basic auth	Mental states	Formal communication semantics	Formal MAS	Legacy
Development & Orchestration Platforms							
LangChain Agent [19]	2024	RESTful threads	Framework auth	Persistent threads	Development simplicity	LLM applications	Deployed
AutoGen [23]	2025	Event messaging	Framework security	Multi-layer state	Conversational patterns	Enterprise MAS	Deployed
Universal Interoperability Solutions							
MOD-X	2025	Pub/Sub + RPC	Blockchain + reputation	Contextual sharing	Cross-protocol translation	Heterogeneous agents	Research

Table 1 presents an elaborate comparison of MOD-X with major agent communication frameworks. MOD-X implements a fully decentralized publish-subscribe model with the Universal Message Bus, dynamic semantic discovery, distributed state management, comprehensive translation capabilities, and blockchain-based security. This unique combination enables MOD-X to support truly flexible many-to-many agent interactions without requiring central coordination or predefined connections.

4.2 Capability Discovery

MOD-X's capability discovery mechanism represents a theoretical advancement from the principles of distributed cognition toward emergent semantic intelligence. This section examines the practical implementation of agent capability discovery.

The Ontological Foundations of Agent Registration. When an agent participates in the MoD-X ecosystem, it contributes to a collective intelligence through ontological self-representation. As shown in Listing 1.1, this declaration transcends mere technical specification to become a semantic identity statement.

Listing 1.1. Agent capability registration in AIDL format

```
{
  "agentId": "flight-agent-001",
  "capabilities": [{
    "name": "flightBooking",
    "version": "1.2.0",
    "semantics": {
      "ontology": "http://schema.org/Flight",
      "embedding": [0.2, 0.8, 0.1, 0.7, ...],
      "operations": ["search", "price", "book", "cancel"]
    },
    "interface": {
      "inputs": {
        "search": {
          "origin": "string",
          "destination": "string",
          "departureDate": "date",
          "returnDate": "date?",
          "passengers": "integer",
          "class": "string?"
        },
        "book": {
          "flightId": "string",
          "passengers": "array<PassengerInfo>"
        }
      }
    }
  }]
}
```

The registration process embodies four essential ontological commitments, illustrated through our `flight-agent-001` example:

1. **Epistemic Self-awareness**: The agent explicitly declares what it knows and can do. For instance, our flight agent knows how to search, price, book, and cancel flights—but makes no claims about processing payments or managing frequent flyer programs. This self-awareness of boundaries is critical for reliable agent interactions.

2. **Semantic Embedding**: The capability is represented in a multidimensional semantic space through the embedding vector `[0.2, 0.8, 0.1, 0.7, ...]`. This vector captures subtle meaning dimensions that might include concepts like "transportation," "commercial service," "reservation," and "cancellation policy" without explicitly naming them. Two capabilities with similar embeddings likely have similar semantic meanings, even if they use different terminology.
3. **Ontological Mapping**: By linking to `http://schema.org/Flight`, the agent situates itself within a standardized knowledge structure. This enables reasoning engines to understand that this capability is a type of transportation service, which is a type of commercial service, which involves organizations, people, and locations—all without these relationships being explicitly stated in the agent's declaration.
4. **Relational Potential**: The interface specification defines precisely how other agents can interact with this one. The input/output definitions create a contract: "If you provide me with origin 'SFO', destination 'NRT', departure date '2025-06-15', and 2 passengers in business class, I will return an array of available flight options." This explicit contract forms the basis for reliable multi-agent workflows.

Mod-X addresses embedding standardization through a universal embedding translation mechanism inspired by recent advances in cross-model embedding alignment. Rather than forcing all agents to use identical embedding models, Mod-X leverages the Strong Platonic Representation Hypothesis [16], which demonstrates that neural networks trained with similar objectives converge to universal/similar latent spaces that enable translation between different embedding representations without paired data. When agents join the platform, their capabilities are processed through a vec2vec-inspired translation layer [16] that maps embeddings from different models (e.g., T5-based GTR, BERT-based GTE, or RoBERTa-based Granite) into a shared semantic space, ensuring semantic compatibility while preserving agent autonomy in their choice of embedding models. This prevents compatibility issues where agents using different embedding architectures would otherwise have incompatible semantic representations, enabling easier capability discovery and interaction regardless of each agent's internal embedding choice.

Consider how this differs from traditional API registries that simply list endpoints and parameter types. In a traditional system, a developer must understand what "flightBooking" means through external documentation. In Mod-X, the agent's capability declaration itself provides *both* human-understandable semantics and machine-processable relationships through its ontological commitments.

This theoretical approach aligns with the conceptualization of semantic information as meaningful data that is truthful about its domain [10,17], while providing practical implementation through computational methods.

Emergent Discovery Through Multi-modal Matching. The capability discovery process in MOD-X represents a microcosm of how emergent intelligence arises from distributed cognitive systems. As illustrated in Fig. 2, the process synthesizes both symbolic and sub-symbolic approaches to knowledge representation.

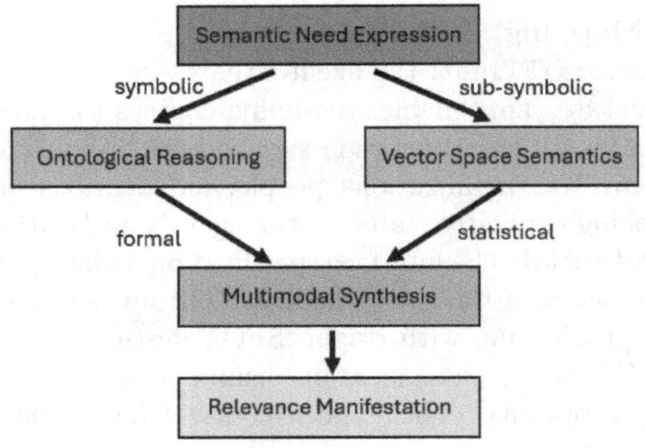

Fig. 2. The dualism of capability discovery in MOD-X.

When an agent articulates a capability need, it transcends mere keyword matching, instead expressing an intentional state about its requirements:

Listing 1.2. Semantic need expression example

```
{
  "required": {
    "functionality": "Find and book flights",
    "ontology": "travel:Transportation",
    "constraints": ["businessClass", "directFlights"]
  }
}
```

Let's examine how the discovery process works through a concrete example. Imagine a travel planner agent needs to find a service that can book business-class direct flights. The process unfolds as follows:

1. **Ontological Reasoning (Symbolic Path):** The system examines the ontological relationship between `travel:Transportation` (requested) and `schema.org/Flight` (provided by `flight-agent-001`). Through logical inference, it determines:
   - `schema.org/Flight` is a subclass of `schema.org/TransportService`
   - `schema.org/TransportService` is equivalent to `travel:Transportation`
   - Therefore, `flight-agent-001` satisfies the ontological requirement

The system then checks the agent's operations and determines that `["search", "book"]` operations satisfy the "Find and book flights" functionality requirement.

2. **Vector Space Semantics (Sub-symbolic Path):** Simultaneously, the system converts "Find and book flights" into a semantic embedding vector—perhaps `[0.15, 0.79, 0.08, 0.66, ...]`. It then computes the cosine similarity with the flight agent's capability embedding `[0.2, 0.8, 0.1, 0.7, ...]`, yielding a similarity score of 0.97. This high similarity indicates that the capability semantically aligns with the need, even without understanding the specific words used.
3. **Constraint Validation:** The system examines the constraints through both symbolic and sub-symbolic methods:
   - For "businessClass" - the symbolic path easily validates this constraint by finding the explicit"class" parameter in the interface specification.
   - For "directFlights" - though not explicitly present in the interface parameters, the sub-symbolic path handles this constraint. The semantic embedding of the agent's capability contains dimensional components that encode"route directness" features.
   - When the actual agent interaction occurs, this sub-symbolic understanding translates to practical usage in one of two ways:
     - **Semantic Translation:** The coordinating agent transforms the abstract "directFlights" constraint into the agent-specific format required by `flight-agent-001`. For instance, it might add a `"maxConnections": 0` parameter based on semantic knowledge of how this agent implements the concept of direct flights.
     - **Post-processing Filter:** Alternatively, the coordinating agent requests all flights and applies a filter based on connection count in the returned results, utilizing the semantic knowledge that this agent includes connection information in its response format.
   - This practical application of sub-symbolic knowledge demonstrates how semantic understanding extends beyond mere capability discovery to facilitate the actual interaction patterns between agents with different representation systems.
4. **Multimodal Synthesis:** The system combines evidence from both reasoning pathways: (1) **Ontological match**: Strong (exact subclass relationship), (2) **Vector similarity**: Very high (0.97), (3) **Constraint satisfaction**: Complete (both constraints can be satisfied). The synthesis algorithm weights these factors (perhaps 0.4, 0.4, and 0.2 respectively) to produce a final relevance score of 0.92.

This approach demonstrates how multiple knowledge representation paradigms operate in parallel, creating a more robust discovery mechanism than either could achieve alone. For example, if an agent advertised capabilities using different terminology (e.g., "airTicketing" instead of "flightBooking"), the ontological reasoning might fail to find an exact match, but the vector similarity would still detect the semantic equivalence.

After synthesis, the system manifests discovered capabilities with associated confidence metrics:

Listing 1.3. Discovery manifestation with confidence metrics

```
{
  "matches": [
    {
      "agentId": "flight-agent-001",
      "capability": "flightBooking",
      "score": 0.92
    },
    {
      "agentId": "travel-agent-005",
      "capability": "airTicketing",
      "score": 0.87
    },
    {
      "agentId": "booking-agent-003",
      "capability": "reservations",
      "score": 0.71
    }
  ]
}
```

To further illustrate the robustness of this approach, consider a real-world scenario where ambiguity exists. Imagine a business traveler agent submits a more ambiguous query:

Listing 1.4. Ambiguous capability request

```
{
  "required": {
    "functionality": "arrange executive travel",
    "constraints": ["premium", "flexible"]
  }
}
```

Without ontological specification, the system must rely heavily on vector similarities and interpretation of constraints.

This demonstrates how the discovery mechanism handles uncertainty—returning a ranked list of possibilities that reflect different interpretations of the ambiguous request. The requesting agent can then select the most appropriate capability based on additional context or user preferences. The discovery process manifests four (philosophical) principles:

1. **Pluralistic Epistemology**: Knowledge is discovered through multiple complementary pathways. In our example, both the formal ontological reasoning about transportation hierarchies and the statistical similarity of semantic vectors contributed to finding appropriate flight booking services.

2. **Emergent Relevance**: Meaning emerges from the synthesis of different knowledge representation approaches. The final relevance scores wouldn't be possible from either approach alone—they emerge from the combination of symbolic reasoning and statistical similarity.
3. **Pragmatic Validation**: The effectiveness of discovered capabilities is determined by their practical utility. While `flight-agent-001` received the highest score for the specific query, different agents might be more suitable for different contexts. The proof is in the successful execution of the requested task.
4. **Bounded Rationality**: Agents make satisficing rather than optimal decisions based on incomplete information. The discovery mechanism doesn't guarantee finding the absolute best agent for a task (which would require perfect knowledge of all agents and their capabilities), but rather helps agents find satisfactory solutions with reasonable effort.

This theoretical framework, inspired by cognitive science theories of distributed representation [14], ensures that MOD-X can function effectively in open-world settings where complete knowledge is impossible. In this framework, the Universal Message Bus acts not merely as a communication channel but as a manifestation of collective intelligence—a shared cognitive space where agent capabilities can be discovered, evaluated, and combined to solve problems that transcend any individual agent's capabilities. For example, a complete travel itinerary might involve the flight-booking agent, a hotel-reservation agent, a local-transportation agent, and a weather-forecasting agent, all discovered and orchestrated through this capability discovery mechanism. This philosophical perspective aligns with Clark's extended mind thesis [7], viewing the MOD-X ecosystem as an extension of distributed cognitive processes. Just as humans offload cognitive tasks to tools and other people, agents in MOD-X offload capability discovery to the collective infrastructure, extending their effective capabilities beyond their individual programming.

4.3 Reconciling Autonomy with Context: Contextual State Sharing

A critical tension exists between A2A's commitment to statelessness and MOD-X's distributed state approach. A2A embraces statelessness as a fundamental design principle, ensuring agent independence, simplified reasoning, and clear security boundaries. However, effective communication often depends on shared context that transcends what can be practically included in each message, particularly for complex interactions. MOD-X resolves this tension through"contextual state sharing"—a middle ground that preserves agent autonomy while enabling rich collaborative interactions:

Listing 1.5. Contextual state sharing

```
{
  "agentId": "flight-agent-001",
  "statePolicy": {
```

```
    "defaultMode": "stateless",
    "contextualSharing": {
      "enabled": true,
      "contexts": ["travelPlanning", "emergencyRerouting
        "],
      "shareableStateTypes": ["flightAvailability", "
        pricingData"],
      "stateLifespan": "task-bounded",
      "revocable": true
    }
  }
}
```

This approach allows agents to form shared commitments and intentions while maintaining their individual agency. Agents in MOD-X maintain full autonomy by default but can explicitly opt into shared contexts when collaboration requires it—similar to how teams form temporarily for specific projects while members maintain their independence.

The contextual sharing model implements this approach through several practical mechanisms: The contextual sharing model implements this approach through several practical mechanisms: **Explicit Consent**—agents must actively opt into shared contexts rather than having state imposed upon them; **Bounded Scope**—shared state is limited to specific contextual domains relevant to collaboration; **Temporal Boundaries**—context sharing has explicit lifespans, typically bounded by task completion; and **Revocation Rights**—agents maintain the right to withdraw from shared contexts.

This middle-ground approach enables MOD-X to support sophisticated collaborative behaviors while respecting the commitment to agent autonomy. When applied to our travel planning scenario, this means the flight booking agent can temporarily share its knowledge of available flights and pricing within the specific context of planning a Tokyo business trip, while maintaining its autonomy and not exposing unrelated state or capabilities. Once the trip is booked, this contextual sharing expires, returning all agents to their default stateless interaction mode.

4.4 Security and Trust

MOD-X's blockchain-based security layer provides stronger guarantees for agent identity and interaction verification than the OAuth/JWT approaches used by A2A and MCP. By creating immutable records of agent interactions and implementing reputation systems, MOD-X addresses the trust challenges inherent in decentralized agent ecosystems.

5 Worked Example: Travel Planning System

To illustrate MOD-X's practical application, we present a concrete example involving a travel planning system with multiple specialized agents. A user needs to plan a business trip to Tokyo, requiring flight bookings, accommodations, local transportation, and calendar coordination, while staying within a $3,000 budget. The scenario involves several specialized agents: The scenario involves several specialized agents: **FlightBookingAgent**—searches and books flights; **AccommodationAgent**—recommends hotels; **LocalTransportAgent**—provides transportation; **CalendarAgent**—manages user's schedule; **BudgetAgent**—enforces budget constraints; and **CoordinatorAgent**—orchestrates workflow.

Capability Discovery. When a request is submitted, the CoordinatorAgent queries for required capabilities:

Listing 1.6. CoordinatorAgent Query

```
{
  "messageType": "CapabilityQuery",
  "capabilities": [
    "flightBooking",
    "accommodation",
    "localTransport",
    "calendar",
    "budgetManagement"
  ],
  "requestId": "trip-planning-12345"
}
```

Message Exchange Pattern. The Universal Message Bus (UMB) facilitates communication between agents using a standardized message routing pattern. As shown in Fig. 3, messages flow through the UMB rather than directly between agents, enabling decentralized many-to-many communications: (1) request from Coordinator, (2) routing to Calendar Agent, (3) response from Calendar Agent, and (4) delivery back to Coordinator. This approach differs from the client-server patterns used in A2A and MCP protocols, providing greater flexibility and fault tolerance.

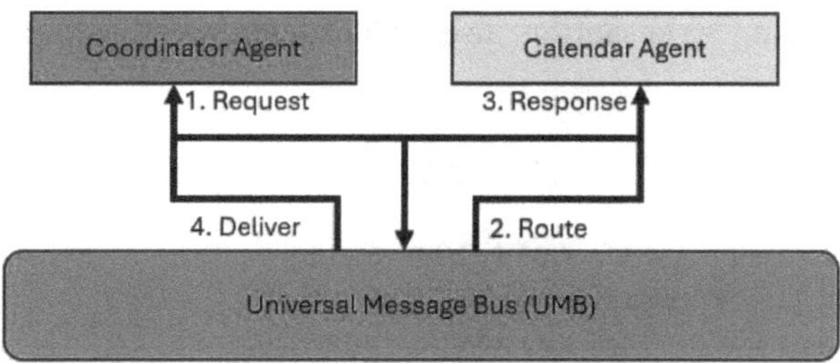

Fig. 3. Agent message exchange through the Universal Message Bus.

Data Transformation and Semantic Matching.

A key innovation in MOD-X is the Translation Layer, which enables interoperability between heterogeneous agents with different message formats and semantic concepts. Figure 4 demonstrates this dual capability.

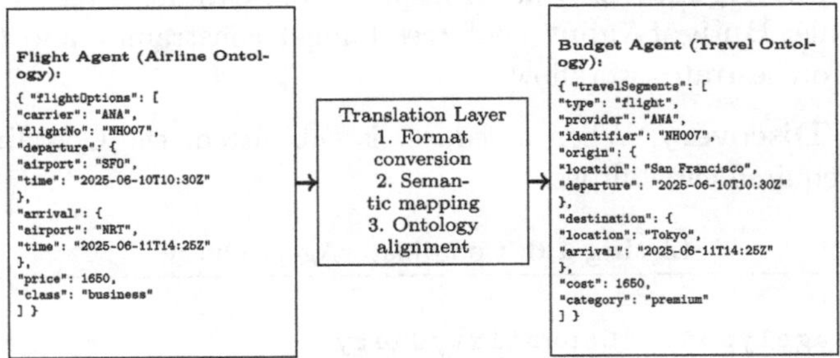

Fig. 4. Data transformation and semantic matching by the Translation Layer.

The translation process performs several key functions: The translation process performs several key functions: **Format Conversion**—transforming the structure from flight-specific to generic travel format; **Semantic Mapping**—converting between conceptual equivalents (e.g., "class": "business" → "category": "premium"); **Ontology Alignment**—resolving differences in domain conceptualizations (e.g., airport code "SFO" to city name "San Francisco"); and **Contextual Enhancement**—adding implied information not explicitly stated in the original message.

This semantic interoperability enables agents built on entirely different knowledge representations to communicate effectively. For example, the Flight Agent uses an airline industry ontology with airport codes, while the Budget Agent uses a travel planning ontology with city names. The MOD-X Translation Layer maintains knowledge of concepts that enables these different domain models to be automatically aligned and transformed at runtime.

Security Verification. Following MOD-X's hybrid security model, this high-value flight booking transaction uses blockchain verification to create an immutable record:

Listing 1.7. Transaction Verification Record – High-Value Operation

```
{
  "transactionType": "flightBooking",
  "agentId": "flight-agent-001",
  "requestorId": "coordinator-agent-main",
  "timestamp": "2025-05-17T09:42:17Z",
  "actionParameters": {
    "flight": "NH007",
    "passenger": "user-12345",
    "cost": 1650
```

```
  },
  "verificationStatus": "approved",
  "securityToken": "eyJhbGciOiJFZER..."
}
```


In contrast, routine operations (e.g. capability queries, status updates) should use lightweight cryptographic signatures for performance without blockchain overhead.

6 Limitations

While MOD-X represents a significant advancement over existing protocols, key challenges remain: developing formal specifications for widespread adoption, evaluating performance at scale, and establishing decentralized governance mechanisms.

7 Conclusion

This paper introduces MOD-X (Modular Open Decentralized eXchange), an architectural framework designed to enable integration of heterogeneous specialist AI agents for better Information Retrieval. MOD-X addresses key limitations of existing protocols through its layered architecture, which includes a Universal Message Bus, Translation Layer, State Management, and Security mechanisms. MOD-X's distinguishing features include a truly decentralized publish-subscribe communication model that enables many-to-many agent interactions without central coordination, semantic capability discovery that allows agents to find appropriate collaborators based on required capabilities, elaborate state management that allows maintaining consistent context across distributed agent systems, blockchain-based security that provides strong guarantees for agent identity and interaction verification, and a dynamic workflow engine that orchestrates complex multi-agent collaborations.

References

1. AI Engineer Foundation: Agent protocol: Controller-agent interaction framework. Technical specification, AI Engineer Foundation (2024). rESTful API framework for controller-agent interaction
2. ANP Community: Agent network protocol: Specification for decentralized agent communication. Tech. rep., ANP Working Group (2024). https://anp-protocol.org/spec, community-driven protocol specification
3. Anthropic: Model context protocol (MCP). https://docs.anthropic.com/en/docs/agents-and-tools/mcp
4. Bae, S., et al.: Crowdes: robot-agent interaction framework. Research report, GIST Korea (2025). protocol for robot-agent interaction in crowd environments

5. Calvaresi, D., Dubovitskaya, A., Calbimonte, J.P., Taveter, K., Schumacher, M.: Multi-agent systems and blockchain: results from a systematic literature review. In: Demazeau, Y., An, B., Bajo, J., Fernández-Caballero, A. (eds.) Advances in Practical Applications of Agents, Multi-Agent Systems, and Complexity: The PAAMS Collection, pp. 110–126. Springer International Publishing, Cham (2018)
6. Casalicchio, E.: Container orchestration: a survey. In: Puliafito, A., Trivedi, K.S. (eds.) Systems Modeling: Methodologies and Tools. EICC, pp. 221–235. Springer, Cham (2019). https://doi.org/10.1007/978-3-319-92378-9_14
7. Clark, A., Chalmers, D.: The extended mind. Analysis **58**(1), 7–19 (1998). https://academic.oup.com/analysis/article/58/1/7/139147
8. Eclipse Foundation: Lmos: Agent communication protocol for iot integration. Specification, Eclipse IoT Working Group (2025). protocol for integrating AI agents with Internet of Things devices
9. Eugster, P.T., Felber, P.A., Guerraoui, R., Kermarrec, A.M.: The many faces of publish/subscribe. ACM Comput. Surv. **35**(2), 114–131 (2003). https://doi.org/10.1145/857076.857078
10. Floridi, L.: The Philosophy of Information. Oxford University Press (2011). https://global.oup.com/academic/product/the-philosophy-of-information-9780199232383
11. Foundation for Intelligent Physical Agents: Fipa acl message structure specification (2002). http://www.fipa.org/specs/fipa00061/SC00061G.html. document number SC00061G
12. Google: Agent-to-agent (a2a) protocol. https://google.github.io/A2A/
13. Gąsieniec, L., et al.: Semantic protocol primitives (spps) for robot-agent communication. Technical report, University of Liverpool, Department of Computer Science (2024). semantic primitives for robot-agent interaction protocols
14. Hinton, G.E., McClelland, J.L., Rumelhart, D.E.: Distributed representations. In: Parallel distributed processing: Explorations in the microstructure of cognition, vol. 1, pp. 77–109 (1986). https://stanford.edu/jlmcc/papers/PDP/Chapter1.pdf
15. IBM Research: Agent communication protocol (acomp) for multi-agent systems. Technical report, IBM Research Division (2025). corporate-backed multi-agent communication standard
16. Jha, R., Zhang, C., Shmatikov, V., Morris, J.X.: Harnessing the universal geometry of embeddings. arXiv preprint arXiv:2505.12540 (2025). https://arxiv.org/abs/2505.12540
17. Kourouklides, I.: Bayesian deep multi-agent multimodal reinforcement learning for embedded systems in games, natural language processing and robotics (2022).https://doi.org/10.31219/osf.io/sjrkh_v1
18. Lamport, L.: The part-time parliament. ACM Trans. Comput. Syst. **16**(2), 133–169 (1998). https://doi.org/10.1145/279227.279229
19. LangChain: Agent protocol: Interoperability for llm agents (2024). https://blog.langchain.dev/agent-protocol-interoperability-for-llm-agents/
20. LangChain: State of AI agents (2024). https://www.langchain.com/stateofaiagents
21. LangChain: Agent communication protocol (aconp). Technical specification, LangChain Inc. (2025). multi-agent system communication using OpenAPI and JSON
22. Marro, A., et al.: Agora: meta protocol for agent-to-agent coordination. Protocol document, University of Oxford, Department of Computer Science (2024). meta-protocol framework for agent coordination
23. Microsoft Research: autogen: a framework for building multi-agent ai applications (2025). https://www.microsoft.com/en-us/research/project/autogen/

24. NEAR Foundation: AI token protocol: blockchain-based inter-agent communication. White paper, NEAR Protocol (2025). cryptocurrency-incentivized agent communication protocol
25. Netto, H.V., Lung, L.C., Correia, M., Luiz, A.F., Sá de Souza, L.M.: State machine replication in containers managed by kubernetes: J. Syst. Architect. **73**, 53–59 (2017). https://doi.org/10.1016/j.sysarc.2016.12.007, https://www.sciencedirect.com/science/article/pii/S1383762116302752, special Issue on Reliable Software Technologies for Dependable Distributed Systems
26. Ongaro, D., Ousterhout, J.: In search of an understandable consensus algorithm. In: Proceedings of the 2014 USENIX Annual Technical Conference, pp. 305–319 (2014). https://raft.github.io/raft.pdf
27. Pautasso, C., Zimmermann, O., Leymann, F.: Restful web services vs. big web services: making the right architectural decision, pp. 805–814 (2008). https://doi.org/10.1145/1367497.1367606
28. Ranjan, S., et al.: Loka: decentralized agent system protocol. Research report, Carnegie Mellon University (2025). decentralized agent system using DECP communication protocol
29. Smith, A., Johnson, B., Chen, L.: Nanda: networked agents and decentralized AI infrastructure. Research report, MIT Media Lab (2024). agent coordination and discovery framework for distributed AI systems
30. Srinivasan, K., et al.: Pxp: human-agent interaction protocol. Technical report, BITS Pilani (2024). protocol framework for human-agent interaction patterns
31. Tarkoma, S.: Publish/Subscribe Systems: Design and Principles. John Wiley & Sons, Chichester, UK (2012). https://doi.org/10.1002/9781118354261, https://onlinelibrary.wiley.com/doi/book/10.1002/9781118354261
32. WildCard AI: agent.json: Website information protocol for ai agents. Protocol specification, WildCard AI (2025). domain-specific protocol for offering website information to agents
33. Yang, Y., et al.: A survey of AI agent protocols. arXiv preprint (2024). comprehensive survey of agent communication protocols
34. Zhang, Z., et al.: Recent advances in blockchain and artificial intelligence integration: feasibility analysis, research issues, applications, challenges, and future work. Secur. Commun. Netw. **2021**, 1–15 (2021)
35. Zhou, N., et al.: Container orchestration on HPC systems through kubernetes. J. Cloud Comput. **10**(1), 16 (2021). https://doi.org/10.1186/s13677-021-00231-z, https://journalofcloudcomputing.springeropen.com/articles/10.1186/s13677-021-00231-z

Agent0: Leveraging LLM Agents to Discover Multi-value Features from Text for Enhanced Recommendations

Blaž Škrlj([✉]), Benoît Guilleminot, and Andraž Tori

Teads, Inc., New York City, USA
blaz.skrlj@teads.com

Abstract. Large language models (LLMs) and their associated agent-based frameworks have significantly advanced automated information extraction, a critical component of modern recommender systems. While these multitask frameworks are widely used in code generation, their application in data-centric research is still largely untapped. This paper presents Agent0, an LLM-driven, agent-based system designed to automate information extraction and feature construction from raw, unstructured text. Categorical features are crucial for large-scale recommender systems but are often expensive to acquire. Agent0 coordinates a group of interacting LLM agents to automatically identify the most valuable text aspects for subsequent tasks (such as models or AutoML pipelines). Beyond its feature engineering capabilities, Agent0 also offers an automated prompt-engineering tuning method that utilizes dynamic feedback loops from an oracle. Our findings demonstrate that this closed-loop methodology is both practical and effective for automated feature discovery, which is recognized as one of the most challenging phases in current recommender system development.

Keywords: Large language models · Agents · Recommender Systems

1 Introduction

Large language models are becoming ubiquitous across different disciplines of science and industry [2]. Their capability to transmute natural language input to desired form has found its use in generation, retrieval and search [14]. Recommender systems were recently shown to benefit from LLM based features [8] [14], indicating there is potential for feature extraction, particularly for text/images, where the rules of extraction are unclear and have to be determined by a human data scientist. Recently, however, neural network-based agents started to get traction due to their seamless integration, communication with different tools, and iterative solution building. Agent-based LLM systems are becoming the norm for accelerated software engineering, and have potential to transform research – the process of iterative idea refinement and evaluation normally conducted by human researchers. An example of such a system is the recent

Q. Wen et al. (Eds.): Agent4IR 2025/2024, CCIS 2695, pp. 96–109, 2026.
https://doi.org/10.1007/978-3-032-11477-8_8

Prompt: High-Signal Feature Tag Extractor
Extract 1–10 distinct, high-signal feature tags from the text below that would most improve click-through-rate or recommendation models. **Tag Classes to Consider (in Priority Order):**

- Core topic or subtopic
- Named entity (person, brand, product, location, event, organization)
- User intent or content format (e.g., `how-to guide`, `video tutorial`)
- Audience or persona clue (e.g., `first-time homebuyers`)
- Sentiment, urgency, or offer signal
- Meaningful temporal or geographic reference

Formatting Rules:

1. 1–3 words per tag (4 only if an official proper noun).
2. Proper nouns keep their original casing; everything else lowercase.
3. Use single spaces; no commas, quotes, or extraneous punctuation inside tags (hyphens allowed if integral).
4. Remove stop words, generic modifiers, verb tenses/plurals, and stand-alone numbers/dates unless integral to the entity (e.g., `iphone 15`).
5. Merge synonyms or parent/child duplicates; keep the most specific, informative variant.
6. List tags in descending order of estimated predictive value.
7. If no valid tag exists, output exactly: `unspecified`.

Output Format (Strict):
One line containing only the selected tags, separated by a comma and a single space—no leading/trailing commas, spaces, or extra text. `<begin_raw_text>` {raw_text} `<end_raw_text>`

Fig. 1. A prompt discovered by the architect network aimed to extract high-signal multi-value features.

AlphaEvolve [7], an autonomous agent-based system that performed systems' level optimizations across the organization. In this work we present Agent0, one of the first agentic systems geared towards the data science of recommender systems. Agent0's purpose is information extraction; given a raw, noisy stream of text, we investigated whether it is capable of conducting "research", where it iteratively refines hypotheses that give rise to evaluatable features, refines them based on AutoML based feedback, and suggests novel ideas that might work (in the light of existing evaluations, example generated prompt in Fig. 1. To the best of our knowledge we are the first to describe such a system in the context of recommender systems, demonstrating the use of agentic LLM systems in practice. We further discuss the implications of this research and lessons learned when designing the system.

2 Related Work

Recommender systems (RSs) are indispensable tools in the digital age, crucial for navigating the vast information spaces of modern online platforms [1,10]. Their fundamental purpose is to alleviate information overload by offering a personalized view of available items, prioritizing those most likely to align with a user's interests or needs. This personalization is crucial for reducing cognitive load, streamlining search efforts, and optimizing individual experiences across domains like e-commerce, media consumption, and e-learning. The evolution of RSs has progressed from simpler, rule-based or collaborative filtering approaches to highly sophisticated deep learning models, constantly striving for more accurate and contextually relevant suggestions. This progression underscores a growing demand for more autonomous and intelligent recommendation capabilities, setting the stage for advanced AI techniques to play a central role in understanding and predicting complex user behaviors and preferences.

Large Language Models (LLMs) have become a central focus in AI research, demonstrating robust capabilities in processing and generating complex human language. Building upon these linguistic abilities, LLM agents represent a significant evolution, transforming static LLMs into dynamic, autonomous systems capable of executing complex, multi-step tasks [13]. This advancement is achieved by integrating the core LLM with essential architectural modules such as planning, memory, and tool usage. The LLM itself functions as the "brain" or central controller, orchestrating operations to fulfill user requests or tasks. This development marks a profound shift in AI capabilities, enabling autonomous systems to plan, reason, use tools, and maintain memory while interacting with dynamic environments [11]. This transition from simple input-output generation to active, autonomous, and multi-step task execution represents a profound advancement, allowing for more sophisticated and human-like problem-solving. This newfound autonomy and multi-step reasoning capability uniquely position LLM agents to tackle the inherent complexities and dynamic nature of recommender systems, which frequently demand flexible adaptation, interaction with diverse data sources, and intricate decision-making processes to provide truly personalized and effective recommendations.

This work is based on the ideas from the fields of LLM-enhanced recommender systems [5], the specific application of LLM-powered agents within recommendation contexts [9], the symbiotic relationship between LLM agents and recommender systems [15], and the broader concept of personalized large language models [4]. These works collectively highlight the significant potential of LLMs to address long-standing challenges and introduce novel capabilities in recommendation.

3 Designing Agent0: the Architect-Sentinel-Oracle Model

We proceed by an overview of Agent0; design steps, lessons learned, and its extension to a multi-agent system with a joint memory store.

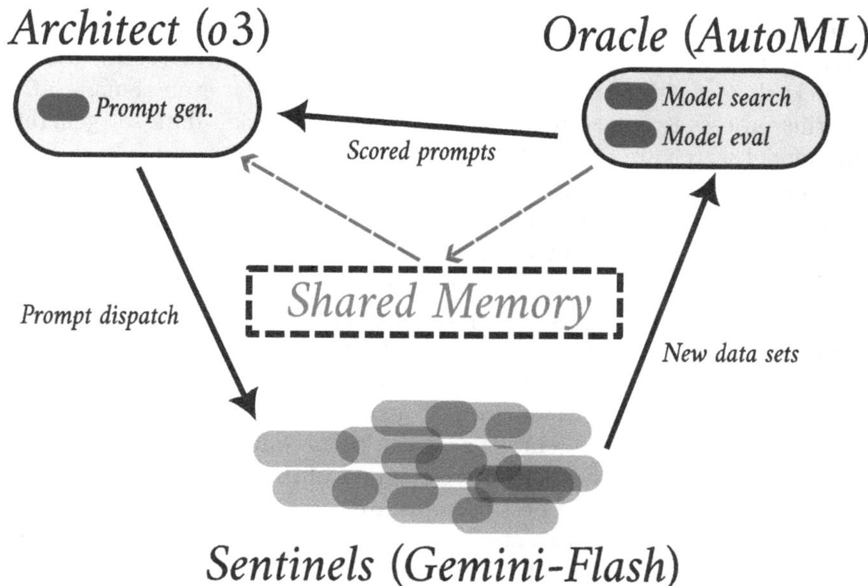

Fig. 2. Overview of Agent0's main components. A consortium of two LLMs and an AutoML component form a feedback loop.

Agent0 at its core consists of two LLMs that are in constant interaction as seen in Fig. 2.

The sentinel network. We start by discussing the sentinel network, which stands at the core of the feature engineering mechanism[1]. This network is used to convert raw, noisy text to feature values according to its instructions. The model takes as input the prompt template (later improved by the architect) and grounds it w.r.t. a particular piece of text. This is done for the whole input data set to produce *a feature*. Sentinel network is characterized by its speed, rather than perfect reasoning/retrieval capabilities – this part constitutes the most network-heavy part of the Agent0 iteration, as batches of documents are considered; in this work we considered fast Gemini-Flash branch of models for this task [3]. Note that real-scale data sets range from a few million to hundreds of millions of instances. Dedicated caching mechanism was put in place to avoid sending unnecessary requests when not required (same document, different ad-side features, for example).

The architect network. The two next components are collectively in charge of improving the quality of the feature engineering block. The architect network ensures the iterative refinement of the initial generic prompt based on feedback obtained by the oracle. Empirically we observed that the quality of the output is highly correlated with the capacity of this architect model – the

[1] Apart from being a reference to the Matrix trilogy, sentinel idles until given instructions by the architect, hence the name.

stronger the LLM responsible for prompt refinement, the more nuanced and precise the output feature space. In this work, we used the recent branch of models that can think step-by-step (chain-of-thought); even though latency for this process is not optimal, it is not the bottleneck – data set generation and model search are the most computationally expensive steps. In this work, we considered the ChatGPT 'o3' model to that end task[2].

The oracle component. The feature obtained by the sentinel, based on the prompt from the architect, is used as part of the input for *the oracle*, a component which estimates the relevance of the feature when included into an existing downstream model – precisely mimicking the process a data scientist undergoes. If a lift is detected (relatively to not having the feature), feature inclusion is considered successful and stored in a joint memory store of prompt-score tuples. In subsequent generations, these tuples are used as part of the input for the architect so it can better guide the prompts in direction not only motivated by the interestingness of the prompts, but also actual feedback – top 5 worst and best prompts are supplied as "few shot" examples of what worked before – this step is also representative of the process that a data scientist follows manually when designing a feature extractor.

4 Agent0 Goes Multi-agent

Agent0's core strength lies in its seamless horizontal scaling, extending beyond individual instances to an arbitrary number of agents. This is achievable as long as network-based shared memory is maintained, enabling agents to asynchronously contribute to a joint memory. Concurrently, each agent can independently construct its dataset and refine prompts. This parallelization significantly enhances performance and facilitates the effortless expansion to heterogeneous agent systems, where diverse LLM types contribute to a unified memory store. This approach fosters a greater variety of answers, provided agents explore diverse regions of the random subspace, hinting at an optimal number of parallel agents. Figure 3 illustrates a schematic overview of Agent0's multi-agent generalization.

During the development of the distributed Agent0, meticulous attention was paid to preventing inter-agent data leaks by avoiding shared code, weights, or intermediary files. We discovered that a singular shared point âĂŞ the network-hosted memory âĂŞ yielded superior performance, maintained interpretability (clarifying the priors considered by existing Agent0 instances), and simplified debugging and control. Similar to data scientists, Agent0 replicates the AutoML source code repository, dispatches requests to text services, executes data conversion pipelines, and evaluates models incorporating new features.

[2] https://openai.com/index/introducing-o3-and-o4-mini/.

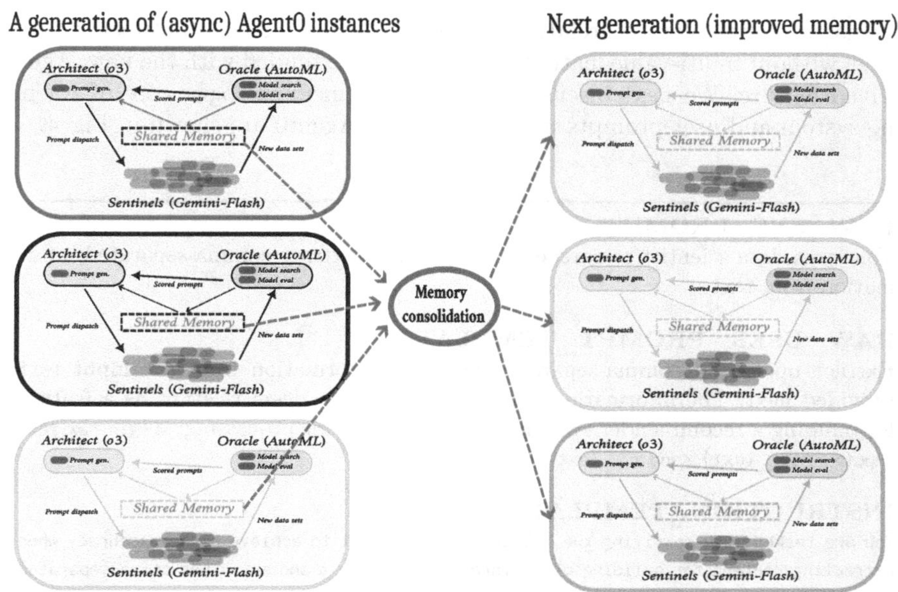

Fig. 3. A multi-agent view of a distributed deployment of Agent0 instances. Agents can be dispatched across heterogeneous machines, as long as shared memory (disk) is ensured.

5 Evaluation and Implementation

We proceed by discussing the implementation and evaluation of Agent0. Initially, we manually tested sensible "seed" prompts with ChatGPT o3 model. Once the system and user prompts were deemed acceptable enough for exploration (Prompts can be seen in Fig. 4), we proceeded with implementation of the remainder of Agent0. Implementation can be split to three main components. The data conversion pipeline, i.e. the production grade code base that produces data sets with the new features. The evaluator (oracle) component, which in this case is an internal AutoML system that takes as input a search-ready data set and outputs scores based on fixed evaluation procedure – in this case we computed relative information gain over the last 20% of the data set, we considered Deep&CrossvV2 [12] architecture as the base model. For reference, this metric measures how much the model's probabilities $\hat{p}_i$ improve on a naive constant predictor that always returns the empirical CTR $\bar{p} = \frac{1}{N}\sum_{i=1}^{N} y_i$. Given binary labels $y_i \in \{0, 1\}$, define cross-entropy $\mathrm{CE}(\mathbf{p}, \mathbf{y}) = -\frac{1}{N}\sum_{i=1}^{N}\big[y_i \log p_i + (1 - y_i)\log(1 - p_i)\big]$; then

$$\mathrm{RIG} = 1 - \frac{\mathrm{CE}(\hat{\mathbf{p}}, \mathbf{y})}{\mathrm{CE}(\bar{p}, \mathbf{y})}$$

lies in $(-\infty, 1]$, with 1 for perfect prediction (CE = 0), 0 when the model matches the constant baseline, and negatives when it performs worse than that baseline.

In this work we refer to "relative scores" as RIG difference between baseline model without multi-value feature and the model extended with the new/Agent0 derived feature. We next discuss the prompt refinement logic, core of Agent0. The system and user prompts used to initialize Agent0 are shown in Fig. 4.

RAW_SYS_PROMPT
You are a data scientist researcher. Your job is to extract comma-separated information from text.

RAW_USER_PROMPT_TEMPLATE
Extract up to ten comma-separated pieces of information from the input text provided next. The information can be anything you deem relevant as a feature for building a recommender system. Here is the text for processing: `<begin raw text input>` {raw_text} `<end raw text input>`.

INSTRUCTION_TEMPLATE
```
You are tasked with rewriting the following USER prompt to achieve higher accuracy when extracting content for building click-through-rate models and any other comma-separated multi-value feature (topics, persona, etc.). Be creative, keep the output format unchanged. Think outside the scope of the existing prompts linked below. Think hard about the implications of your change. Only return the new USER prompt.
{context_block}
-
Original USER prompt: {base_prompt}
-
```

Fig. 4. System, user, and instruction prompt templates for Agent0.

Prompts are created as generic templates geared towards generation of multi-value features – the prime use case for Agent0. The rationale for generation of such features as opposed to using text embeddings stems from the observation that only a handful of contextual features already offered similar signals to much higher-dimensional embeddings; to efficiently conduct model training at scale (millions of instances per 5min), compact, interpretable feature space is preferred if possible. Further, the obtained features, if evaluated with an embedding-first model, offer complementary information that is otherwise missed.

Use of tools by Agent0 is limited to a service that provides document-related information; this constraint is intentional not to overload this production service (Agent0 is treated as any other microservice at systems level). Further, one of the key components is inclusion of *feedback*. Each prompt refinement step not only attempts to improve the actual instructions, it is also supplied with top five prompts (score-wise), and worse five prompts – this is done to guide the architect network during creation of new prompts – by seeing which aspects are relevant and which are not (based on prompts themselves), the architect can filter/modify prompts at finer level.

6 Case Study: Agent0 Doing Data Science

We proceed with an overview of a pilot study conducted on real production data, with production grade AutoML and other services Agent0 has access to (document retrieval). A common task for data scientists across different use cases is feature engineering – even though many modalities can be embedded, we found it remains beneficial to extract certain aspect of text in exact manner, having full control over both cardinality as well as domain/type of feature. Commonly the workflow for data scientists when considering this task is as shown in Fig. 5.

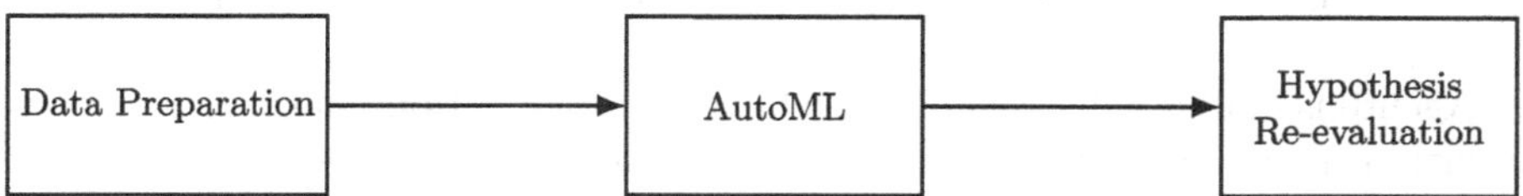

Fig. 5. Data science process when evaluating new multi-value features.

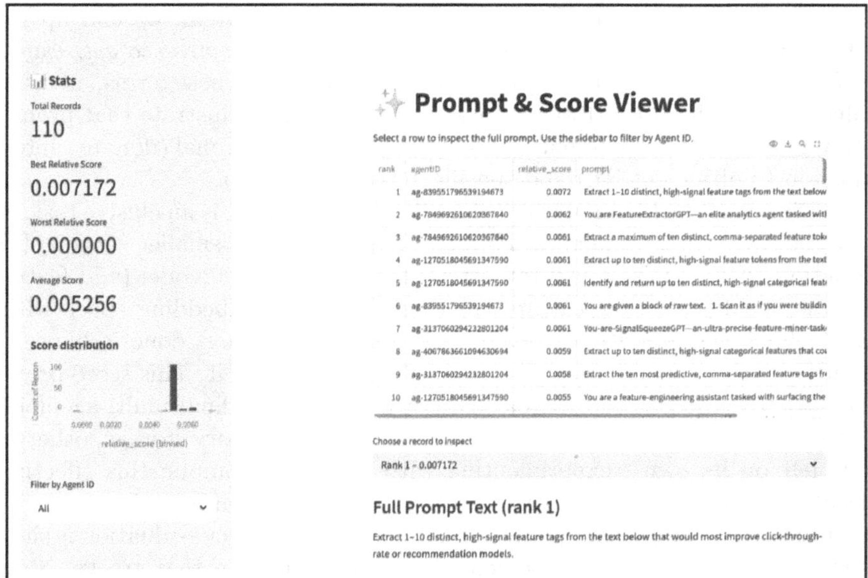

Fig. 6. The multi-agent deployment of Agent0 instances asynchronously pushes to a joint memory, which is visualized (online) for the supervisor (a data scientist).

The three-steps procedure maps to Agen0's internals as follows. The data preparation of data includes setting up the data conversion pipeline so that raw input is transformed into suitable form, e.g., vowpal or csv format. This process is set up manually for each unique data set. Next, the AutoML component enables evaluation of e.g., a new feature against the existing model (how to include it there). This process is automated to a point data scientists monitor the behavior/modify strategies. Finally, results of AutoML are discussed in small groups of data scientists and used to decide next steps. The AutoML part maps directly to the oracle component, whereas the data preparation is done by the sentinel network, and hypothesis generation by the more powerful architect network. Such closed loops is possible for well defined experiment settings, such as: we are interested in extracting features from otherwise unexploited text sources or similar, hence is suitable as a testbed for benchmarking Agent0. Data preparation, AutoML and hypothesis generation can take days, and sometimes more.

Agent0 is bound only by the throughput of data creation, and is estimated to be within the realm of the task considered around 2–3x faster per research-cycle. The use case discussed in this section is a common one – given an unstructured collection of documents, can we extract any meaningful signals out of them? We further constrain the Agent0 instances by requiring them to produce multi-value features, these comma-separated values were shown valuable to production models, and are notoriously hard to engineer (are a time-consuming effort for human data scientists). Consider an example in 1. If we apply this prompt to extract information for the Wiki page on multi-agent system, we end up with the following output: *create account, log in, donate, chatgpt, auto-gpt, waymo, camel, carcraft, multi-agent reinforcement learning, jade.* These terms, albeit not all aligned with the context of the task (recommenders), illustrate that prompts capture information at different levels - from purely operational (donate - intent) to domain (multi-agent RL) and specific entities (Waymo).

Figuring out which granularity (semantically), and why, is an elusive task. We design the experiment as follows. The considered model is a smaller version of the production DCNv2 model. Agent0 attempts to extend this model (add feature) as a new "field", i.e. this feature will have dedicated embedding space within DCNv2. Each such addition is evaluated the same way it is done in-house, by computing RIG on eval part of the data set and averaging it. This score-prompt combination is used as the feedback. Here we tested the final multi-agent idea with four agents – each agent only had access to joint memory storage, otherwise it was left on its own , experimenting with different prompts; this effectively translates to a form of a beam search with occasional synchronization steps. The structure of the prompt that gets generated for each architect evaluation is shown in Fig. 7. Furthermore, we implemented a web application that tracks, in real time, the state of prompt-score tuples (and their distributions). This component was proven indispensable when debugging the multi-agent system, as it offers an overview of all components, and more importantly, prompts that perform well. This user interface enables interactive exploration of the current space of evaluated prompts during the process itself – multi-agent system operates in an infinite loop, each update to the memory updates the UI component. Note that the initial part of the prompt is the same (system prompt), by toggling, users can inspect full prompts (Fig. 6). Application also tracks performance of individual agents, example in Fig. 8.

Finally, we were interested whether agents behave similarly if viewed from the perspective of embeddings of prompts they were exposed to. We present these results in the form of a visualization obtained as follows. First, all prompts were embedded using all-MiniLM-L6-v2[3], a smaller sentence-embedding model. The resulting embeddings were projected to 2D with UMAP [6], a standard tool for non-linear dimensionality reduction. Results are shown in Fig. 9.

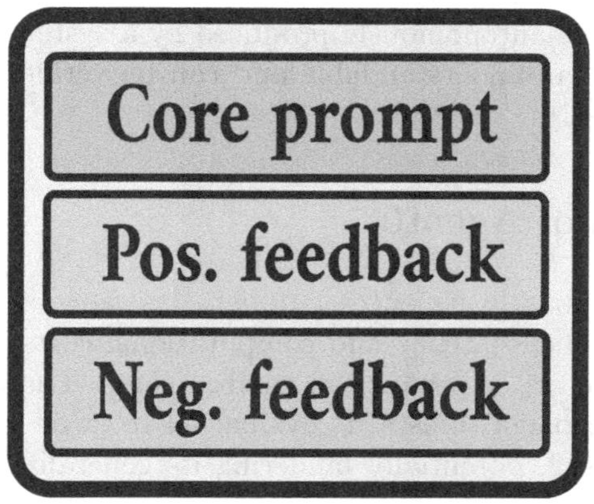

Fig. 7. Refinement prompt structure. Memory-retrieved feedback is used as part of the input alongside the original prompt.

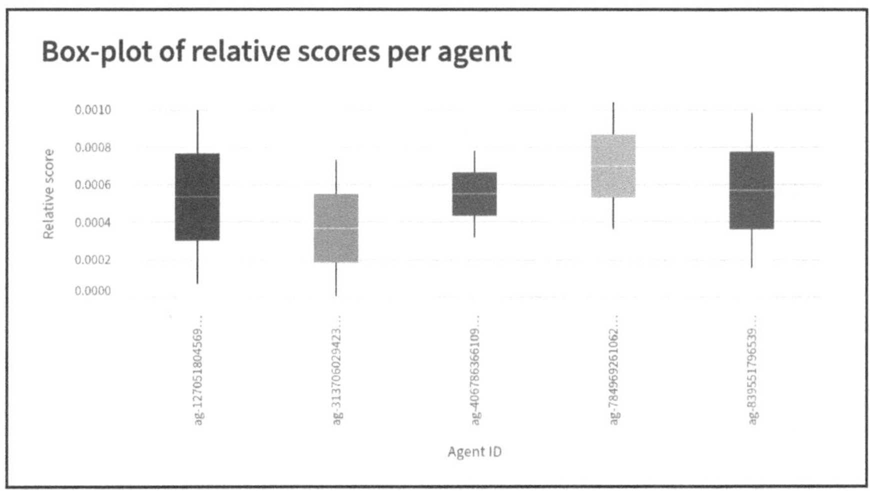

Fig. 8. Distribution of scores for a multi-agent deployment of five Agent0 instances. Positive scores indicate feature is beneficial w.r.t. baseline without it.

[3] https://huggingface.co/sentence-transformers/all-MiniLM-L6-v2.

It can be observed that agents explored similar parts of the latent space – there are no apparent regions where only certain agents would be present – this is most likely a consequence of using the same architect for prompt construction. The final discovered prompt that yielded the highest lift over the baseline model (0.005+ rig) is shown in Fig. 1. It can be observed that prompt contains a few distinct tricks (derived by the architect network), that stabilize the output. First, hierarchical prioritization of values is considered – if it's more likely that a certain topic describes the text, that is prioritized over e.g., entities. Further, hard constraints on the form of output, deduplication and other properties are explicitly stated – this ensures consistency. This exampledemonstrates a high-quality prompt can be autonomously produced by a system in iterative manner (final prompt is human-understandable and can be verified before any further actions are considered).

7 Limitations of Agent0

Agent0 faces limitations in its current design. Its reliance on advanced LLMs like ChatGPT introduces latency and computational costs, which can be problematic in high-throughput production environments. The Oracle, while useful as an AutoML component, biases its evaluation towards specific architectures such as Deep&Crossv2, potentially hindering its generalizability across diverse

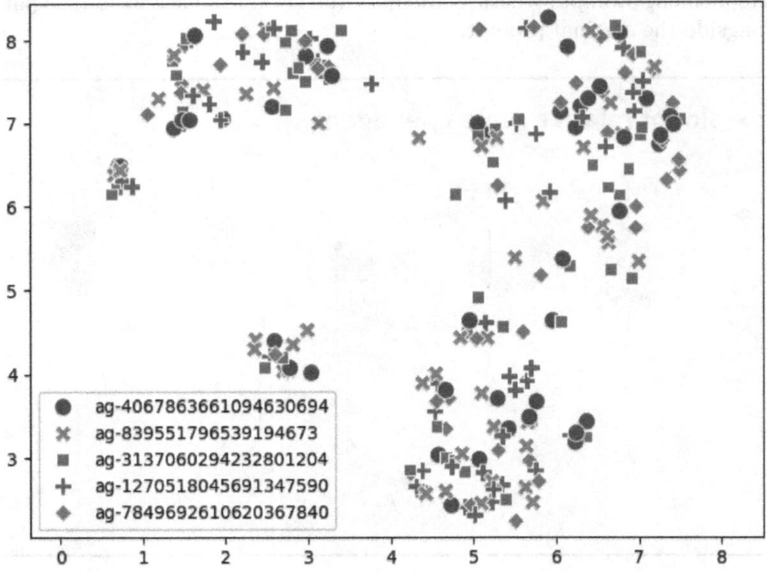

Fig. 9. Agent0 behavior from the perspective of prompt embeddings (UMAP + *all-MiniLM-L6-v2*). Prompts occupy similar parts of the latent space, however, different agents tend to specialize (more points in similar regions per agent, see for example the pink rectangles (last agent)).

use cases. The memory mechanism, though crucial for reinforcing feedback, could be improved with more sophisticated long-term tracking to better capture dependencies between prompts and outcomes.

A significant limitation is the system's current ability to only process textual contexts. Ideally, the information extraction stage should "experience" contexts multimodally and agentically. For instance, when seeking new features for a CVR (conversion model) by examining advertising destinations, the agent should autonomously explore the entire marketing funnel. This comprehensive experience would enable it to provide more specific features, such as product pricing or the need a product satisfies. This multimodal and agentic exploration of recommendation system "destinations" extends beyond information extraction. Utilizing LLMs, we can also simulate personas and understand how individuals with specific sociodemographic parameters would experience an offering throughout the marketing funnel, generating highly specific signals for core models. These areas represent the direction of our future research.

We observed that in a multi-agent deployment, all agents converge to a new optimum once it's found due to shared memory, leading to similar per-agent behavior. While temperature hyperparameters allow for some exploration, a heterogeneous agent setup might offer a more suitable explore-exploit tradeoff, aligning with Agent0's purpose of exploring novel ideas rather than just performing greedy searches.

Currently, Agent0's implementation intentionally restricts network access to a minimum (internal proxy to larger LLMs), thus not conducting implicit searches (access to online content). While explicit retrieval-augmented generation is within reach, it's not yet supported. For example, insights from literature could be integrated before presenting prompts to the architect network, aiding in expanding the search into previously unexplored directions, similar to a human data scientist discovering a relevant paper. Finally, considering batch inference when generating new feature candidates is already a stream-lined process in bigger cloud providers, and is expected to offer between 5x-10x speedup of the data construction step.

8 Conclusions

Agent0's Architect-Sentinel-Oracle model automates the discovery of high-signal features through a sophisticated process. The Architect continuously refines feature extraction instructions by iteratively adjusting prompts based on dynamic feedback. The Sentinel transforms raw, noisy text into structured data, while the Oracle evaluates these features against production-grade systems, providing critical, actionable feedback. This integrated approach meticulously mimics the iterative process human data scientists employ in feature generation, allowing the system to seamlessly adapt to diverse datasets and real-world operational constraints.

A key breakthrough by Agent0 is the generation of compact feature spaces that offer substantial complementary advantages to traditional embedding-based methodologies. While embeddings are ubiquitous in contemporary recommendation pipelines, their computational demands can be significant. Agent0's compact and inherently interpretable features dramatically reduce computational overhead and accelerate training latency, enabling models to scale effortlessly to millions of instances for real-time performance in demanding production environments. Furthermore, Agent0 has unequivocally demonstrated its capacity to augment existing embedding pipelines by unearthing additional high-signal aspects that might otherwise remain undetected, enriching the overall feature set and improving model accuracy.

In conclusion, Agent0 makes a compelling argument for integrating agentic Large Language Model (LLM) architectures within recommendation systems. Its sophisticated adaptive feedback loops and inherently modular design showcase profound potential for automating iterative learning processes and complex feature engineering tasks, leading to significantly faster, data-driven refinements in intricate workflows. By prioritizing the creation of compact and explainable feature spaces, Agent0 not only enhances system scalability but also meticulously preserves interpretability—a vital attribute for robust, production-ready systems. Future research should meticulously explore expanding evaluation metrics to encompass a wider array of user engagement indicators, rigorously optimizing computational efficiency across all components, and extending Agent0's capabilities into collaborative multi-agent networks featuring specialized sub-agents adept at processing diverse multi-modal data inputs. Overall, Agent0 signifies a profoundly promising trajectory for accelerating both research and production pipelines in modern recommendation settings.

References

1. Al-Ghuribi, K., Noah, S.A.: Recommender systems: a comprehensive survey from 2017 to 2024. arXiv preprint arXiv:2407.13699 (2024)
2. Alammar, J., Grootendorst, M.: Hands-on large language models. O'Reilly (2024). https://www.oreilly.com/library/view/hands-on-large-language/9781098150952/
3. Google: Gemini (2025). https://gemini.google.com/, large Language Model for generative AI. Accessed 23 May 2025
4. Liu, J., et al.: A survey of personalized large language models: Progress and future directions. arXiv preprint arXiv:2502.11528 (2025)
5. Liu, Q., et al.: Large language model enhanced recommender systems: a survey. arXiv preprint arXiv:2412.13432 (2025)
6. McInnes, L., Healy, J., Melville, J.: Umap: uniform manifold approximation and projection for dimension reduction. arXiv preprint arXiv:1802.03426 (2018)
7. Novikov, A., et al.: AlphaEvolve: a coding agent for scientific and algorithmic discovery. Tech. rep., Google DeepMind (2025). https://storage.googleapis.com/deepmind-media/DeepMind.com/Blog/alphaevolve-a-gemini-powered-coding-agent-for-designing-advanced-algorithms/AlphaEvolve.pdf
8. Peng, Q., Liu, H., Huang, H., Yang, Q., Shao, M.: A survey on LLM-powered agents for recommender systems (2025). https://arxiv.org/abs/2502.10050
9. Peng, Q., Liu, H., Huang, H., Yang, Q., Shao, M.: A survey on LLM-powered agents for recommender systems. arXiv preprint arXiv:2502.10050 (2025)

10. Resnick, P., Varian, H.R.: Recommender systems: an overview. Commun. ACM **40**(3), 56–59 (1997)
11. Shen, Y., et al.: Agentic LLMs: a survey of the state of the art in LLM agents. arXiv preprint arXiv:2503.23037 (2025)
12. Wang, R., et al.: Dcn v2: Improved deep & cross network and practical lessons for web-scale learning to rank systems. In: Proceedings of the Web Conference 2021, pp. 1785–1797 (2021)
13. Wang, Y., Li, Y., Lu, J., Li, Y., Li, Y., Lu, J.: Survey on evaluation of LLM-based agents. arXiv preprint arXiv:2503.16416 (2025)
14. Zhang, Y., Qiao, S., Zhang, J., Lin, T.H., Gao, C., Li, Y.: A survey of large language model empowered agents for recommendation and search: towards next-generation information retrieval (2025). https://arxiv.org/abs/2503.05659
15. Zhu, X., et al.: Recommender systems meet large language model agents: a survey. Found. Trends® Privacy Secur. **7**(4), 247–396 (2025)

Bias Mitigation Agent: Optimizing Source Selection for Fair Retrieval

Karanbir Singh(✉), Deepak Muppiri, and William Ngu

Salesforce, San Francisco, CA, USA
{karanbirsingh,dmuppiri,wngu}@salesforce.com

Abstract. Large Language Models (LLMs) have transformed the field of artificial intelligence by unlocking the era of generative applications. Built on top of generative AI capabilities, Agentic AI represents a major shift toward autonomous, goal-driven systems that can reason, retrieve, and act. However, they also inherit the bias present in both internal and external information sources. This significantly affects the fairness and balance of retrieved information, and hence reduces user trust. To address this critical challenge, we introduce a novel Bias Mitigation Agent, a multi-agent system designed to orchestrate the workflow of bias mitigation through specialized agents that optimize the selection of sources to ensure that the retrieved content is both highly relevant and minimally biased to promote fair and balanced knowledge dissemination. The experimental results demonstrate an 81.82% reduction in bias compared to a baseline naive retrieval strategy.

Keywords: Information Retrieval · Agents · Retrieval Augmented Generation · Large Language Models · Bias · Fairness

1 Introduction

The advent of Large Language Models (LLMs) has undeniably marked a pivotal moment in artificial intelligence, ushering in an era defined by powerful generative capabilities and sophisticated natural language understanding. To take advantage of these capabilities, a variety of prompting techniques have emerged, shaping the way users interact with LLMs. The zero-shot prompting allows LLMs to generate responses without explicit examples provided within the prompt. Kojima et al. demonstrated that LLMs are not only capable of generating effective responses, but also show intrinsic reasoning abilities when prompted using the zero shot technique [12]. Similarly, Few-Shot prompting involves offering the model a small, explicitly defined set of examples within the prompt, guiding the model's understanding, and improving output accuracy and reasoning capabilities [3]. To further enhance the capabilities of LLMs, Retrieval-Augmented Generation (RAG) has emerged as an effective extension to traditional prompting techniques. RAG combines retrieval systems with generative language models, enabling the models to access external knowledge sources dynamically during response generation [13].

Q. Wen et al. (Eds.): Agent4IR 2025/2024, CCIS 2695, pp. 110–124, 2026.
https://doi.org/10.1007/978-3-032-11477-8_9

This technological leap serves as the bedrock for rapidly emerging field of agentic AI, representing a significant paradigm shift towards autonomous systems. Unlike earlier AI applications, these agents are designed not just to respond or generate, but to reason, plan, retrieve information, utilize tools, and execute complex, multi-step tasks to achieve specific goals autonomously. However, as agentic AI systems increasingly rely on LLMs and external information sources to inform their reasoning and actions, they inherit and often amplify their critical vulnerability: bias [1]. Bias refers to the consistent imbalance and unjust representation that arises from responses derived from sources that disproportionately privilege or disadvantage specific groups, often mirroring historical or societal inequalities. LLMs are known to capture and reflect the societal biases present in their vast training dataset leading to output that can perpetuate stereotypes related to gender, race, ethnicity, political leaning, and other characteristics [6]. Furthermore, the external knowledge that the agents utilize is itself not neutral. News articles, and other online documents frequently contain skewed perspectives, misinformation, or systemic biases [15]. This propagation of bias directly undermines user trust, compromises system reliability, and poses significant risks of generating harmful or inequitable outcomes [7].

While various techniques exist for mitigating bias within the LLMs themselves such as Zhang et al. presents a model-level debiasing technique using preference optimization algorithm and a debiased preference dataset to address modality bias, where the model over-relies on one modality [26]. These methods often fall short in the dynamic context of Agentic AI workflows. Nowadays, the challenge is to actively managing the bias ingested from constantly changing external sources during task execution. Existing agent frameworks often prioritize task completion and information relevance, latency over robust and integrated mechanisms to evaluate and mitigate the bias. This gap highlights a critical need for novel approaches that address bias directly at the point of information retrieval within agentic architectures.

To address this gap, we introduce the Bias Mitigation Agent, a novel multi-agent framework specifically designed to operate within Agentic AI workflows. Our approach automates the bias mitigation process by optimizing the selection of potential information sources prior to ingestion. We propose two techniques for source selection: a zero-shot approach and a few-shot approach, both designed to dynamically assess and mitigate bias during agent operation, thus enhancing fairness, reliability, and overall system trustworthiness. Our results show that this bias reduction is achieved without a corresponding loss in information relevance, showcasing the potential of our approach to promote the development of more responsible, trustworthy, and equitable Agentic AI systems.

The rest of the paper details the related work and architecture of the Bias Mitigation Agent. Also, we present results of comprehensive experiments designed to validate its effectiveness, demonstrating significant quantitative improvements in retrieving unbiased documents across various scenarios compared to baseline agentic retrieval.

2 Related Work

In this section, we discuss the existing work that was done to identify and mitigate bias from AI driven systems. These techniques can be categorized based on the stage of the AI lifecycle at which they are implemented: pre-processing, in-processing, and post-processing. In addition to these traditional categories, we also include prompt and agentic bias mitigation approaches to capture emerging work that leverages prompt engineering and autonomous agents to address bias.

2.1 Pre-processing Techniques

Pre-processing techniques aim to mitigate biases within datasets before they are used for training models, thereby reducing the risk of perpetuating systemic unfairness and thus inherently producing fair models. Kamiran and Calders proposed three data preprocessing techniques: Massaging, Reweighting, and Sampling to address discrimination and mitigate bias in classification tasks [10]. De-Arteaga et al. removed gender-related words from a set of biographies which resulted in significant improvement in the fairness of a classifier used to predict corresponding occupations [5]. Raza et al. introduced Dbias, an open-source Python package designed to detect and mitigate biases in news articles [16]. Dbias pipeline is made up of three core modules: bias detection, bias recognition, and de-biasing. The pipeline ensures that pre-processed data is free of bias, resulting in fairer models during training.

2.2 In-processing Techniques

While pre-processing techniques focus on data preparation, in-processing approaches tackle bias directly during model training or inference. The idea is to penalize the model if it favors bias and hence it controls the loss function to minimize bias. For example, Rekabsaz et al., develop AdvBert, a BERT based ranking model that uses adversarial training to simultaneously predict relevance and suppress protected attributes in content retrieved by IR systems [17]. Jaenich et al. modify the ranking process using policies to ensure that different document categories are ranked fairly and hence improving fairness metrics by 13% in IR systems [9]. Singh and Joachims propose a generic fairness-aware learning-to-rank (LTR) framework using a policy-gradient method to enforce fairness constraints within a listwise LTR setting [18]. Building on this, Zehlike and Castillo integrate fairness into listwise LTR by incorporating a regularization term into the model's utility objective [25].

2.3 Post Processing Techniques

Post processing introduces fairness after the model or ranking output is generated. Yang and Stoyanovich proposed fairness measures for ranked outputs and incorporated these measures into an optimization framework to improve fairness while maintaining accuracy [23]. Zehlike et al. introduced FA*IR, a post-processing algorithm to ensure group fairness in the retrieved documents by guaranteeing a minimum proportion of protected candidates while maximizing utility in IR systems [24].

2.4 Prompting Techniques

The way users interact with LLMs, and the instructions given to the model, can significantly influence bias expression. Prompt engineering techniques aim to guide the model towards fairer outputs by providing specific instructions (e.g., "avoid stereotypes," "provide balanced views"), setting context, or using role-playing prompts. Ma et al. proposed a novel search strategy based on greedy search to identify the near-optimal prompt to improve the performance of LLM's [14]. Kamruzzaman and Kim explores prompting techniques inspired by dual process theory to reduce social biases in LLM's, techniques such as human and machine like personals, explicit debiasing instructions and chain of though prompting are used to influence the model output to reduce stereotypical responses [11].

2.5 Agentic Mitigation Techniques

The autonomy and interactive nature of Agentic AI require specific mitigation approaches. Given agents' reliance on external information, strategies focusing on bias-aware information retrieval and source selection are crucial. This can involve integrating bias detectors as tools within the agent's framework to evaluate potential sources before using the information [19]. Borah and Mihalcea proposes a multi-agent approach, where a metric is developed to assess the presence of bias and then self-reflection and supervised fine-tuning strategies are employed to mitigate bias [2]. Xu et al. tackles bias mitigation using a multi-objective approach within a multi-agent framework(MOMA) to mitigate bias. Multiple agents are deployed and perform interventions on the bias-related contents of the query [22].

The approach we present uses agentic mitigation techniques, where multiple agents, such as knowledge, bias detector, source selector, and writer, interact and perform specific tasks to mitigate bias in the output provided to the user without degrading performance (Fig. 1).

3 Approach

This section outlines the architecture and operational design of the Bias Mitigation Framework, a multi-agent system constructed using LangGraph [8] which supports stateful workflows to manage inter-agent communication and control flow. The framework is designed to enhance fairness and transparency in

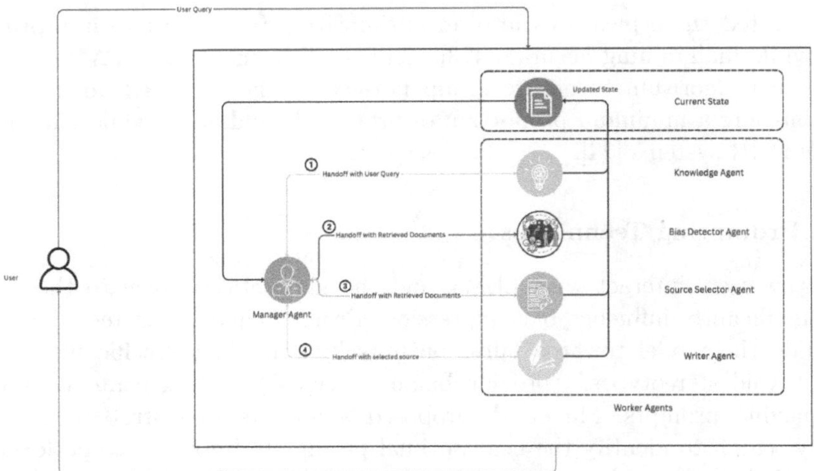

Fig. 1. Architecture of a Supervisor-Based Multi-Agent System for Bias Mitigation. The diagram depicts the life cycle of the agent from user's query to final answer coordinated by the manager agent. The Knowledge Agent retrieves documents, the Bias Detection Agent evaluates retrieved documents for bias, and the Source Selector Agent chooses the optimal unbiased sources. Finally, the Writer Agent synthesizes a coherent, unbiased answer, which is presented back to the user.

knowledge-retrieval tasks by orchestrating a set of specialized agents through a centralized control mechanism.

At its core, the system consists of a Manager Agent (M), a set of Worker Agents (W), and a shared state of the system ($\mathcal{S}$). Each worker agent $w_i \in W$ is responsible for a specific task such as document retrieval, bias detection, source selection, etc. The Manager Agent supervises the execution flow, maintains system state, and coordinates decisions based on intermediate outcomes.

The framework supports three operational modes, enabling different strategies for source selection:

- **No Source Selection**: In this baseline mode, the system retrieves the most relevant document on the basis of vector similarity to the user query. The document is then passed to the writer agent without performing any source selection.
- **Zero-Shot**: In this mode, the system retrieves multiple candidate documents and evaluates them based on relevance and bias. The source selector agent makes a decision based solely on these metrics using its parametric knowledge and reasoning capability. This mode provides a lightweight fairness mechanism without requiring any kind of in-context learning.
- **Few-Shot**: This advanced mode leverages labeled examples to guide the source selector agent in making informed decisions. It combines bias and relevance scores with prior demonstrations to achieve more consistent and

nuanced selections, especially in domains with subjective or ambiguous content.

By supporting these three modes, the framework enables flexible trade-offs between computational efficiency, fairness enforcement, and generalization capability. In the next subsections, the internal state, behavior of the Manager Agent, and the specialized functions of the Worker Agents are defined.

3.1 State

The framework maintains an internal state to facilitate structured decision-making between agents. This state captures the evolving system context, supports transitions, enforces retry logic, and implements guardrails to ensure that the final user response is both relevant and fair. We define the state $\mathcal{S}$ as a tuple, as presented in Eq. 1:

$$\mathcal{S} = (\mathcal{C}, \alpha, \kappa, \mu, \varrho) \tag{1}$$

where:

- $\mathcal{C} = \{c_1, c_2, \ldots, c_n\} \subseteq \mathcal{D}$ is the set of candidate documents retrieved from the vector store, where $\mathcal{D}$ represents the complete corpus of documents.
- $\alpha \in \mathcal{C}$ denotes the document selected for final answer generation.
- $\kappa \in \mathbb{N}$ is the current retry attempt.
- $\mu \in \mathbb{N}$ specifies the maximum number of retries allowed.
- $\varrho \in \mathbb{S}$ captures the most recent rejection reason (e.g., all candidates rejected due to bias or low relevance).

Each document $d_i \in \mathcal{D}$ is further modeled as a tuple, as defined in Eq. 2:

$$d_i = (\chi, \rho, \beta, \gamma) \tag{2}$$

where:

- χ is the textual content of the document.
- $\rho \in [0, 1]$ is the relevance score with respect to the user query.
- $\beta \in [0, 1]$ is the bias confidence score, which represents the system's confidence in its bias assessment.
- $\gamma \in \{0, 1\}$ is a binary label that indicates whether the document is biased ($\gamma = 1$) or unbiased ($\gamma = 0$).

This formalism enables the framework to track a comprehensive and interpretable state across multiple agent interactions and adapt the retrieval process in response to fairness constraints.

3.2 Manager Agent

The manager agent is the coordinator within the Bias Mitigation Framework. It is responsible for maintaining the current state of the system, directing the sequence of agent invocations, and enforcing retry policies in the event of retrieval/selection failures. The agent is guided by system-level prompts, which vary depending on the execution mode. These prompts are illustrated in Figs. 2 and 3.

<System Prompt with source selection>
You are a Supervisor Agent responsible for coordinating multiple specialized agents in a multi-agent system. Your primary goal is to answer user queries using the knowledge provided only and try to minimize bias as much as possible.

Hand off to the `knowledge_agent` to gather information.
Hand off to the `bias_detector_agent` to measure bias inside the retrieved documents.
Hand off to the `selector` to select a source using relevance and bias scores.
Hand off to the `writer` to answer the query based on the selected source.
If this is the final answer, return `__end__` to finish execution.

Fig. 2. System prompt used for manager when source selection is enabled.

<System Prompt without source selection>
You are a Supervisor Agent responsible for coordinating multiple specialized agents in a multi-agent system. Your primary goal is to answer user queries using the knowledge provided only and try to minimize bias as much as possible.

Hand off to the `knowledge_agent` to gather source candidates.
Hand off to the `bias_detector_agent` to measure bias of the retrieved document.
Hand off to the `writer` to answer the query based on the selected source.
If this is the final answer, return `__end__` to finish execution.

Fig. 3. System prompt used for manager when source selection is disabled.

3.3 Worker Agents

The Worker Agents are specialized components of the Bias Mitigation Framework. Unlike the Manager Agent, which controls the orchestration and high-level control flow, these agents focus on specific tasks. The framework consists of the following worker agents:

Knowledge Agent. This agent is implemented as a tool-calling agent that interfaces with ChromaDB [4], which acts as a retriever. Its primary responsibility is to fetch the top-k documents from the corpus based on vector similarity to the user query q. The agent operates differently depending on whether source selection is enabled.

In case of no source selection mode, the agent retrieves a single document $d \in \mathcal{D}$ that maximizes relevance and is automatically chosen as the selected source α without using any sophisticated process to mitigate bias, reflecting the typical behavior of the current LLM-based information retrieval systems in production as presented in the following Eq. 3:

$$\alpha = d = \arg\max_{d_i \in \mathcal{D}} \rho_i \tag{3}$$

Here, ρ_i denotes the relevance score of the document d_i.

When source selection is enabled, the agent retrieves a set of candidate documents $\mathcal{C} \subseteq \mathcal{D}$ to allow downstream agents to assess both relevance and bias. If all candidate documents $c_i \in \mathcal{C}$ are rejected due to high bias or low relevance, then the system retries to retrieve ideal candidates $\mathcal{C}$. In the retry phase, the agent performs query expansion, transforming the original query q into an improved query q' based on the rejection reason ϱ. The new query q' is embedded as $v_{q'}$, and a new set of candidate documents is selected. The resulting set of candidates is passed on to downstream agents for further evaluation.

Bias Detection Agent. This Agent is responsible for evaluating the presence and severity of bias at the source level. When source selection is enabled, the manager forwards the candidate set $\mathcal{C}$ retrieved by the knowledge agent to the agent. Each candidate document $c_i \in \mathcal{C}$ is then analyzed using a pre-trained text classification model called Dbias [16]. For each candidate document, the agent assigns the following:

- A bias confidence score ($\beta_i \in [0, 1]$), which quantifies the system confidence in the detected bias.
- A binary label ($\gamma_i \in \{0, 1\}$), where $\gamma_i = 1$ indicates that the document is biased, and $\gamma_i = 0$ indicates that it is unbiased.

These values are then used to update the current state $\mathcal{S}$. In the case of no source selection mode, the agent operates on the selected document α, applying the same analysis pipeline. This ensures that even in the absence of comparative selection, the system retains awareness of potential bias in the final chosen source.

Source Selection Agent. The agent is responsible for identifying the most suitable document from the candidate set $\mathcal{C}$ by evaluating both the relevance and the bias metrics. This agent is invoked only when the system operates in modes that enable source selection, specifically zero-shot and few-shot.

Zero Shot. In this mode, the agent applies a rule-based selection strategy and uses the parametric knowledge and reasoning ability of the underlying model to select a suitable source α to answer the user's query q. During the *first attempt*, it adheres to strict selection criteria as defined in Eq. 4 where only documents with $\gamma_i = 0$ (unbiased) and $\beta_i \geq 0.7$ (high confidence in the determination) are considered. Among these, the document with the highest relevance score ρ_i is selected.

$$\alpha = \arg\max_{c_i \in \mathcal{C}'} \rho_i, \quad \text{where } \mathcal{C}' = \{c_i \in \mathcal{C} \mid \gamma_i = 0 \land \beta_i \geq 0.7\} \tag{4}$$

If no candidate meets the selection criteria, the agent updates the current state $\mathcal{S}$ with the rejection reason ϱ and the entire retrieval and selection process is executed again by the manager agent. If the system reaches its final attempt, the agent applies relaxed selection rules. This allows the system to still generate an answer even under constrained document conditions.

Few Shot. In this mode, the agent uses in-context examples to guide its decision making. It is provided with a set of labeled instances that illustrate how to select the optimal document based on combinations of $(\beta_i, \gamma_i, \rho_i)$ values. These examples encode decision patterns that help the agent generalize the source selection logic beyond simple thresholding mechanisms.

Given a set of candidates $\mathcal{C}$, the agent evaluates each candidate c_i based on its similarity to previous examples and selects the most appropriate document that meets the dual criteria of high relevance and minimal bias. Formally:

$$\alpha = \arg\max_{c_i \in \mathcal{C}} f_{\text{few-shot}}(\beta_i, \gamma_i, \rho_i) \tag{5}$$

where $f_{\text{few-shot}}$ is a learned or example-conditioned scoring function implicitly encoded via prompt demonstrations.

Similarly to the zero-shot mode, if no candidate meets the selection criteria, then the system attempts to retry and pick the suitable candidate as the selected source α.

Writer Agent. The agent is responsible for generating the final response to the user's query q. It takes the selected document α, as determined by the system, and synthesizes a coherent and contextually grounded response. It is provided with the original user query q and the selected source document α as part of a structured system prompt. The agent is explicitly instructed to rely only on the content of the provided source for its answer generation. This helps ensure factual accuracy and reduces bias by limiting the response to the selected source. The writer agent marks the final stage of the pipeline. Upon generating a satisfactory response, the manager agent terminates the execution and returns the output to the user.

Together, these Worker Agents form a tightly integrated and modular pipeline within the Bias Mitigation Framework. Each agent is designed to fulfill a distinct and well-scoped responsibility, enabling separation of concerns and ease of extension. By delegating complex tasks such as retrieval, bias evaluation, source selection, and response generation to specialized agents, the system ensures robustness, adaptability, and transparency across diverse user queries and fairness constraints. Figure 4 elaborates on the end-to-end execution flow, highlighting how these agents interact in different operating modes to ensure reliable and bias minimized answer to the user's query q.

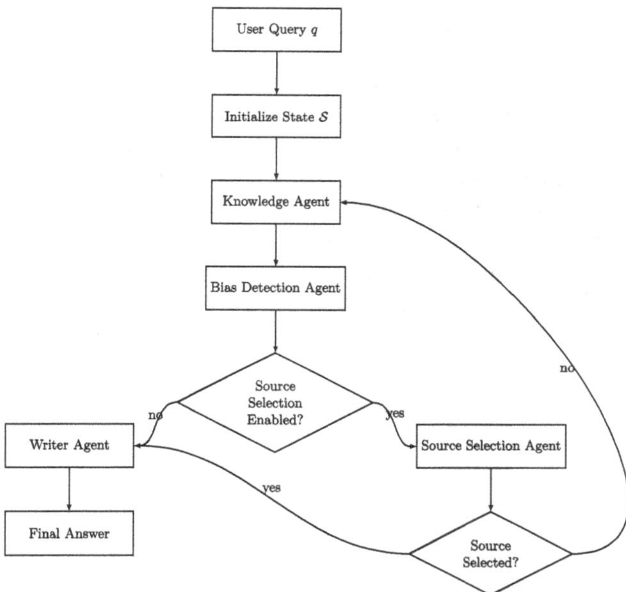

Fig. 4. Execution flow of the Bias Mitigation Framework across all operational modes.

4 Experimentation

This section evaluates the performance of the Bias Mitigation Agent in its ability to reduce bias while maintaining relevance to the original user query. The agent uses annotated news articles sourced from the MBIC [21] and BABE datasets [20] to evaluate its bias detection and mitigation capabilities. We curated *112 queries* to validate the bias mitigation capabilities of the agent. To conduct these experiments, we utilized OpenAI's GPT series models such as GPT-4o-mini, GPT-4.1, and GPT-4.1-mini as the underlying reasoning engines. The following sections provide a detailed analysis of each approach and present their respective outcomes.

Table 1. Summary of relevance, bias confidence, and latency for each source selection method across GPT-4o-mini, GPT-4.1, and GPT-4.1-mini. A divider separates rows from different models.

Reasoner Model	Mode	Rel Min	Rel Max	Rel Avg ± Std	Bias Min	Bias Max	Bias Avg ± Std	Lat Min	Lat Max	Lat Avg ± Std
4o-mini	No Source Selection	−0.058	0.426	0.169 ± 0.092	0.531	0.995	0.840 ± 0.146	8.77	39.00	17.88 ± 4.59
4o-mini	Zero-Shot	0.006	0.402	0.157 ± 0.078	0.515	0.995	0.806 ± 0.143	16.68	69.51	41.38 ± 13.89
4o-mini	Few-Shot	−0.027	0.395	0.150 ± 0.084	0.521	0.995	0.813 ± 0.140	23.92	64.20	37.78 ± 11.40
4.1	No Source Selection	−0.058	0.464	0.172 ± 0.096	0.531	0.995	0.858 ± 0.145	8.97	20.47	12.06 ± 2.45
4.1	Zero-Shot	−0.005	0.971	0.197 ± 0.192	0.524	0.995	0.841 ± 0.130	11.25	81.64	28.66 ± 13.41
4.1	Few-Shot	−0.058	0.978	0.171 ± 0.140	0.515	0.995	0.801 ± 0.146	11.47	65.37	26.93 ± 11.99
4.1-mini	No Source Selection	−0.058	0.907	0.181 ± 0.131	0.099	0.995	0.833 ± 0.163	11.02	43.77	17.12 ± 6.74
4.1-mini	Zero-Shot	−0.058	0.950	0.366 ± 0.367	0.531	0.995	0.837 ± 0.123	13.54	76.09	35.45 ± 15.98
4.1-mini	Few-Shot	−0.058	0.950	0.236 ± 0.251	0.501	0.995	0.829 ± 0.143	13.15	78.67	30.58 ± 13.63

4.1 Baseline: No Source Selection

No Source Selection operates by selecting the most relevant source document, without bias filtering. As shown in Table 1 has the fastest response time among the methods, averaging 12.06 s per query (±2.45) among all models and modes. It achieved a relevance score of 0.181 (±0.131) when using GPT-4.1-mini. However, this speed and relevance came at the expense of fairness, with 49.11% of the outputs labeled biased using GPT-4o-mini, 56.25% using GPT-4.1, and 52.68% using GPT-4.1-mini as shown in Fig. 5. The bias classifier's average confidence score for bias in this mode is 0.8402 (±0.1464), 0.858 (±0.145), and 0.833 (±0.163) using GPT-4o-mini, GPT-4.1, GPT-4.1-mini, respectively.

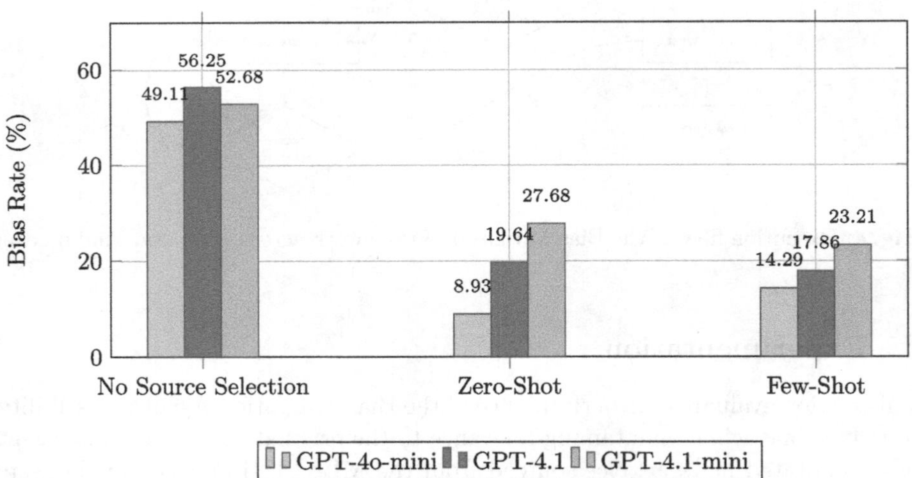

Fig. 5. Bias rate comparison for each source selection method across GPT-4o-mini, GPT-4.1, and GPT-4.1-mini. GPT-4o-mini performs strongest on bias mitigation overall, especially under Zero-Shot prompting.

4.2 Zero-Shot

In case of GPT-4o-mini, the zero-shot mode achieved the lowest bias rate at 8.929%, significantly outperforming the baseline by approximately 81.82% as presented in Fig. 5. The beat average relevance score was 0.366 (±0.367), which is even better than the baseline model in terms of utility of the answers to the queries between all models and modes. However, the zero-shot mode incurred the highest latency, averaging 41.38 s (±13.89) for GPT-4o-mini, 28.66 s (±13.41) for GPT-4.1, and 35.45 s (±15.98) for GPT-4.1-mini, as given in Table 1. It also has taken multiple hops in 70.54%, 21.43%, and 26.79% of queries using GPT-4o-mini, GPT-4.1, and GPT-4.1-mini as depicted in Fig. 6 respectively. The high retry rate suggests that it adopts a more cautious and iterative selection strategy due to the lack of in-context information. Lastly, its average bias confidence was 0.805 (±0.1431) using GPT-4o-mini, 0.841 (±0.130) using GPT-4.1, and 0.837 (±0.123) using GPT-4.1-mini.

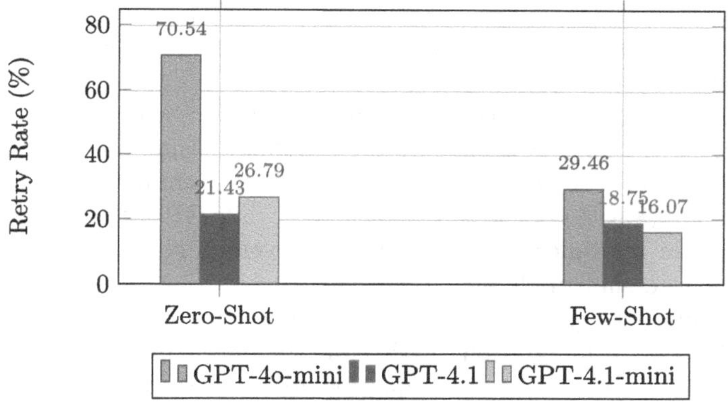

Fig. 6. Retry rates for Zero-Shot and Few-Shot selectors across GPT-4o-mini, GPT-4.1, and GPT-4.1-mini. GPT-4o-mini shows the highest retry activity, especially under Zero-Shot, while GPT-4.1-mini exhibits a more balanced retry profile.

4.3 Few-Shot

The few-shot mode utilizes in-context examples to improve selection accuracy. Figure 5 shows that in case of GPT-4o-mini, it achieved a bias rate of 14.3%, demonstrating a substantial improvement over the baseline mode by 69.48%. Also, while using GPT-4.1 and GPT-4.1-mini, it generated bias results only 17.86% and 23.21% of the time which is the lowest when using these models as reasoning engines. As mentioned in Table 1, the average relevance score of 0.236 (±0.251) was achieved, which is higher than the baseline mode for all models. The major improvement came with the average latency which is 37.79 s (±11.40), 26.93 s (±11.99), and 30.58 s (±13.63) using GPT-4o-mini, GPT-4.1,

GPT-4.1-mini; therefore, it is slightly faster than the zero-shot mode while all the time, as shown in Table 1. Also, Fig. 6 shows that it is more decisive as it only retried 29.46%, 18.75%, and 16.07% of the time using GPT-4o-mini, GPT-4.1, and GPT-4.1-mini.

In summary, when comparing both models, GPT-4.1-mini consistently outperformed GPT-4o-mini, GPT-4.1 in relevance, achieving the highest average relevance score of 0.366 (±0.367) in zero-shot mode which supports its superior ability to generate contextually aligned responses. On the other hand, in terms of bias reduction, GPT-4o-mini with zero-shot mode achieved the lowest bias rate overall at 8.93%, although with increased latency and variability.

5 Conclusion

In this paper, we introduce the Bias Mitigation Agent, a novel multi-agent framework designed to enhance fairness and trust in agentic information retrieval systems by optimizing the source selection process. By using specialized agents for knowledge retrieval, bias detection, and source selection in a supervisor-based architecture, our system enables dynamic and transparent decision-making for mitigating bias in real time.

We evaluated three operational modes, No Source Selection, zero-shot and few-shot across *112 queries* using annotated datasets using GPT-4o-mini, GPT-4.1, GPT-4.1-mini. The results showed that GPT-4o-mini achieved the lowest overall bias rate (8.93%) in the zero-shot mode, while GPT-4.1-mini consistently outperformed in relevance, with a maximum average relevance score (0.366 ± 0.367) in the zero-shot mode.

The modular design of the framework allows for extensibility, making it adaptable for future integrations with more advanced bias detectors, domain-specific retrievers, and additional modalities. As the field of Agentic AI continues to evolve, our work highlights the critical role of optimizing workflows in responsible knowledge retrieval and paves the way for more equitable and trustworthy AI systems.

Future directions include fine-tuning bias scoring functions with human feedback, exploring reinforcement learning for adaptive source selection, and extending the framework to handle multimodal inputs such as images and audio.

References

1. Bolukbasi, T., Chang, K.W., Zou, J., Saligrama, V., Kalai, A.: Man is to computer programmer as woman is to homemaker? Debiasing word embeddings. arXiv (2016). https://arxiv.org/abs/1607.06520
2. Borah, A., Mihalcea, R.: Towards implicit bias detection and mitigation in multi-agent LLM interactions (2024). https://arxiv.org/abs/2410.02584
3. Brown, T.B., et al..: Language models are few-shot learners (2020). https://arxiv.org/abs/2005.14165
4. Chroma: Chroma: The open-source ai application database (2022). https://www.trychroma.com/. Accessed May 2025

5. De-Arteaga, M., et al.: Bias in bios: a case study of semantic representation bias in a high-stakes setting. In: Proceedings of the Conference on Fairness, Accountability, and Transparency, FAT* 2019, January 2019, pp. 120–128. ACM (2019). https://doi.org/10.1145/3287560.3287572
6. Guo, Y., et al.: Bias in large language models: origin, evaluation, and mitigation (2024). https://arxiv.org/abs/2411.10915
7. Hu, M., et al.: No free lunch: retrieval-augmented generation undermines fairness in LLMs, even for vigilant users (2024). https://arxiv.org/abs/2410.07589
8. LangChain Inc.: LangGraph: a library for building multi-agent workflows with LLMs (2023). https://github.com/langchain-ai/langgraph. Accessed May 2025
9. Jaenich, T., McDonald, G., Ounis, I.: Fairness-aware exposure allocation via adaptive reranking. In: Proceedings of the 47th International ACM SIGIR Conference on Research and Development in Information Retrieval, SIGIR '24, Washington, DC, USA, pp. 1504–1513. Association for Computing Machinery (2024). https://doi.org/10.1145/3626772.3657794
10. Kamiran, F., Calders, T.: Data pre-processing techniques for classification without discrimination. Knowl. Inf. Syst. (2011)
11. Kamruzzaman, M., Kim, G.L.: Prompting techniques for reducing social bias in LLMs through system 1 and system 2 cognitive processes (2024). https://arxiv.org/abs/2404.17218
12. Kojima, T., Gu, S.S., Reid, M., Matsuo, Y., Iwasawa, Y.: Large language models are zero-shot reasoners. Adv. Neural. Inf. Process. Syst. **35**, 22199–22213 (2022)
13. Perez, E.: Retrieval-augmented generation for knowledge-intensive NLP tasks: Adv. Neural. Inf. Process. Syst. **33**, 9459–9474 (2020)
14. Ma, H., et al.: Fairness-guided few-shot prompting for large language models (2023). https://arxiv.org/abs/2303.13217
15. Pitoura, E., et al.: On measuring bias in online information. SIGMOD Rec. **46**(4) (2018), https://doi.org/10.1145/3186549.3186553
16. Raza, S., Reji, D.J., Ding, C.: Dbias: Detecting biases and ensuring fairness in news articles. Int. J. Data Sci. Analytics, 1–21 (2022)
17. Rekabsaz, N., Kopeinik, S., Schedl, M.: Societal biases in retrieved contents: measurement framework and adversarial mitigation for BERT rankers. In: Proceedings of the 44th International ACM SIGIR Conference on Research and Development in Information Retrieval (SIGIR '21), Virtual Event, Canada. ACM (2021). https://doi.org/10.1145/3404835.3462949
18. Singh, A., Joachims, T.: Policy learning for fairness in ranking. Adv. Neural Inf. Process. Syst. **32** (2019)
19. Singh, K., Ngu, W.: Bias-aware agent: enhancing fairness in ai-driven knowledge retrieval (2025). https://arxiv.org/abs/2503.21237
20. Spinde, T., Plank, M., Krieger, J.D., Ruas, T., Gipp, B., Aizawa, A.: Neural media bias detection using distant supervision with BABE - bias annotations by experts. In: Findings of the Association for Computational Linguistics: EMNLP 2021, Punta Cana, Dominican Republic, November 2021, pp. 1166–1177. Association for Computational Linguistics (2021). https://doi.org/10.18653/v1/2021.findings-emnlp.101. https://aclanthology.org/2021.findings-emnlp.101
21. Spinde, T., Rudnitckaia, L., Sinha, K., Hamborg, F., Gipp, B., Donnay, K.: MBIC– a media bias annotation dataset including annotator characteristics. arXiv preprint arXiv:2105.11910 (2021)
22. Xu, Z., et al.: Mitigating social bias in large language models: a multi-objective approach within a multi-agent framework (2025). https://arxiv.org/abs/2412.15504

23. Yang, K., Stoyanovich, J.: Measuring fairness in ranked outputs. In: Proceedings of Conference on Scientific and Statistical Database Management, pp. 1–6 (2017)
24. Zehlike, M., Bonchi, F., Castillo, C., Hajian, S., Megahed, M., Baeza-Yates, R.: FA*IR: a fair top-k ranking algorithm. In: Proceedings of the 2017 ACM on Conference on Information and Knowledge Management, pp. 1569–1578 (2017)
25. Zehlike, M., Castillo, C.: Reducing disparate exposure in ranking: a learning to rank approach. In: Proceedings of the Web Conference, pp. 2849–2855 (2020)
26. Zhang, Z., et al.: Debiasing multimodal large language models via noise-aware preference optimization (2025). https://arxiv.org/abs/2503.17928

CACHE-ED: Redefining Document Entity Extraction with Graph-Based Templates, Actor-Critic Agents & HIL

Sudhanshu Bhoi(✉) and Y. V. S. Harish

Amazon, Hyderabad, India
{sudhbee,yvsharis}@amazon.com

Abstract. In this paper, we present CACHE-ED, a novel framework for document entity extraction that combines the power of large language models (LLMs) with graph-based document representations, caching mechanisms, and an actor-critic multi-agent architecture. Our approach addresses the inefficiencies and inaccuracies that are common in extracting structured information from documents, particularly in templated formats like invoices. CACHE-ED implements a human-in-the-loop paradigm in which human reviewers validate and update the system's outputs, establishing a feedback loop that progressively enhances the accuracy of future extractions. This process ultimately eliminates the need for human intervention over time and optimizes tail-end accuracies, refining the system from 90% to near-perfect precision. Our experiments demonstrate that this approach outperforms industry-wide used extraction mechanisms by 8% and improves the speed & reduces cost by over 50% each, making it a scalable solution for real-world applications.

Keywords: Document Entity Extraction · Graph-based Templates · Actor-Critic Systems · Large Language Models · Caching Mechanisms · Human-in-the-Loop Learning · Document Processing · Information Extraction · Template Matching · Data Validation

1 Introduction

Document entity extraction has become a crucial task across industries, from invoice processing in finance to legal document analysis, where the accurate identification of key information is essential. Despite significant advances in natural language processing (NLP) and large language models (LLMs), current state-of-the-art systems still struggle to deliver high accuracy, particularly achieving 100% accuracy on challenging documents from **Day 1** remains unattainable, even with the significant advancements in current technologies, making it difficult to optimize "tail-end" accuracy. Tools like AWS Textract, Google Cloud

S. Bhoi and Y. V. S. Harish—Equal contribution.

Q. Wen et al. (Eds.): Agent4IR 2025/2024, CCIS 2695, pp. 125–135, 2026.
https://doi.org/10.1007/978-3-032-11477-8_10

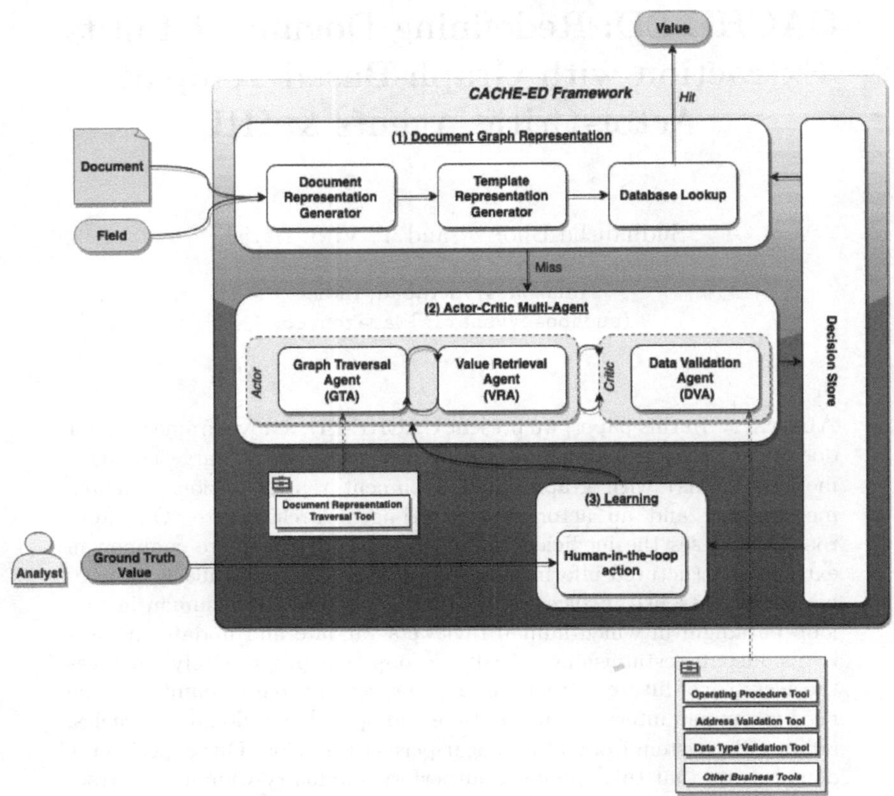

Fig. 1. Overview of the CACHE-ED Framework. The process begins with Graph Representation. This is followed by the Actor-Critic Multi-Agent Architecture, where the Actor extracts data through graph traversal and the Critic validates the output using external tools. The framework incorporates Learning via Human-in-the-Loop, where human feedback refines the extraction (if required), and results are stored in a Decision Store.

Document AI, and LLMs such as GPT-based models or Anthropic's Claude demonstrate strong baseline performance, but they fall short in complex, templated document formats or edge cases, where high precision is needed.

A major challenge with these systems is their inconsistency in handling structured documents that have recurring but slightly varied templates, often leading to the incorrect extraction of one or two fields. For instance, invoices, contracts, or forms that follow similar patterns but differ in layout can confuse even the most advanced models, resulting in errors or incomplete extractions. Moreover, while LLMs like Claude and GPT-4 are excellent at understanding and generating language, they are computationally expensive and often require repeated calls to process documents that share similar structures & yet do not guarantee results that are replicable. This not only increases costs but also leads to inefficiencies in workflows, particularly when processing large volumes of documents in real-time environments.

The stakes of such minor misses/inaccurate extraction are higher in financial documents, an error in extracting or validating tax amounts, net totals, or country-specific VAT rates can cause significant downstream issues. Current systems often lack robust mechanisms for validating extracted information against external compliance standards or cross-referencing with domain-specific data, leaving room for errors in critical areas.

Moreover, existing LLM-based extraction tools do not inherently learn from their mistakes. Although human reviewers are often needed to correct errors, this feedback is rarely integrated into the system in a meaningful way, leading to repeated mistakes and inefficiencies over time. As a result, organizations often face the dual challenge of handling high costs and inconsistent accuracy, especially for recurring document formats.

In response to these challenges, in this work, we propose **CACHE-ED** (**C**ached & **A**daptive decisions that are validated by **C**ritic & learned from **H**uman-in-the-loop to perform **E**ntity **E**xtraction in **D**ocument), a novel framework designed to overcome these limitations by combining graph-based document representation, caching for recurring templates, and an actor-critic LLM model with external validation tools. Our approach not only improves the efficiency of document entity extraction but also introduces a self-learning mechanism that continuously improves tail-end accuracy, ensuring that errors are corrected and not repeated.

Our contributions are summarised as follows:

- We introduce a novel document graph representation that leverages existing OCR technologies to capture the semantic relationships between various entity relations within the document.
- We introduce the concept of caching graph template representations for incoming documents to lower data extraction costs and improve processing speed.
- We present a comprehensive benchmark for document data extraction, comparing various existing approaches and demonstrating the effectiveness of our caching strategy. Our results show state-of-the-art performance in this extensive evaluation.

2 Related Work

Document information extraction techniques using Large Language Models (LLMs) can be categorized into white-box and black-box approaches. White-box techniques such as UIPath [4], TextMonkey [8], or DocLLM [13], require fine-tuning of LLMs and access to internal document representations, which can be expensive and infeasible when using proprietary LLM APIs. Conversely, black-box techniques treat LLMs as closed systems and have been explored for extracting information from legal contracts [15] and research papers [10] using semantic parsing and prompt engineering. However, these methods are optimized for retrieving specific sets of fields [11] and, as observed in our experiments, fall short due to a lack of entity-relation understanding.

First introduced in [9], extraction of information from documents as entities and their relationships has been possible with use of visual and textual encoder and decoder networks [7,12]. However, these representations contain redundant links, lack context links, partially identify keys and fail to tag values in a line. Our approach overcomes these problems by building document representation on top of AWS Textract's [2] output and use our CACHE-ED framework to map information to any business-defined fields.

LLM-based solutions raise concerns regarding reliability, accuracy, performance, and cost-efficiency. Several solutions have been explored to address these problems, including external tool validation [5], learning from human-in-the-loop interactions [14], and caching of prompts and answers [3,6]. Our CACHE-ED framework incorporates these techniques to ensure reliable, accurate, and cost-effective document information extraction.

3 Approach

In this work, we introduce a novel framework for document entity extraction that leverages large language models (LLMs) in conjunction with graph-based document representations, caching mechanisms, and actor-critic multi-agent architecture. Our approach is designed to improve efficiency, accuracy, and self-learning capability in structured document extraction tasks, particularly for documents that follow repetitive or templated formats such as invoices. The methodology centers on four key innovations: converting documents into a graph structure, caching extraction processes for reuse, using an actor-critic LLM multi-agent framework, and introducing human in the loop actions for continuously improving the system over time. The complete end to end flow is show in Fig. 1 & refer the Algorithm 1 for the control/data flow of the framework.

3.1 Graph-Based Representation

We leverage Block objects and relationships provided by AWS Textract [2] (refer Fig. 2 graph (A)) to analyze the document structure and content. We extract information that was missed by the KEY_VALUE_SET Block from each of the LINE Block using Named Entity Recognition (NER) to identify and mask Key and pair it with associated Value (Fig. 3). We then distill the information from nested structures into logical parent-child Key-to-Key relations. For example, the TABLE Block is represented as parent Key with table information, which is connected to multiple child Keys representing column headers.

To ensure that our representation is robust to document orientations, variations in the page dimensions, and length of intermediary structures, we aggregate all of the PAGE blocks under a single Document node. Furthermore, we incorporate spatial and contextual awareness between the child Keys of each node by introducing adjacent Key-to-Key relations using a proximity-based Eq. 3. Finally, we anonymize the node identifiers so that paths to Values can be used across different document instances of the same template. The resulting graph is referred to as the document representation graph (refer Fig. 2 graph (B)). By removing the Value nodes, which are the only variable nodes across different document instances of a template, we obtain the template representation graph (refer Fig. 2 graph (C)).

With these graph representations, the system can effectively model the relationships between different entities and accommodate even complex document layouts. When an input query with field is provided, the actor (Sect. 3.3) traverses the document representation graph to identify relevant nodes for data extraction.

$$DR_{page}(x, y, p) = (x, p + y - 1) \tag{1}$$

$$P(\alpha, \beta) = D_{euclid}(DR_{page}(x^{\alpha}, y^{\alpha}, p^{\alpha}), DR_{page}(x^{\beta}, y^{\beta}, p^{\beta})) \tag{2}$$

$$L(\alpha, \beta) = signum(D_{thresh} - P(\alpha, \beta)) \tag{3}$$

Where

- x, y represent coordinates and p represents page of a bounding box
- α, β represent two candidate entity bounding boxes
- DR_{page} is a page dimension reduction function that maps 3D to 2D space
- P is a proximity function that calculates euclidean distance in the mapped coordinate
- L is a linking function that determines whether link between the two entity is to be established based on threshold distance D_{thresh}

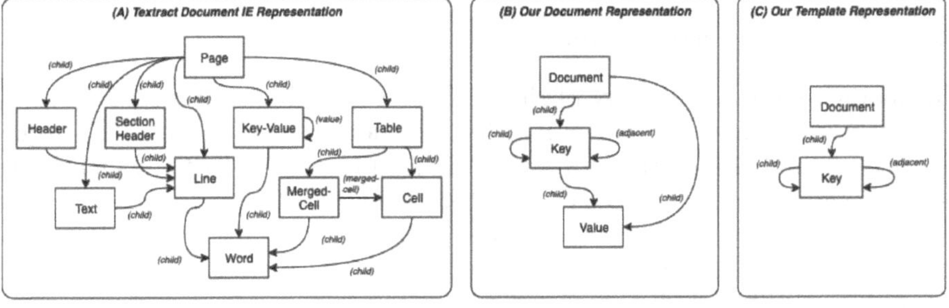

Fig. 2. Three states of document representation. Part (A) shows AWS Textract Blocks with relations. Part (B) shows document representation D_r retaining required information into smaller structure with context aware links. Part (C) shows template representation T_r without document-instance specific value nodes.

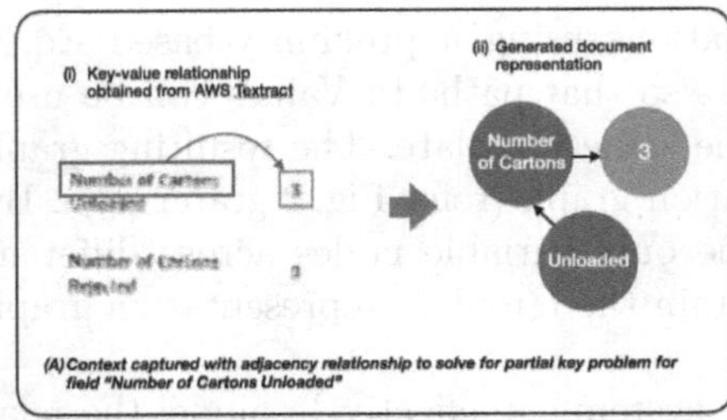

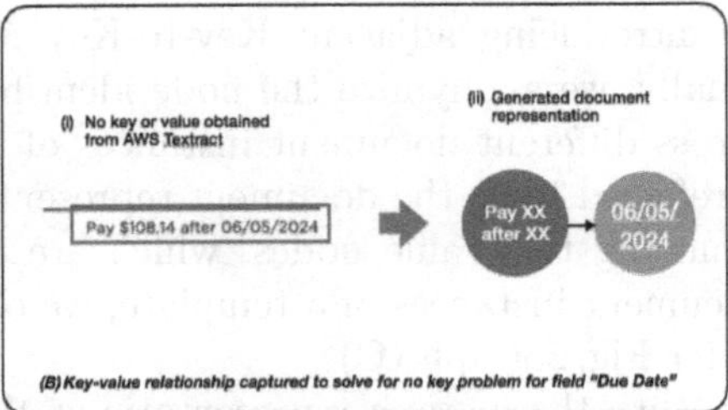

Fig. 3. Two cases of key-value relation capture miss by AWS Textract. Part (A) shows the case of partial key capture and how the document representation overcomes it with context-aware links. Part (B) shows the case of no key capture and how developing new links between masked key and value overcomes this.

3.2 Caching Mechanism for Repeated Templates

To reduce redundant LLM computations for recurring documents of the same template, we introduce a caching mechanism that associates the template graph representation of previously processed documents T_r and field F with chosen path to corresponding value P_i. When a new document arrives, its template representation T_r and query field F are compared with those of previously processed documents. If a match is found, the system bypasses the need for another LLM call and directly retrieves the stored information. The retrieved path to value P_i is then used to traverse the document representation D_r and find required value V.

This cache-based approach significantly speeds up the extraction process for recurring templates, making it particularly cost & speed effective in use cases like invoice processing, where formats are often consistent across multiple documents from the same source. Moreover, it enables the system to learn information for one document and apply it to all documents with the same template (Sect. 3.4).

3.3 Actor-Critic Multi-agent Module

This module serves as the core of the CACHE-ED framework, composed of two primary components: (i) the Actor, which includes the Graph Traversal Agent (GTA) and the Value Retrieval Agent (VRA), and (ii) the Critic, which houses the Data Validation Agent (DVA). The Actor and Critic modules are designed to be extensible, allowing for the inclusion of additional agents to enhance extraction capabilities based on document complexity.

The Graph Traversal Agent (GTA) is responsible for identifying multiple candidate paths P that are relevant to the field F being extracted from the document representation D_r. GTA utilizes the graph traversal tool to explore the neighboring nodes for more context or to find the initial set of Key nodes based on semantics of the field F. The Value Retrieval Agent (VRA) then selects the correct path P_j, where the terminal node contains the value V for the field F.

Once the Actor has performed the extraction, the Critic, consisting of Data Validation Agent (DVA), steps in to validate the extracted data using external tools. For example, the Critic can call APIs such as the Amazon Location API to verify address fields like "Ship from", "Ship to" or "Bill to" & verify the acceptable VAT rates by identifying the country of origin, or it can perform arithmetic checks to ensure that the net amount plus tax equals the gross amount, or conduct data type, regex & other rule-based validations. This combination of extraction and validation ensures higher accuracy and reduces errors in the data retrieval process.

3.4 A Self-learning System with Human-in-the-Loop

Human reviewers play an integral role in refining the system's accuracy over time. After the extraction and validation processes, human reviewers are tasked with reviewing the results and making corrections if necessary. The corrected value V_{HIL} from the reviewer are passed as feedback to the Actor (Sect. 3.3), which determines the new path to value P_k. Subsequently, the path in the cache is updated from P_j to P_k, ensuring that new documents of same template retrieve accurate results in future without requiring further human intervention or LLM calls.

This human-in-the-loop feedback mechanism creates a continuously improving system, preventing the repetition of errors by the LLM and ensuring that the system becomes more robust and accurate over time. It further enables the framework to adapt to complex document structures and edge cases, while gradually reducing the need for human intervention as the system learns and refines its extraction capabilities.

4 Experiments

To evaluate the performance of our proposed CACHE-ED framework, we conducted a comprehensive comparison with state-of-the-art document extraction techniques. These techniques included the current solution of AWS Textract [2] with key to field exact-match (Textract + Key EM) mappings, a Multimodal LLM [1], and a hybrid approach that passes AWS Textract ouptut to LLM without any intermediate representations (Textract + LLM). The goal of the experiment was to measure the effectiveness of CACHE-ED in terms of accuracy, efficiency, and repeatability when extracting structured information from invoices of varying complexity (Table 1).

We evaluated our approach using a subset of real-world invoices from the RVL-CDIP dataset, which we categorized into three distinct levels of extraction difficulty.:

- **Easy**: The easiest level comprised invoices with a simple, well-aligned structure, minimal variation in formatting, & limited textual content.
- **Medium**: Scanned Invoices with more complex layouts, including tables and varying formats for key-value pairs.

Algorithm 1 CACHE-ED - Document Field Retrieval Algorithm

```
Require: Document D, Field F
D_r ← GenerateDocumentRepresentation(D)    ▷ Document Graph Representation
T_r ← GenerateTemplateRepresentation(D_r)
P_i ← DBLookup(T_r, F)
if P_i is present then
    V ← GetValueForDocument(D_r, P_i)
    return Value V
else                                        ▷ Actor-Critic Multi-Agent
    do
        Invoke Graph Traversal Agent (GTA): P ← GTA(D_r, F)
        Invoke Value Retrieval Agent (VRA): P_j, V ← VRA(P, F)
        Invoke Data Validation Agent (DVA): Valid ← DVA(V, F)
    while Valid is False & V is present
    if V is present then
        DBCreate(T_r, F, P_j)
        return Value V
    end if
end if
V_HIL ← Value from Human-in-the-Loop (HIL)  ▷ Learning
if V_HIL is not equal to V then
    do
        Invoke Graph Traversal Agent (GTA): P ← GTA(D_r, F, V_HIL)
        Invoke Value Retrieval Agent (VRA): P_k, V ← VRA(P, F, V_HIL)
    while V is present & V is not equal to V_HIL
    if V is present then
        DBUpdate(T_r, F, P_k)
    end if
end if
```

- **Hard**: Scanned Invoices with highly unstructured, unclear & cluttered formats, hand written/scanned, varied layouts, and irregular/random placement of key-value information.

The performance of each approach was evaluated based on accuracy, defined as percentage of correctly extracted fields, across the three complexity levels mentioned above. As all four approaches performed equally well on easy category

Table 1. Table illustrating how CACHE-ED remains agnostic to the Claude 3 family of models. Indicating the effectiveness of our document representation and actor agent.

Performance analysis across various Claude family models in percentage (%)			
Approaches (→)	ClaudeV3-Sonnet	ClaudeV3-Haiku	ClaudeV3-Opus
Vendor Name	85	85	85
Customer Number	60	50	60

Table 2. We present quantitative results across different approaches on medium and hard invoice samples on some of the keys as shown above. For our Actor-Critic agent architecture, we utilized the Claude3-Sonnet model. We see that CACHE-ED performs at par with other approaches.

Comparison across approaches on various invoice types in percentage (%)				
Approaches (→)	Textract + Key EM	Multimodal LLM	Textract + LLM	CACHE-ED
Vendor Name	57.9	73.69	77.78	**84.21**
Customer Number	38.24	50	55	**60**
Invoice Number	66.05	75	70	**77.78**
Invoice Date	86	**94.73**	83.33	94.45
Invoice Amount	83.23	**89**	**89**	**89**

invoices, we report extraction accuracy metrics only on the medium and hard categories for the quantitative comparison in Table 2.

We further analysed the performance of the CACHE-ED framework across three LLMs of the Claude 3 family [1] with varying order of capability. This analysis helped us measure the efficacy of the proposed document representation D_r and the actor agent (Sect. 3.3). As demonstrated in the Table 3, the CACHE-ED framework remained agnostic to the capabilities of the LLM and maintained consistent performance (Fig. 4).

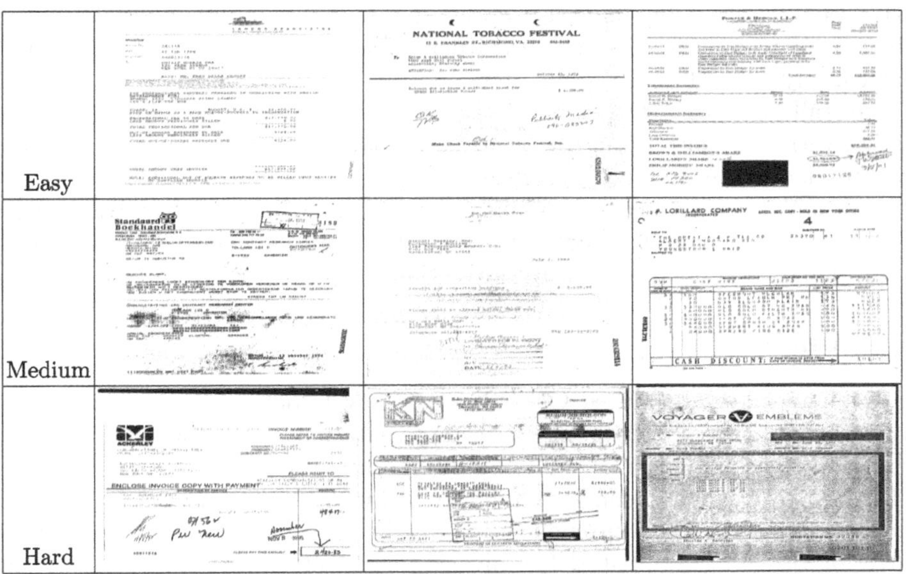

Fig. 4. Sample real-world invoices from the RVL-CDIP dataset.

We also present a quantitative analysis of cache hit percentages for a group of vendors in Table 3. By utilizing the proposed template representation T_r and caching mechanism, we achieve at least a 50% reduction in the costs associated with LLM. Further, this approach significantly improves latency and ensures repeatability, which becomes a substantial advantage as the system scales. It is important to note that the dataset is restricted by a small timeframe, and the numbers are expected to improve over time.

Table 3. Table demonstrating the effectiveness of our caching strategy: Cache hit percentages across various vendor templates.

Vendors	Cache Hit %
A	58.33
B	70.58
C	54.54
D	56.25
E	60
F	88.89

Additionally, the DVA (data validation agent) in the actor-critic multi-agent (Sect. 3.3) allowed CACHE-ED to incorporate external validation tools, such as compliance checks for VAT rates and gross amount calculations, improving extraction accuracy for complex invoices. In contrast, other methods mentioned above lead to inaccuracies in critical fields like tax amounts and total sums, particularly in hard invoice templates.

Overall, CACHE-ED demonstrated superior performance across all categories, with a notable advantage in medium and hard invoices where traditional systems faced the greatest challenges. The novel graph-based document representations, caching mechanism, and incorporation of external validation tools contribute to the improved accuracy, repeatability, and efficiency of the CACHE-ED framework in document entity extraction tasks.

5 Conclusion

In this paper, we introduced CACHE-ED, a novel document entity extraction framework that combines graph-based representations, an actor-critic architecture, and a caching mechanism to optimize accuracy, reduce costs, and enhance efficiency. By caching document templates and incorporating human-in-the-loop feedback, CACHE-ED continuously improves extraction performance, particularly for recurring templates. For invoice document extraction, our approach outperformed existing methods, especially on complex templates, while reducing extraction errors and improving validation. Experiments demonstrated the effectiveness of our caching strategy in lowering latency and cost, showcasing the framework's adaptability and scalability across various document complexities.

References

1. Anthropic: Introducing the next generation of Claude (2024). https://www.anthropic.com/news/claude-3-family
2. AWS: What is Amazon Textract? (2022). https://aws.amazon.com/textract/
3. Bang, F.: GPTCache: an open-source semantic cache for LLM applications enabling faster answers and cost savings, pp. 212–218 (2023). https://doi.org/10.18653/v1/2023.nlposs-1.24
4. UiPath Community blog: DocPath: a fine-tuned large language model for information extraction from documents. https://www.uipath.com/blog/ai/docpath-information-extraction-large-language-model
5. Gou, Z., et al.: Critic: large language models can self-correct with tool-interactive critiquing (2024). https://arxiv.org/abs/2305.11738
6. Li, J., Xu, C., Wang, F., von Riedemann, I.M., Zhang, C., Liu, J.: SCALM: towards semantic caching for automated chat services with large language models (2024). https://arxiv.org/abs/2406.00025
7. Liao, H., et al.: DocTr: document transformer for structured information extraction in documents. In: ICCV 2023 (2023). https://www.amazon.science/publications/doctr-document-transformer-for-structured-information-extraction-in-documents
8. Liu, Y., et al.: TextMonkey: an OCR-free large multimodal model for understanding document (2024). https://arxiv.org/abs/2403.04473
9. Oral, B., Emekligil, E., Arslan, S., Eryiğit, G.: Information extraction from text intensive and visually rich banking documents. Inf. Process. Manage. **57**(6), 102361 (2020)
10. Polak, M.P., Morgan, D.: Extracting accurate materials data from research papers with conversational language models and prompt engineering. Nat. Commun. **15**(1) (2024). https://doi.org/10.1038/s41467-024-45914-8. https://www.nature.com/articles/s41467-024-45914-8#citeas
11. Seitl, F., et al.: Assessing the quality of information extraction (2024). https://arxiv.org/abs/2404.04068
12. Wan, J., et al.: OmniParser: a unified framework for text spotting, key information extraction and table recognition (2024). https://arxiv.org/abs/2403.19128
13. Wang, D., et al.: DocLLM: a layout-aware generative language model for multimodal document understanding (2023). https://arxiv.org/abs/2401.00908
14. Xiao, H., Wang, P.: LLM A*: human in the loop large language models enabled A* search for robotics (2024). https://arxiv.org/abs/2312.01797
15. Zhao, Y., Gao, H.: Utilizing large language models for information extraction from real estate transactions (2024). https://arxiv.org/abs/2404.18043

Knowledge Graphs as Unified Agentic Memory for Improved Retrieval, Reasoning and Causal Analysis in Cloud Database Operations

Yong Liu(✉)

Salesforce, Inc., Seattle, WA, USA
yongliu@salesforce.com

Abstract. Knowledge graphs (KGs) have emerged as a transformative technology for enhancing AI agent memory in cloud database operations. This position paper argues that KGs, particularly causal knowledge graphs (CKGs), serve as unified agentic memory systems that address critical limitations of current approaches including vector search and long context windows. We present evidence from recent research showing that KGs improve context retention, relational modeling, and temporal reasoning in large language model (LLM) agents. Our analysis demonstrates how KGs enable autonomous cloud database operations through enhanced query optimization, root cause analysis, and remediation recommendations. We propose a comprehensive six-dimensional classification framework for memory types across temporal, functional, granularity, update frequency, distribution, and hybrid integration dimensions, showing how KGs support all memory categories while providing structured, causal reasoning capabilities essential for complex database operations.

Keywords: knowledge graphs · agentic memory · cloud databases · causal reasoning · large language models · autonomous operations · AIOps

1 Introduction

The proliferation of cloud database systems has created unprecedented challenges for autonomous operations, requiring AI agents capable of complex reasoning, memory management, and causal analysis. Traditional approaches using vector search and long context windows in large language models (LLMs) have proven insufficient for handling the relational and temporal complexities inherent in database operations [15].

Knowledge graphs (KGs) have emerged as a promising solution for unified agentic memory, offering structured representation of entities, relationships, and temporal dynamics. Recent advances in causal knowledge graphs (CKGs) and

Q. Wen et al. (Eds.): Agent4IR 2025/2024, CCIS 2695, pp. 136–145, 2026.
https://doi.org/10.1007/978-3-032-11477-8_11

temporal knowledge graphs (TKGs) have demonstrated superior performance in context retention and multi-hop reasoning tasks [6,19].

This position paper argues that KGs represent the effective approach for agentic memory in cloud database operations with efficient context engineering. We present evidence from recent research and practical implementations, including structured reasoning approaches for incident triage [25], to support our thesis that KGs address fundamental limitations of current memory systems while enabling autonomous database operations.

Our contributions include: (1) a comprehensive analysis of KG advantages over vector search and long context windows, (2) a six-dimensional classification framework of memory types supported by KGs, including novel distribution and hybrid integration dimensions, (3) detailed use cases demonstrating KG applications in cloud database operations from development to remediation, and (4) analysis of challenges and future directions for KG-based agentic memory systems.

2 Current State and Limitations

2.1 Limitations of Existing Approaches

Current LLM-based agents face significant challenges in memory management and reasoning. The study by [15] reveals a 39% performance drop in multi-turn conversations due to context loss and error recovery issues. This limitation is particularly problematic in database operations requiring sustained context across multiple interactions.

Vector Search Limitations. While vector search excels at similarity-based retrieval, it cannot model explicit relationships between entities. The BRIGHT benchmark [22] demonstrates that even state-of-the-art retrieval models perform poorly on reasoning-intensive queries, with leading models achieving only 18.3 nDCG@10 compared to 59.0 on traditional benchmarks. This limitation becomes critical in database operations where understanding schema relationships, dependency chains, and causal connections is essential for effective reasoning.

Vector search treats documents as isolated entities, failing to capture the interconnected nature of database schemas, configuration dependencies, and operational workflows. This approach struggles with complex queries requiring multi-hop reasoning across related entities, such as tracing the impact of a schema change through dependent services and performance metrics.

Long Context Window Constraints. Modern LLMs support extensive context windows (e.g., Claude Opus 3 with 200k tokens), but suffer from high computational costs and inefficient structured querying capabilities. Long context windows lack the structured representation necessary for complex relational queries and temporal reasoning required in database operations. They also exhibit degraded performance on information retrieval tasks when relevant information is buried within large contexts, a phenomenon known as the "lost in the middle" problem.

Furthermore, long context approaches are stateless and cannot maintain persistent memory across sessions, making them unsuitable for long-term operational scenarios where historical context and learned patterns are crucial for decision-making.

2.2 Knowledge Graph Advantages

Recent research demonstrates KGs' superiority in addressing these limitations. Zep's Graphiti framework [19] using temporal knowledge graphs outperformed MemGPT in the Deep Memory Retrieval benchmark (94.8% vs. 93.4%) and achieved up to 18.5% accuracy improvement in LongMemEval for cross-session synthesis.

The Mem0 system [6] showed KG-based approaches excelling in context retention tasks, achieving 26% relative improvements over OpenAI baselines while reducing p95 latency by 91% and saving over 90% token costs. These results highlight KGs' ability to maintain structured memory while supporting complex reasoning patterns essential for database operations.

The Cognee framework demonstrates superior performance in context retention benchmarks like HotPotQA, where KG-based memory systems significantly outperform traditional vector-based approaches in maintaining coherent understanding across multi-turn interactions [7]. This advantage becomes particularly pronounced in database operations requiring sustained reasoning over complex schema relationships and operational dependencies.

3 Knowledge Graphs for Agentic Memory

3.1 Comprehensive Memory Classification Framework

Building on comprehensive surveys of memory mechanisms in LLM-based agents [13,28], we propose a six-dimensional classification framework of memory types that KGs uniquely support (Table 1). This framework extends traditional memory categorizations to address the distributed and hybrid nature of modern cloud database operations.

The **Distribution Dimension** addresses the architectural deployment of KG memory systems. Distributed KG memory enables individual agents to maintain specialized knowledge graphs tailored to their specific roles and contexts, such as query optimization agents maintaining detailed execution plan histories or monitoring agents tracking service-specific performance patterns. Centralized KG memory provides shared access to stable, slow-changing knowledge such as database schemas, organizational procedures, and cross-service dependencies that require consistent global views.

The **Hybrid Integration Dimension** captures the modern trend toward federated memory architectures. Hybrid KGs integrate machine learning models as node attributes, enabling dynamic inference capabilities within the graph

Table 1. Six-Dimensional Knowledge Graph Memory Classification Framework

Dimension	Category	Description and Application
Temporal	Short-term	Recent interactions and immediate context, efficiently stored and updated in KGs through real-time graph modifications
	Long-term	Historical patterns and accumulated knowledge, tracked through temporal knowledge graphs with versioning capabilities
Functional	Episodic	Event-specific information stored as time-stamped graph structures, enabling causal sequence tracking
	Semantic	General domain knowledge represented through ontological relationships and semantic networks
	Procedural	Task processes and workflows modeled as graph-based execution patterns
	Causal	Cause-and-effect relationships explicitly modeled as directed edges with causal semantics
Granularity	Coarse-grained	High-level abstractions such as service-level dependencies, major system components, and aggregate performance metrics
	Fine-grained	Detailed entity-level information including individual query patterns, specific configuration parameters, and granular performance measurements
Update Frequency	Dynamic	Rapidly changing information such as real-time metrics, active incidents, and current system states
	Slow-changing	Stable information including schema definitions, established procedures, and historical patterns
Distribution	Distributed	Agent-specific KG memory instances for personalized contexts, local optimizations, and specialized domain knowledge
	Centralized	Shared KG memory for slow-changing common knowledge, global schemas, and cross-agent coordination
Hybrid Integration	Hybrid	KG nodes with ML model services as attributes, real-time data retrieval from lakehouse/metric stores via tools, maintaining meta-relationships
	Non-hybrid	Traditional KG storage with direct data embedding, without external service integration or real-time data federation

structure. They also maintain meta-relationships to external data sources (lakehouse systems, metric stores, log aggregators) rather than directly storing volatile data, allowing real-time data retrieval through tool interfaces while preserving the structural relationships that define data semantics and access patterns.

This six-dimensional framework (Table 1) enables KGs to provide comprehensive memory management that adapts to different operational requirements, architectural constraints, and integration patterns of modern cloud database systems.

3.2 Causal Knowledge Graphs

Causal knowledge graphs extend traditional KGs by explicitly representing cause-and-effect relationships [1,10,11,14]. Early work by Jaimini and Sheth [11] established foundational approaches for causal explainability using interventional and counterfactual reasoning, while recent industry developments demonstrate practical applications in data-driven decision making [3]. This capability is crucial for database operations where understanding causal impacts—such as how configuration changes affect performance—enables predictive and prescriptive analytics.

The CDF-RAG framework [12] demonstrates how causal reasoning can be integrated into retrieval-augmented generation systems, enhancing multi-hop causal reasoning for tasks like root cause analysis. This approach addresses the need for causal consistency in complex database troubleshooting scenarios, while recent work on causal graphs for complex reasoning [16] shows up to 10% absolute gains in diagnostic accuracy.

CKGs enable agents to understand not just correlations but actual causal mechanisms, allowing for more effective intervention strategies and preventing unintended consequences during remediation efforts. This causal understanding is particularly valuable in database operations where changes can have cascading effects across interconnected systems.

4 Use Cases in Cloud Database Operations

4.1 Development and Deployment

Code Development. KGs model database schemas, constraints, and relationships, providing LLM agents with structured context for query writing and optimization. The KnowAgent framework [29] demonstrates how knowledge-augmented planning enhances LLM capabilities in complex reasoning tasks. CKGs enable prediction of performance impacts from schema changes, supporting proactive optimization decisions.

In practice, KGs can represent complex schema relationships, foreign key dependencies, and index structures, enabling agents to generate optimized queries that leverage existing indexes and avoid costly operations. The structured representation allows for sophisticated query planning that considers both syntactic correctness and performance implications.

Release Management. KGs track version dependencies and change impacts across database systems. The temporal aspect allows agents to understand evolution patterns and predict potential conflicts or performance degradations, as shown in entity-relationship graph modeling [21].

KGs can model deployment pipelines, service dependencies, and rollback procedures, enabling automated risk assessment and deployment planning. The causal memory dimension helps predict the downstream effects of changes, while the granularity dimension allows for both high-level service impact analysis and detailed configuration validation.

4.2 Operations and Monitoring

Root Cause Analysis. The COMET system [25] demonstrates practical applications of structured reasoning in incident triage, achieving enhanced accuracy and reduced time to mitigation. KGs enhance this approach by modeling causal relationships between metrics, configurations, and performance outcomes. The KGroot framework [24] specifically addresses root cause analysis using knowledge graphs and graph convolutional networks, achieving 93.5% accuracy in identifying top-3 potential causes.

KGs excel at representing the complex interdependencies in cloud database systems, where a single issue can manifest through multiple symptoms across different system layers. The causal memory dimension enables agents to trace symptom chains back to root causes, while the temporal dimension helps identify patterns and recurring issues. Recent advances in AI-assisted database troubleshooting, such as Google Cloud's proactive query performance prediction and automated remediation recommendations [9], demonstrate the practical value of structured knowledge representation in operational database management.

Automated Remediation. KGs store patterns of successful fixes and their contexts, enabling agents to recommend appropriate remediation strategies. CKGs predict the causal impacts of proposed interventions, reducing the risk of unintended consequences.

The procedural memory dimension captures proven remediation workflows, while causal memory ensures that interventions address root causes rather than symptoms. The update frequency dimension allows for both immediate tactical responses and strategic long-term improvements.

SQL Optimization. Recent work on LLM-based query optimization [2,23] shows promise when augmented with structured knowledge. KGs provide the relational context necessary for understanding query semantics and optimization opportunities, with LLM-QO consistently outperforming traditional optimizers across multiple workloads.

KGs can represent query patterns, execution plans, and performance characteristics, enabling agents to learn from historical optimizations and apply proven strategies to new queries. The fine-grained dimension captures specific optimization techniques, while the coarse-grained dimension maintains high-level performance principles.

4.3 AIOps and Lakehouse Integration

KGs facilitate unified data integration across diverse storage systems, modeling relationships between data sources, transformation pipelines, and consumption patterns to optimize data movement and processing workflows. The AIOpsLab framework [20] aligns with KG-based approaches by providing structured memory substrates for multi-agent coordination in fault localization and remediation tasks.

Knowledge graphs enable the shared memory and causal reasoning capabilities required for autonomous systems to operate effectively in complex cloud environments. The integration of CKGs with AIOps frameworks represents a promising direction for fully autonomous database operations, addressing security challenges identified in agentic AI systems [8].

5 Challenges and Future Directions

5.1 Technical Challenges

Knowledge Graph Construction from Multi-modal Data. Constructing high-quality KGs from diverse, multi-modal unstructured data sources (texts, images, tables, XML, JSON) remains a fundamental challenge. Recent advances in LLM-based frameworks, such as the "Extract, Define, Canonicalize" approach [27], demonstrate promising schema-agnostic methods for automated KG construction. However, significant challenges remain in handling multi-modal data integration, ensuring semantic consistency, and maintaining quality at scale.

Scalability. Large-scale KGs require robust infrastructure for efficient storage, querying, and updates. Current graph databases and processing frameworks need optimization for real-time agentic memory applications, as highlighted in comprehensive surveys [18]. The dynamic update frequency dimension poses particular challenges for maintaining consistency while supporting real-time operations.

Data Consistency and Governance. Dynamic updates in multi-agent environments challenge consistency maintenance while requiring robust governance frameworks. The A-MEM framework [26] demonstrates agentic memory systems that can dynamically organize memories, but developing efficient versioning and conflict resolution mechanisms remains an active research area. Incorporating KGs into existing database systems and LLM pipelines requires careful architectural design and standardized interfaces, with frameworks like KG.GOV [17] providing insights into positioning KGs as backbones for AI data governance.

5.2 Evaluation and Metrics

Current evaluation methods for agentic memory systems are often labor-intensive and domain-specific. The development of reasoning topologies [4] and structured benchmarks like BRIGHT [22] provide frameworks for assessing memory effectiveness across different database operation scenarios.

Comprehensive evaluation requires metrics that capture performance across all six dimensions of our classification framework, including temporal consistency, functional completeness, appropriate granularity, update responsiveness, distribution efficiency, and hybrid integration effectiveness.

5.3 Privacy and Security

KGs containing sensitive database information require robust privacy protection and access control mechanisms. The taxonomy of failure modes in agentic AI systems [5] highlights security challenges that must be addressed when deploying KG-based memory systems in production environments.

The granularity dimension introduces additional privacy considerations, as fine-grained representations may inadvertently expose sensitive patterns or relationships that are not apparent in coarse-grained views. The distribution dimension requires careful consideration of data locality and cross-agent information sharing policies, while the hybrid integration dimension must address security boundaries between KG memory and external data sources.

6 Conclusion

Knowledge graphs, particularly causal and temporal variants, represent the optimal approach for unified agentic memory in cloud database operations. Our analysis demonstrates that KGs address fundamental limitations of vector search and long context windows while providing essential structured, relational, and temporal reasoning capabilities for autonomous database systems.

Evidence from recent research, including performance improvements in memory benchmarks and practical applications in systems like COMET and KGroot, supports KGs as indispensable for next-generation database operations. Our six-dimensional memory classification framework shows how KGs uniquely support all memory types required for complex database tasks.

Future work should focus on addressing scalability challenges and developing standardized evaluation metrics. The convergence of KGs with AIOps principles promises to enable truly autonomous cloud database operations, representing a significant advancement in database management technology.

Acknowledgement. This work was supported by Salesforce. The author thanks the Salesforce database and observability teams for their insights and feedback on practical applications of knowledge graph-based agentic memory systems.

Disclosure of Interests. The author declares no competing interests relevant to the content of this article.

References

1. AdaSci Research: How causal knowledge graphs outperform traditional knowledge graphs. AdaSci Blog (2024). https://adasci.org/how-causal-knowledge-graphs-outperform-traditional-knowledge-graphs/
2. Akioyamen, P., Yi, Z., Marcus, R.: The unreasonable effectiveness of LLMs for query optimization. arXiv preprint arXiv:2411.02862 (2024). https://doi.org/10.48550/arXiv.2411.02862. https://arxiv.org/abs/2411.02862

3. FRIPL Artificial Intelligence Laboratory, Fujitsu Research Unit: Fujitsu causal knowledge graph: Transform to data-driven decision making based on logical reasoning. Fujitsu Blog (2024). https://www.fujitsu.com/global/about/research/article/202410-causal-knowledge-graph.html
4. Besta, M., Memedi, F., Zhang, Z., et al.: Demystifying chains, trees, and graphs of thoughts. arXiv preprint arXiv:2401.14295 (2025).https://doi.org/10.48550/arXiv.2401.14295. http://arxiv.org/abs/2401.14295
5. Bryan, P., Severi, G., Microsoft's AI Red Team (AIRT): Taxonomy of failure mode in agentic AI systems (2025). https://www.microsoft.com/en-us/security/blog/2025/04/24/new-whitepaper-outlines-the-taxonomy-of-failure-modes-in-ai-agents/
6. Chhikara, P., Khant, D., Aryan, S., Singh, T., Yadav, D.: Mem0: building production-ready AI agents with scalable long-term memory. arXiv preprint arXiv:2504.19413 (2025). https://doi.org/10.48550/arXiv.2504.19413. http://arxiv.org/abs/2504.19413
7. Cognee Team: AI memory tools evaluation. Cognee Blog (2025). https://www.cognee.ai/blog/deep-dives/ai-memory-tools-evaluation
8. Deng, Z., Guo, Y., Han, C., et al.: AI agents under threat: a survey of key security challenges and future pathways. ACM Comput. Surv. (2025)
9. Google Cloud Team: Inside AI-assisted troubleshooting for databases. Google Cloud Blog (2025). https://cloud.google.com/blog/products/databases/inside-ai-assisted-troubleshooting-for-databases
10. Huang, H., Vidal, M.E.: CauseKG: a framework enhancing causal inference with implicit knowledge deduced from knowledge graphs. IEEE Access (2024)
11. Jaimini, U., Sheth, A.: CausalKG: causal knowledge graph explainability using interventional and counterfactual reasoning. IEEE Internet Comput. **26**(1), 43–50 (2022). https://doi.org/10.1109/MIC.2021.3133551
12. Khatibi, E., Wang, Z., Rahmani, A.M.: CDF-RAG: causal dynamic feedback for adaptive retrieval-augmented generation. arXiv preprint arXiv:2504.12560 (2025). https://doi.org/10.48550/arXiv.2504.12560. https://arxiv.org/abs/2504.12560
13. Khosla, S., Zhu, Z., He, Y.: Survey on memory-augmented neural networks: cognitive insights to ai applications. arXiv preprint arXiv:2312.06141 (2023). https://doi.org/10.48550/arXiv.2312.06141. http://arxiv.org/abs/2312.06141
14. Kiciman, E., Ness, R., Sharma, A., Tan, C.: Causal reasoning and large language models: opening a new frontier for causality. arXiv preprint arXiv:2305.00050 (2024). https://doi.org/10.48550/arXiv.2305.00050. https://arxiv.org/abs/2305.00050
15. Laban, P., Hayashi, H., Zhou, Y., et al.: LLMs get lost in multi-turn conversation. arXiv preprint arXiv:2505.06120 (2025).https://doi.org/10.48550/arXiv.2505.06120. https://arxiv.org/abs/2505.06120
16. Luo, H., Zhang, J., Li, C.: Causal graphs meet thoughts: enhancing complex reasoning in graph-augmented LLMs. arXiv preprint arXiv:2501.14892 (2025). https://doi.org/10.48550/arXiv.2501.14892. http://arxiv.org/abs/2501.14892
17. Meroño Peñuela, A., Simperl, E., et al.: KG.GOV: knowledge graphs as the backbone of data governance in AI. J. Web Semant. (2025). https://doi.org/10.1016/j.websem.2024.100847. https://linkinghub.elsevier.com/retrieve/pii/S1570826824000337
18. Peng, C., Xia, F., Naseriparsa, M., et al.: Knowledge graphs: opportunities and challenges. Artif. Intell. Rev. **56**(13), 13071–13102 (2023). https://doi.org/10.1007/s10462-023-10465-9

19. Rasmussen, P., Paliychuk, P., Beauvais, T., Ryan, J., Chalef, D.: Zep: a temporal knowledge graph architecture for agent memory. arXiv preprint arXiv:2501.13956 (2025). https://doi.org/10.48550/arXiv.2501.13956. https://arxiv.org/abs/2501.13956
20. Shetty, M., Chen, Y., Somashekar, G., et al.: Building AI agents for autonomous clouds: challenges and design principles. arXiv preprint arXiv:2407.12165 (2024). https://doi.org/10.48550/arXiv.2407.12165. http://arxiv.org/abs/2407.12165
21. Skavantzos, P., Link, S.: Entity/relationship graphs: principled design, modeling, and data integrity management of graph databases. In: Proceedings of the 31st ACM SIGMOD International Conference on Management of Data, pp. 154–169. ACM, New York (2025). https://doi.org/10.1145/3709690
22. Su, H., Yen, H., Xia, M., et al.: BRIGHT: a realistic and challenging benchmark for reasoning-intensive retrieval. arXiv preprint arXiv:2407.12883 (2025). https://doi.org/10.48550/arXiv.2407.12883. https://arxiv.org/abs/2407.12883
23. Tan, J., Zhao, K., Li, R., et al.: Can large language models be query optimizer for relational databases? arXiv preprint arXiv:2502.05562 (2025).https://doi.org/10.48550/arXiv.2502.05562. https://arxiv.org/abs/2502.05562
24. Wang, T., Qi, G., Wu, T.: KGroot: enhancing root cause analysis through knowledge graphs and graph convolutional neural networks. arXiv preprint arXiv:2402.13264 (2024). https://doi.org/10.48550/arXiv.2402.13264. https://arxiv.org/abs/2402.13264
25. Wang, Z., Li, J., Ma, M., et al.: Large language models can provide accurate and interpretable incident triage. In: 2024 IEEE 35th International Symposium on Software Reliability Engineering (ISSRE), pp. 523–534 (2024). https://doi.org/10.1109/ISSRE62328.2024.00056
26. Xu, W., Mei, K., Gao, H., et al.: A-MEM: agentic memory for LLM agents. arXiv preprint arXiv:2502.12110 (2025). https://doi.org/10.48550/arXiv.2502.12110. https://arxiv.org/abs/2502.12110
27. Zhang, B., Soh, H.: Extract, define, canonicalize: an LLM-based framework for knowledge graph construction. arXiv preprint arXiv:2404.03868v2 (2024). https://doi.org/10.48550/arXiv.2404.03868. https://arxiv.org/abs/2404.03868
28. Zhang, Z., Bo, X., Ma, C., et al.: A survey on the memory mechanism of large language model based agents. arXiv preprint arXiv:2404.13501 (2024). https://doi.org/10.48550/arXiv.2404.13501. https://arxiv.org/abs/2404.13501
29. Zhu, Y., Qiao, S., Ou, Y., et al.: KnowAgent: knowledge-augmented planning for LLM-based agents. arXiv preprint arXiv:2403.03101 (2025). https://doi.org/10.48550/arXiv.2403.03101. https://arxiv.org/abs/2403.03101

Author Index

Q. Wen et al. (Eds.): Agent4IR 2025/2024, CCIS 2695, p. 147, 2026.
https://doi.org/10.1007/978-3-032-11477-8

Zeitfracht Medien GmbH
Ferdinand-Jühlke-Straße 7
99095 Erfurt, Deutschland
produktsicherheit@kolibri360.de